FLIGHT C

FLIGHT OF THE TITAN

THE STORY OF THE R34

George Rosie

BIRLINN

First published in 2010 by
Birlinn Limited
West Newington House
10 Newington Road
Edinburgh
EH9 1QS

www.birlinn.co.uk

Copyright © George Rosie 2010

ISBN: 978 1 84158 863 6

British Library Cataloguing-in-Publication Data
A catalogue record for this book is available from the British Library

Typeset by Iolaire Typesetting, Newtonmore
Printed and bound by Cox & Wyman Ltd, Reading

For Marcus George Rosie

Contents

Contents

List of Illustrations

1. Pride of the Clyde. The R34 leaves the airship shed at Inchinnan where she was built.
2. Cathedral in the sky. A rare image of the R34's lofty interior.
3. Brigadier-General Edward Maitland, the driving force behind the R34's transatlantic journey.
4. Major George Herbert Scott and Lieutenant-Commander Zachary Lansdowne.
5. Watercolour painting of the R34 taking off from East Fortune airfield in the early hours of 2 July 1919.
6. The kitten 'Whoopsie' with engineer George Graham.
7. Billy Ballantyne is quizzed by officers in the control car.
8. Punishment duties. Ballantyne doing the ship's dirty work for stowing away.
9. Lieutenant John Shotter, the R34's engineering officer.
10. Sunday, 6 July 1919 and the R34 touches down at Roosevelt Field, Mineola, Long Island with the help of the US Army.
11. The R34's skipper George Herbert Scott takes questions from the press after the R34 touched down at Pulham in Norfolk.
12. Lady Sybil Grant, the beautiful if raffish daughter of the Earl of Rosebery and a close friend of Edward Maitland.

Acknowledgements

No one writes this kind of book without piling up debts to other people in various corners of the world. This venture into early twentieth-century aviation history is no exception. My heartfelt thanks, then, to the following: the librarians of the National Library of Scotland in Edinburgh and the British Library in London; the staff of the National Archives at Kew; the archivists at the Royal Aeronautical Society in London and Farnborough; the Royal Air Force Museum at Hendon, the Fleet Air Arm Museum at Yeovilton in Somerset; the Royal Institute of Navigation, London; the University of Glasgow Archive, Glasgow; the Mitchell Library, Glasgow; the National Museum of Scotland's Museum of Flight at East Fortune.

And on the other side of the Atlantic my gratitude to: the US Naval Academy, Annapolis; the Cradle of Aviation Museum, Garden City, Long Island, New York; the Mineola Memorial Library, Mineola, Long Island, New York; the Long Island Studies Institute, Hempstead, Long Island, New York; the librarians of the *New York Times* and the Museum and Library of Greenville, Ohio.

These days, no researcher worth his or her salt can afford to ignore the wealth of material – personal, local, national, international – available on internet websites. All of which has to be checked, of course, but these sites do represent a new dimension that deserves to be acknowledged. So my thanks to, among others, the websites of *Flight International*, the Airship Foundation, Airships Online, Renfrewshire Portal, the National Hydrogen Association, the Essex Police and St Nicholas Church, Little Wigborough, Essex.

I'd also like to thank Hugh Andrew of Birlinn for taking a flier on this one (no pun intended) and my ever-encouraging agent David Godwin and the staff at DGA. Also my friends Ian Jack and Harry Reid for taking a look at one particularly difficult and crucial chapter and reassuring me it wasn't boring. And thanks and love, as ever, to my patient wife Liz for putting up with the writing of yet another book.

Introduction

It was like something from another world. A huge, stream-lined, silvery-blue shape caught in the crossbeams of powerful searchlights, prowling slowly over the Manhattan skyscrapers. In the early hours of Thursday, 10 July 1919, hundreds of thousands of New Yorkers rushed out onto the streets and rooftops and gaped up into the sky as the great ship, hundreds of feet long, rolled slowly across the city. Restaurants, hotels, theatres, nightclubs and bars emptied as people took to the street to gaze upwards. The sight was one of the great events of the summer of 1919.

None of them had seen anything like it. The vast ship, as long as an ocean liner, three times the size of a modern jumbo jet, shimmered against the dark sky like some vision out of the future. Its majestic progress down Manhattan halted over the *New York Times* building at the corner of 42nd Street and Times Square. Then, very slowly, it turned its bow east and headed off over the East River towards Long Island and the Atlantic. New Yorkers were left to wonder as the thrum of the ship's engines died away to the east.

But it was no alien visitation or vision of the future. The Leviathan in the sky was the Scottish-built airship R34. It was manned by a 30-strong crew of World War I veterans and a few days earlier had made the first-ever east–west flight across the Atlantic against headwinds and electrical storms. Now, after four days of being wined, dined and courted by New York's finest and sharing a platform with the president himself, the crew were on their way home – to make the first-ever return flight from Europe to North America.

The flight of the R34 in July 1919 was one of the great feats of British aviation and it has been largely forgotten. All the

glory has been attached to Alcock and Brown's flight which
took place a few weeks earlier which was not only more than
1,000 miles shorter than the R34's but was only one way
and had the huge benefit of a following wind. But the R34
did it the long, hard way, flying almost 4,000 miles from an
airfield east of Edinburgh to an airfield east of New York City
– and then back again to Britain. It was the longest flight ever
by any aircraft and the longest time any airship had spent in
the air.

And in the eyes of many it proved – or at least strongly
suggested – that passenger flights across the Atlantic were
possible and that lighter-than-air ships were the way ahead.
Many (maybe even most) aviation experts in 1919 regarded
heavier-than-air aeroplanes as being too limited in their range
and too small in size ever to carry enough passengers to make
long flights profitable. The R34's transatlantic flight seemed,
at least, to have settled the argument.

Aeroplanes would make the short hops, the conventional
thinking ran, but the long, intercontinental flights, would be
left to the big 'dirigibles'. And the R34 was, at the time, one of
the biggest dirigibles on the planet. The R34 seemed to bring to
life the picture drawn by Kipling in his 1905 story 'With the
Night Mail' of fleets of fast-flying commercial and passenger
airships criss-crossing the Atlantic every day, shepherded on
their way by a system of searchlights and radio beacons.

There's something about the story of the R34 that appeals to
me in ways that the stories of the other transatlantic projects
do not. Partly it is because most of the others – the successful
ones at least – are well known. Almost everyone in Britain
knows the tale of Alcock and Brown, who made the first flight
from Newfoundland to the west coast of Ireland. Most aviation buffs are familiar with the attempt by Harry Hawker and
Mackenzie Grieve and how that attempt came to grief and
almost cost the men their lives. A few know of the failed efforts
of Rear-Admiral Mark Kerr and Freddie Raynham.

But hardly anyone in Britain remembers the saga of the R34,

the great Clyde-built airship that made the journey from East Fortune in East Lothian to Mineola in Long Island with thirty-one men aboard, one of them a stowaway, two carrier pigeons and a cat who shouldn't have been there. The R34 has left few overt traces: a plaque in a shopping mall in Mineola; some photographs, crew items and a plaque at the Museum of Flight in East Fortune; a café/restaurant of the same name on the site where the R34 was built at Inchinnan near Glasgow airport. There used to be a model of the R34 in one of the terminals at Heathrow but it is long gone.

The R34 also carried an extraordinary aviator who had seen the R34 through from its inception to its moment of triumph in the USA. He was Brigadier-General Edward Maitland Maitland, veteran of the Boer War and World War I and a man of many accomplishments. He was one of Britain's first aeroplane pilots, a world-class balloonist, an experimental parachutist and a zealot in the cause of lighter-than-air flight. Maitland was an Edwardian man of action with a taste for high-bred ladies, fanciful fiction and transcendental poetry, and a passionate supporter of airships. He's been described (aptly, I think) as 'T.E. Lawrence with his head in the clouds'.

To me, the R34 itself seems to represent something strange: a huge flying machine that stretches backwards to the days of ballooning yet forwards into the future of long-distance, transcontinental flight. The principles that held the R34 aloft had been familiar since the end of the eighteenth century, but the R34's latticed structure of lightweight aluminium alloy reaches into the twenty-first century. On her journey across the Atlantic the R34 kept in touch with London via a network of recently built radio stations but steered her course by magnetic compasses and naval sextants that would have been familiar to Captain James Cook.

The R34 wasn't much faster than the ocean-going liners battering across the Atlantic thousands of feet below, but her five aero engines represented the technology that would eventually make the passenger-carrying luxury liner obsolete. The

men aboard the R34 were seeing mid-Atlantic cloudscapes that
no one had seen before but relying for explanations on Luke
Howard, an early nineteenth-century Quaker whose work was
admired by Goethe.

It was also 'walked out' of its shed near Glasgow when the
world was about to change. The R34 first saw the light of day
on 20 December 1918, a few weeks after the war had ground
to halt but half a year before the Germans signed the Treaty of
Versailles. In those crucial six months no one was sure whether
the Germans would accept defeat. Not long before the treaty
was signed the R34 was ordered to patrol the German coast of
the North Sea and the Baltic in a display of British air power
(although everyone who ordered the mission knew it would
only take one incendiary bullet to reduce the R34 to burning
ruin).

The R34 was also caught up in the rivalry between the USA
and the UK, the only two serious contenders in the race to be
first across the Atlantic. The nominal prize was the £10,000 on
offer from the London-based *Daily Mail* but the real prize was
the kudos and prestige that would attend the winning entry.
One American venture involved three flying boats, each with a
crew of six, and more than 20 warships strung out in a line
across the Atlantic. It was an operation that cost far more than
could ever have been recovered from the *Daily Mail*.

It has long seemed to me that, in a strange way, the R34 and
the airships that followed were spiritual ancestors of the
Anglo-French 'Concorde'. Both were apparently advanced,
world-changing technologies that lasted for a few decades
(two in the case of the airships) until their problems and costs
rendered them obsolete. Both were brought shudderingly to a
halt by disasters: a crash in Paris in 2000 in the case of
Concorde; an explosion in New Jersey in 1937 in the case
of the airship. But both Concorde and the airship have large
bands of admirers who would dearly love to see them return to
the sky.

The story of the R34 reaches into many corners of the early

twentieth-century world: Great Power politics and the Peace Conference in Paris; the humiliation of the German aviation industry; the creation of new materials and new instrumentation; the internal politics of the British defence bureaucracies; the slow, gradual understanding of the Atlantic weather systems. And, of course, the beginnings of the transatlantic aviation that so many of us now take for granted. What we regard as 'pond-hopping' the aviators of 1919 saw as a seriously grim challenge.

There's also something Edwardian, perhaps even Victorian, about the saga of the R34. Many of the men involved in the R34 project, on the ship or in the ministries, were veterans of the Boer War or some other military venture by imperial Britain. Some had been wounded while confronting outraged Dutch farmers in Natal or hostile 'natives' in the Gambia. Almost all had experienced the horrors of World War I, some of them in the mud and blood of the trenches, others in aeroplanes above the trenches or in airships loitering over the Atlantic. A few led extraordinary lives that are worthy of serious biographies.

And then there is the airship itself, an elaborate and truly marvellous creation. I've only ever seen photographs and drawings of the interior of the R34 but I couldn't help being struck by the resemblance to one of the great cathedrals. The way in which the lattice of aluminium girders soars upwards nearly 100 feet (the ceiling height of many cathedrals) reminded me of the vaults and traceries of a great church. I'm certainly not the first to make the comparison. In his 1978 book *Airship Wreck*, the British author Len Deighton wrote:

> For me the airship has a magic that the aeroplane cannot replace. The size is awesome, the shape Gothic; a pointed arch twirled into a tracery of aluminium. And the reality is not disappointing. No one present ever forgot the day a concert pianist sat down and gave his fellow passengers a recital while the airship moved through the cloudy skies of

the Atlantic . . . the airship remains one of the greatest triumphs of structural engineering the world has ever seen . . . It was almost impossible to make a rigid airship that was light enough to lift into the sky yet strong enough to endure the forces of nature it would encounter there.

But it happened. It was made.

In many ways rigid airships were paradoxical. They were a new technology – controlled from 'gondolas' that looked like something out of a novel by Jules Verne, complete with voice tubes, dials for 'ringing down' to the engine rooms and a helmsman at the ship's steering wheel. It's not hard to imagine Captain Nemo in the R34's control car, standing over the chart table plotting a route through the clouds instead of under the sea and signalling down to the engine cars to give him 'full ahead'. It's hard to look at the drawings of the R34's control car without smiling.

And, coming from a seagoing family, I found myself intrigued by the maritime language used by the aeronauts of 1919. An airship had no fuselage, but a 'hull'. The living quarters and the petrol were stored along the 'keel'. The front was the 'bow' and the rear was the 'stern'. Right was 'starboard' and left was 'port'. Steering was done by a wheel. The men who worked high up in the girders tending to the ship's gas bags and outer cover were known as 'riggers', the men in the rigging.

But flying an airship all the way across the Atlantic in the year 1919 was nothing to smile about. No one knew if it could be done. Seagoing vessels had been doing it for centuries, of course, but they usually had a horizon from which to take a sextant bearing to fix their position while airships often found themselves totally enveloped by cloud, with crude altimeters that were notoriously inaccurate. Aerial navigation was in its infancy. During the war one seasoned Zeppelin skipper who set out to bomb Edinburgh found himself being forced down in Norway.

Also, ocean-going ships floated on top of the fluid on which they moved, not completely immersed in it like an airship which was subject to downdraughts and updraughts as well as headwinds, following winds and crosswinds. No one knew what perils lurked in the upper air above the Atlantic. No one had the means to study the high atmosphere for the direction or speed of the winds. No one knew how they might be influenced by the currents or temperature of the oceans. The best the officers of the R34 could do was watch the clouds around them and listen to the weather information coming in on the radio from ships down below.

From the R34's crew of 30 (31 in the event) the transatlantic flight required faith in the technology, patience, a high degree of skill and a talent for improvisation. Plus an ability to rough it on minimal rations in a chilly interior that reeked of petrol and vibrated ceaselessly to five unsynchronised aero engines. They had to try to snatch some sleep between four-hour watches in narrow hammocks that were swaying between the girders. All this had to be suffered for days on end without even the comfort of a cigarette (most were smokers). And with the ever-present prospect that they might have to 'ditch' in the Atlantic and hope (rather than expect) to be rescued by one of their two attendant warships.

There are, alas, no survivors of the R34's epic flight of July 1919. Some of them were later killed in other airships and the others died many years ago. But there is a large store of information about the epic flight. Some of it is in the log-cum-diary kept by General Edward Maitland, which was later published (with a foreword by Rudyard Kipling). Other material comes from the flight reports of the airship's officers, crew diaries, press interviews and information buried in the National Archives in Kew, the records of the RAF Museum at Hendon, the Royal Aeronautical Society in London and the Museum of Flight at East Fortune.

And the R34's brief sojourn in New York was heavily documented by the US press, in particular the *New York*

Times and the *Brooklyn Eagle*. Both newspapers saw the first-ever aircraft to fly into the USA from abroad as a huge event (and used it to chide their own government for tardiness). Also available are photographs taken on the voyage, manufacturers' material and working drawings and photographs of the airship sheds from the archive of the Royal Commission on Ancient and Historical Monuments of Scotland (RCAHMS) in Edinburgh.

Taken together, these diverse sources paint a vivid picture of one of the great feats of early aviation and one of which Britain, and Scotland in particular, should be proud. It certainly deserves to be better known than it is. The great Clyde-built airship made its crossing of the Atlantic and back with the red-on-gold Lion Rampant of the King of Scots painted on its bow and above it the motto: 'Pro Patria Volans' – flying for my country.

1

Building the R34

The R34 might never have been built if Second Lieutenant Alfred Brandon's machine guns had worked properly in the early hours of Sunday, 24 September 1916. Brandon, a New Zealander, was one of the Royal Flying Corp's handiest pilots. He was attached to No. 39 (Home Defence) squadron operating out of the airfield at Hainault Farm a few miles from Romford in Essex and had won the Military Cross for a daring attack on Zeppelin L13 earlier in the year. That September evening Brandon's squadron was scrambled to intercept a flight of German Zeppelins that had been bombing around the east end of London. Four of the enemy raiders – L30, L31, L32, L33 – were from the new breed of 'Super-Zeppelins' for which the German navy had high hopes.

But it was to be a bad night for the German navy. By 1916 the British air defences were in good shape, with a reasonably efficient network of fighter bases, barrage balloons, searchlights and anti-aircraft artillery that was strung from Edinburgh down to the Channel coast and a cluster around London. It was ready and waiting for the fleet of Zeppelins as they came in across the North Sea. The first to go was L32 which was jumped at 13,000 feet by an RFC pilot called Fred Sowrey who, as he wrote in his report of the engagement, 'poured in three drums of Brock and Pomeroy, resulting in the start of another explosion'.

'Brock' and 'Pomeroy' were the names of explosive ammunition rounds called after their inventors. They were part of a lethal mix of ordnance that British interceptors used against German airships. The others were magnesium tracers called 'Sparklets' and flat-nosed phosphorus rounds known as 'Buckingham'. All of them could light up an airship's hydrogen-filled

gas bags and turn the ship into a mass of flame that killed
everyone aboard. The Brock was particularly effective, as it
was sensitive enough to explode on contact with fabric. But
they were all lethal, and by 1916 the casualty rate among
Zeppelin crews was atrocious. It was the reason why the
German army preferred to have little or nothing to do with
Zeppelins.

But when Alfred Brandon made his run against Zeppelin
L33 just after midnight and raked its hull with his Lewis gun,
for some reason the hydrogen in the airship's bags failed to
ignite. The Zeppelin seemed to be defying the laws of physics
and chemistry. Time after time Brandon ran at the L33,
shredding its outer cover and gas bags with explosive rounds
and ripping chunks off the airship's engine cars and control
car, but the Zeppelin resolutely refused to explode.

'The Brock ammunition seemed to be bursting all along it,'
Brandon reported later, 'but the Zepp did not catch fire. I was
using Brock, Pomeroy and Sparklets. I turned again and put on
a fresh drum and came up from behind and fired again. The
gun jammed after about nine rounds.' Brandon's attack lasted
30 minutes and all that time the German crew resisted firing
back. They knew that with hydrogen leaking all around them
one spark from their own machine guns could do Brandon's
job for him.

With his Lewis gun finally out of action Brandon broke off
the attack and returned to his base, leaving the 22-strong crew
of the L33 struggling to keep their ship in the air. The L33 was
losing hydrogen and height fast. The crew shed anything they
could find – ammunition boxes, a machine gun, shell casings,
boots, water canisters, books, anything – in a desperate
attempt to gain enough height to make it to the North Sea.
Once there they could ditch the airship, send out a distress call
and, with a bit of luck, be picked up by a German patrol boat.

But there was no luck to be had that night. The trail of
equipment they left across the Essex countryside failed to do the
trick. Brandon's mauling had taken its toll. The L33 had lost too

much hydrogen to stay in the air. The stricken Zeppelin sank to the ground near the Essex village of Little Wigborough where, thanks to skilful airmanship by the skipper, Kapitänleutnant Alois Bocker, the crew emerged from the crash landing unharmed. They came down on Copt Hall Lane at half past midnight on Sunday, 24 September.

There then followed one of those odd sequences of events that seemed to occur in World War I. Bocker knocked on the door of the nearest cottage, politely warned the inhabitants that he was about to set fire to the crashed airship and advised them to vacate the premises. Then he collected all the ship's papers and code books, tossed them into the control car, fired a signal flare into the interior and watched the L33 go up in a blaze of hydrogen. But by then the ship had lost so much gas and fuel that the blaze was not nearly enough to reduce the airship to cinders. Most of the ship's structure and at least one of the engines remained intact.

Having done his best, Bocker then knocked on the door of another cottage and asked 14-year-old George Rout the way to Colchester. The startled boy told him, at which the Germans marched off, in good military order. At the nearby village of Peldon they ran into the local bobby – one Special Constable Edgar Nicholas – who arrested them. Nicholas took his 22 prisoners to the local post office, where they were joined by PC Charles Smith, who telephoned the army at Mersea. Eventually the military came and took the Germans away for interrogation in London. The other ranks ended in a prisoner-of-war camp at Stobo in the Scottish Borders and the officers in more comfortable quarters at Donington Hall near Leeds.

The descent of the ruined Zeppelin was a big event in the history of Little Wigborough. Small parts of the L33 are now built into the tower of the fifteenth-century church of St Nicholas, and an account of the event hangs in the church in a frame made from some of the L33's aluminium. For his part rounding up the Germans, local bobby Charles Smith was made a sergeant and known thereafter as 'Zeppie'. And after

Mrs Clark of Little Wigborough delivered a daughter the night the L33 descended on the village the child was christened Zeppelina.

The L33 was far from intact, but there was more than enough left of her to be of great interest to the British. The L33 was a genuine prize. She was the first 'Super Zeppelin' to be downed on British land. Designed by Ludwig Dürr and built at the Luftschiffbau Zeppelin works at Friedrichshafen on the Bodensee (Lake Constantine), the L33 was only three weeks old, having first flown on Wednesday, 30 August 1916. More than 640 feet long and powered by six 240-horsepower, six-cylinder Maybach engines, the L33 was one of the latest and most powerful ships in the German navy's Zeppelin fleet.

The British acted quickly to stop the ship being pillaged by souvenir hunters. The area around the wreckage was secured and put under armed guard, and no one was allowed near it without a pass from the military (something that irritated local farmers and carters no end). Colonel Edward Maitland, the commander of the airship base at Pulham in Norfolk was put in charge of the wreckage, while a string of military brass and VIP visitors came down from London to see what had fallen into Britain's lap.

One of the visitors was Prime Minister Lloyd George, who was given a tour of the crashed Zeppelin and an explanation of its technical importance. Impressed, Lloyd George returned to Downing Street and instructed Brigadier-General Hugh Trenchard, then responsible for Britain's air forces, that the country needed its own version of the L33. Trenchard agreed, consulted the Admiralty (who were responsible for airships), and the machinery was set in motion to create Britain's own 'Super Zeppelin'.

The job of extracting what the ruins of the L33 had to offer was given to the Royal Corps of Naval Constructors (RCNC), whose airship group was run by a flinty Scotsman named Commander Charles Ivor Rae Campbell RN. Campbell's passion for airships was once described as 'almost a faith'.

A brilliant engineer, and originally a designer of submarines, Campbell switched to airships early in his career and worked on Britain's very first dirigible (imaginatively entitled Airship No. 1). Campbell and his team were based at 10 Smith Square in Westminster, from where he oversaw the design and construction of every one of Britain's wartime airships

The business of making sense of the wreckage of the L33, however, was given to three of the RCNC's 'assistant constructors', A.P. Cole, F. Sutcliffe and H. May, all lieutenant commanders. The group were despatched to Little Wigborough with orders to stay there until they understood every detail of the structure and workings of the L33. They headed a little squad of draughtsmen and engineers who were to crawl over every inch of the wreckage and re-create the L33 on paper.

Many years later Cole told the aviation historian Geoffrey Chamberlain that 'Sutcliffe, May and I were immediately sent down to the wreck, and together with all the draughtsmen, were able to make detailed drawings of the structure and reconstruct the complete ship'. It was a complicated business that took the group almost five months. 'The main problem confronting us was the correct tensioning of the bracing wires,' Cole said. 'I ultimately solved this problem, for which I received the MBE.' Cole's gong was well-deserved. The bracing wires were what held the ship together.

The design that Cole and his team teased out of the charred remains of the L33 was simple in principle but complex in detail. With triangular girders made from lightweight aluminium, the structure comprised a series of 25-sided polygonal, transverse girders, like giant hoops, that were held 24 feet apart by a system of 'longitudinal' girders (13 main girders and 12 intermediate). They were the 'cage' of the airship and each of the 'panels' they created was braced by diagonally-arranged steel wires of varying diameters.

It was a beautifully efficient cat's cradle of light metal and wire, flexible enough to accommodate 19 huge gas bags and strong enough to carry the load of a 50-foot long control car plus six engines and thousands of gallons of water, oil and petrol. In a paper published in *Flight* magazine a few years later, Cole claimed that 'This scheme of construction has been found to give the lightest ship and to be most readily adaptable to use in very large ships'.

By February 1917 the work of Cole and his colleagues was complete, and everything had been approved by Campbell. The designs and specifications were collected into a document numbered CB1265, stamped 'top secret' and delivered to the Admiralty. The document confirmed what everyone by then knew – that German airship technology was a long way ahead of anything being produced in Britain or France. There were rumours that the Germans would soon have the long-distance capability to hit any part of Britain or Ireland, even the Home Fleet at Scapa Flow.

But it took the Cabinet another nine months to act. That may have been due to opposition from Winston Churchill, who regarded big airships as a dangerous waste of money. But in November 1917, the Cabinet gave the Admiralty the go-ahead to produce three ships based on the design that Campbell's RCNC team had teased out of the German L33. The orders were placed with Sir W.G. Armstrong Whitworth & Co. at Selby in Yorkshire (R33), William Beardmore & Co. at Inchinnan in Renfrewshire (R34) and Short Brothers at Cardington in Bedfordshire (R35). All three firms swung quickly into action.

And none with more enthusiasm than Beardmore's, then one of the most enterprising and diverse engineering firms in Britain. Beardmore's was Clydeside heavy engineering at its innovative best. From their workshops and shipyards at Dalmuir on the north bank of the Clyde and the Parkhead Forge in the east end of Glasgow the company turned out warships, cargo vessels, ferries, aeroplanes, armour plate, motor vehicles, gun barrels, artillery shells, marine boilers, aero engines, tanks, tank engines, even tin helmets for the infantry. By 1916 the firm was employing around 15,000 men and women.

The firm was run by the autocratic engineer-businessman William Beardmore, an offspring of the family who had bought into the Parkhead Forge in 1868 and had grown over the years to become an industrial power in Scotland. It's been said of William Beardmore that he couldn't see a product without wanting to manufacture it. His upbringing was unusual. Born in London but educated at Glasgow and Ayr academies, young Beardmore began his working life as an apprentice in the heat and clamour of the Parkhead Forge.

Ambitious, shrewd and well-connected, in just over a decade Beardmore had built a huge engineering and shipbuilding conglomerate (stretching from Clydebank to London via Dumfries and Manchester) which, by 1900, was operating one of the most efficient naval shipyards in Britain. The shipyard produced, among many others, His Majesty's Ships *Conqueror, Benbow, Ramillies* and *Argus*, the world's first purpose-built aircraft carrier.

By 1917 the firm also had experience of building airships, having already completed the R24 and the R27. To build the dirigibles, Beardmore's had acquired (with the help of the Defence of the Realm regulations) a 600-acre site at Inchinnan on the south side of the River Clyde, near the point where the Clyde meets the Black Cart. And to accommodate their key personnel Beardmore's built an estate of sixty comfortable two-storey houses (paid for by the Admiralty) and bussed the rest of the workforce in from Renfrew and Glasgow.

And to house the airships, in 1916 Beardmore's commissioned the engineering consultancy of Sir William Arrol & Co (the designers of the Forth Railway Bridge and Tower Bridge in London) to construct a huge airship shed at Inchinnan. The working drawings, now in the archives of RCAHMS, show an enormous steel-framed structure 720 feet long, 270 feet wide and 122 feet high.

The legs of the shed were bolted onto pairs of reinforced concrete foundations that were buried deep in the boulder clay. The building's steel columns, or at least the ones that lined the erection bay, were lined with padded canvas to prevent them damaging the outer covers of the airships. The whole structure was clad in steel plate and lined with 'blast flaps' and 'panic doors' to cope with the effects of a possible explosion of hydrogen. Windows were fitted with tinted glass and a system of air-raid blackout blinds operated by a central control.

At each end of the shed were massive sliding doors, the leaves of which parted to create an opening of 152 feet. The great doors were counterbalanced with concrete to prevent them blowing over as they slid open. According to calculations on the working drawings it took about 13 minutes to shift a single door leaf 76 feet.

Running at right angles to the doors at either end of the shed were two windscreens, each 650 feet long and 60 feet high, designed to shelter airships entering or exiting the shed. The Admiralty had learned from bitter experience that it didn't take much of a crosswind to damage an airship by banging it against its shed. Work began on the vast structure at the beginning of January 1916 and was completed by the end of September – nine months to build what, almost a hundred years later, looks like a marvel of civil engineering.

On the other side of the Glasgow to Greenock road the company built a cluster of low buildings as quarters for Royal Naval Air Service personnel. And strung out along the few hundred yards that separated the naval quarters from the airship shed were all the ancillary buildings: paint store, petrol stores, paraffin store, frame shop, girder shop, fabric shop, boiler house, hydrogen generator, power station, garage and a canteen for the workforce. By the time the order for the R34 came down from the Admiralty the Beardmore airship division had the workforce, the equipment and the experience to build the giant dirigible.

Three crucial elements were needed to keep a rigid airship flying. One was hydrogen, the explosive but lighter-than-air gas with which the ship's gas bags were filled. The second was a strange material known as 'goldbeaters' skins' with which the gas bags were lined and which was the only thing known to be virtually (but not quite) impervious to hydrogen. The third was the hard, light aluminium alloy known as 'duraluminium' from which the airship's skeleton was crafted. Almost all the rigid airships built before and during World War I owed their existence to these three materials. The exceptions were the laminated timber airships built by the German company Schütte-Lanz.

Just who realised that hydrogen was something special is unknown, but the laurels probably belong to that sixteenth-century Swiss-German genius known as Paracelsus. In his day, Paracelsus was regarded as a warlock, which was probably why he was beaten to death in Salzburg in 1541 and why it was later believed that his half-decayed corpse stalked the country-side of central Europe. The legend of Paracelsus is eerily similar to the fable of Victor Frankenstein's monster dreamed up by Mary Shelley during a wet weekend in a villa near Geneva.

Hydrogen was rediscovered by Robert Boyle in 1671, identified as 'inflammable air' by Henry Cavendish in 1766 and named hydro-gen (Greek – 'creator of water') by Antoine Lavoisier, the brilliant French chemist and all-round genius who was guillotined in May 1794 for being one of Louis XVI's tax collectors. There's a story (probably apocryphal) that the judge at Lavoisier's trial told him that 'The Republic has no need of scientists'.

It was Lavoisier's countryman Jacques Charles who first got a hydrogen-filled balloon into the air in December 1783, although the idea had already occurred to the Scots chemist Joseph Black. In 1766, while ruminating on the possible uses of Cavendish's 'inflammable air', Black suggested that if the vapour were used to inflate a 'sufficiently light bladder' then that bladder 'would necessarily form a mass lighter than the bulk of the atmosphere and would rise in it'.

What makes hydrogen special, of course, is its extraordinary lightness. It is, in fact, the lightest element in the known universe. Where 1,000 cubic feet of air weighs around 75 pounds, the same quantity of hydrogen weighs 5 pounds. Which means that 1,000 cubic feet of hydrogen has a 'gross lift' of 70 pounds, i.e. the weight of the air minus the weight of the hydrogen. It is also the simplest element known to exist, consisting of one proton and one electron, makes up 90 per cent of the known universe and produces the energy that drives our sun.

For many years hydrogen was thought to be irreducible. The British chemist and physicist John Dalton (the Quaker genius who developed the atomic theory of matter) wrote in 1808 that 'We might as well attempt to introduce a new planet into the solar system, or to annihilate one already in existence, as to create or destroy a particle of hydrogen'. More than 100 years later the American physicist Victor Weisskopf remarked 'To understand hydrogen is to understand all of physics'.

Most of the hydrogen gas used in British airships was conjured up by the 'Lane Hydrogen Producer'. The name of the Birmingham engineer Howard Lane is not as well-known as it should be, but without the 'Lane process' and its ability to turn out huge quantities of (relatively) low-cost hydrogen it's hard to see how airships as big as the R34 could have taken to the air. There were other ways of making hydrogen, but they were either a lot more expensive (e.g. electrolysis) or produced impure hydrogen (sulphuric acid on zinc).

But creating hydrogen by the Lane process required a formidable array of equipment: retort-furnace, washers, purifiers, fan, steam engine, condenser, gas holders etc. As Lane himself admitted in the magazine *Flight,* 'The initial cost of the plant is fairly high, although the gas produced is cheap. On account of the massive nature of the apparatus it is desirable that the installation should be established in a permanent position, suitable for its local use . . .' All the airship stations in Britain had their own hydrogen-producing stations manned by specially trained staff.

The Lane system was simple in essence and complex in

practice. It devoured huge amounts of water (hydrogen dioxide) and fuel (usually coal or coke). Large quantities of deoxidised iron were heated to enormous temperatures and once the iron was white-hot, steam was pumped across it. The process broke the steam down into its component parts, i.e. hydrogen and oxygen. The hydrogen was then drawn off and stored while the iron was deoxidised again, and reused again and again.

The process was never perfect, and the machinery was both difficult to maintain and had a tendency to break down. But it did produce hydrogen that was usually 95 per cent pure and cost (at 1909 prices) around 5 shillings (25 pence) per 1,000 cubic feet. Even before World War I, Lane hydrogen producers were in operation across Europe and were creating hydrogen gas at rates that varied from 500 cubic feet to 10,000 cubic feet an hour.

But hydrogen gas is a very difficult vapour to contain. As mentioned above, the only material known at the time that did the job was known as 'goldbeaters' skins'. As the name suggests, these skins were a device used by goldsmiths to separate fragile leaves of beaten gold. They were the inner membranes of the caecum, or blind gut, of the large intestine of the ox. Most of the UK's supply came from the abattoirs of Australia and South America but under wartime regulations every killing house in Britain was obliged to supply them to the country's airship builders. German abattoir owners and butchers worked under similar rules. More than 600,000 goldbeaters' skins were required to line the R34's 19 gas bags, at a cost of around £40,000 (nearly £1.5 million in modern terms, according to the retail price index).

Slaughtered oxen were carefully disembowelled and the lining of the gut separated out by hand. It was normally in the shape of a cylindrical bag between 3 feet and 18 inches long and 6 inches in diameter. It was then cleaned, covered with fine salt, rolled up and packed in barrels, often 3,000 to 5,000 per barrel, for transport to a processor who passed it through baths of potash or soda to remove any grease. The skins were then stretched on boards to be dried, each forming a rectangular sheet of (roughly) 3 feet by 18 inches and less than half a millimetre thick.

For years gas bags had to be lined with two or more layers of goldbeaters' skins to guarantee the hydrogen wouldn't seep out. That continued until one Alfred Ryan of Vickers came up with the idea of rubberising the gas bag fabric, coating the interior with *one* layer of skins, and then varnishing them with a 'special' linseed oil. It worked a treat, and after the war Vickers claimed that Ryan's technique had saved the government almost a £1 million by reducing the consumption of goldbeaters' skins by airships.

This strange commodity has a fascinating history. In 1881, one Walter Powell, the Tory MP for Malmesbury in Wiltshire, came across a family from Alsace called Weinling living in the East End of London, who processed goldbeaters' skins for the jewellery trade. Powell, who was a keen balloonist and had heard about the skins' imperviousness to hydrogen, introduced the Weinlings to Captain James Templer, who ran the army's balloon factory at Chatham. Thanks to Templer, the Weinlings and their process were eventually hired by the British government for the strategic purpose of lining the gas bags of military balloons.

At one point during World War I the skins became a political issue when an MP claimed that the trade was 'in the hands of a ring composed of Germans, American-Germans and Jews of German extraction' and that before and at the beginning of the war this ring exported the skins to Germany, 'receiving in return manufactured goods'. He was assured by the president of the Board of Trade that the Admiralty now had a lock on all goldbeaters' skins and that 'no firm can do business in that commodity without a permit'.

The third essential material was the light, hard, aluminium alloy the Germans marketed as 'duraluminium'. The alloy was the creation of the Prussian metallurgist Alfred Wilm, who ran a laboratory near Potsdam. In 1902 Wilm was commissioned by the military to try to find a form of aluminium hard enough to make cartridge cases to replace the heavy (and expensive) brass ones. One Saturday morning Wilm was experimenting with an alloy of 95 per cent aluminium, 4 per cent copper, and the rest magnesium and manganese, which he heated to 525° Celsius and then drenched with water (a process used to harden some steels). When that failed to produce the desired results Wilm gave up and went sailing on the Havel River.

When he returned on Monday morning, he was amazed to find that the alloy had hardened by a factor of at least three. Simple 'ageing' at room temperature had done the trick. Wilm experimented some more and found that it worked every time. In 1903 he applied for the patent and then licensed the idea to the firm of Dürener Metallwerke, who marketed it as 'duraluminium'. One of the first customers was the Zeppelin company. When war broke out British and American metallurgists 'reverse-engineered' the alloy for their own industries. But without Wilm's accidental discovery, the giant rigid airships might never have flown.

Alfred Wilm received little credit and even less money for his creation. After the war his patent was hijacked by anyone who could make money from it. For example, the 'airship catalogue' for 1920–21 of the British company Vickers boasts that, 'All rigid airships built for HM Navy are constructed of Vickers' special alloy "Duraluminium"'. In 1919 a disillusioned Alfred Wilm abandoned metallurgy and took to farming, which occupied him until his death in 1937.

But it was the combination of duraluminium, hydrogen gas and goldbeaters' skins that enabled Ferdinand von Zeppelin to realise his dreams, first by flying civilian passengers around Germany for a few years before the outbreak of hostilities in 1914 and then building the airships that flew over the North Sea to bomb cities on the east coast of Britain. They were all kept in the air by highly inflammable hydrogen. (Only the Americans ever flew rigid dirigibles inflated by the inert gas helium. It was a product they regarded as a strategic asset and kept to themselves.)

One of the most frustrating aspects of the story of the R34 is that relatively little information remains about its creation. Many of the records of William Beardmore & Co. were destroyed during the blitz on Clydebank in May 1941. Fortunately, the National Museums of Scotland have a set of Beardmore's colour-coded working drawings (plans, elevations and cross-sections) of the R34. Dated 27 October 1917 and marked 'Secret and Confidential', they offer a fascinating glimpse into the sheer engineering complexity of the great ship.

And the January 1920 issue of the lively company journal, *Beardmore News,* carries an article by Charles V. Wallace, one of the firm's engineers, who was plainly involved in building the airship in some senior capacity. His article is entitled 'A Giant Airship in the Making', and offers some real insights into the construction of the R34.

Wallace begins by claiming that everyone's priority was to keep the aircraft as light as possible. 'Not only in the designing office, where all the main scantlings (i.e. dimensions, sizes) are settled, but in the workshops and erection sheds, every worker, however unimportant his bit may be, must keep the great ideal of saving weight ever in front of him.' He describes in some detail two more or less simultaneous operations – the metal work and the gas bags

The process began with engineering the 'hundreds of thousands' of bracing pieces that made up the triangular and box-like girders which were then taken to the girder shop where they were 'assembled inside wooden formers', riveted up, cut to length and then their ends fitted with angle pieces 'ready to be assembled into the main frame rings'. Meanwhile, a jig in the polygonal shape of the frame ring was laid down on the floor of the airship shed into which the girders were 'choked' into position, riveted and then spliced with metal wires which were carefully tensioned.

When the ring (about 80 feet in diameter) was complete it was hoisted upright by an overhead gantry crane which moved along the roof of the shed. 'This operation is a very ticklish one,' Wallace writes, 'as the frame is not stiff enough to lift as one would a cycle wheel, although it is very similar in general style and appearance. It is indeed an important day in an airship building shed when a main frame is to be lifted, and all hands in the shed have to be prepared to lend their aid.'

The frame was then lifted into the air and lowered carefully into its place on a long timber-built cradle. It was held in that place from the roof gantry until the longitudinal girders had been inserted into the frame and then riveted. Once the frames were firmly attached to one another by the longitudinal girders thousands of feet of diagonal wiring, all of it carefully tensioned, was strung along the outer plane.

'This wiring is designed to meet the main stresses which arise in treating the whole hull as a beam,' Wallace explains, 'and also to distribute the effect of the local loads applied to the ship, such as cars, engines etc.' It was onto that system of wires that the ship's outer cover was fitted. On the inside plane of the ship, about 9 inches away from the outer plane, another elaborate network of wire was fitted, this one to contain the giant gas bags.

From bow to stern (or nose to tail) the R34 measured 643 feet and along most of that ran a triangular corridor along which, in Wallace's words, were fitted 'all the working accessories of an airship': petrol tanks, water ballast bags, reserve feed water for engines, stores, mooring ropes, crew spaces.

The work of assembling the corridor can be proceeded with concurrently with the ship . . . The stabilising fins, fitted on all four sides of the ship at the tail end, and composed of the same class of girders as the hull frames, are rigidly braced together and to one another. They are built into the main ship girders and are securely attached to them, afterwards being covered in fabric, exactly the same as the main hull. At

the aftermost main frame there is fitted a cruciform girder
which takes the inner bearings of the rudders or elevators.

While all this engineering was proceeding, hundreds of workers,
most of them women, were putting together the 19 giant fabric
gas bags that held the R34 in the air. It was one of the most
unpleasant jobs of all. 'When the bag has been all joined up and
finally closed off,' Wallace explains 'it has always to be inflated
with hot air in the workshops, and carefully gone over and
defects remedied, especially in the region of the closing seams.'
Which, of course, meant that the women checking the seams
inside the gas bags had to breathe in hot air for hours on end.

When the managers were happy with the state of the gas
bags (each of which was around 80 feet in diameter and 30 feet
long) they were transported to the main shed and fitted into the
interior of the ship. They were not secured in any way, but held
in their position by the pressure of the hydrogen in the bags.
But organising this, according to Wallace, was a very tricky
business, 'owing to the delicacy of the material, they are
manhandled all the time, and the operation of fitting, it cannot
be rushed, but must be carried out with great care'.

Once in place the bags were inflated some more and the
airship allowed to float off its cradles. Then it was moored in
position (from the roof and the floor) for the control car and
engine cars to be attached to the structure by their suspension
tubes and wires. 'The cars themselves are built of the same
metal as the main hull, but more the style of small ships, being
fitted with rigid transverse frames, intercostal longitudinals to
carry engines, etc., and plated over.'

Wallace stresses the importance of the control car:

The foremost car of all is probably the most interesting to
the casual visitor, as it is the one from which all the
navigation of the ship is carried out. Here in one little space
the commander is able to control everything on the ship,
from the mooring ropes right in the bow to the rudders and

elevators in the stern. All his navigating instruments, steering gear, voice pipes, telephones, lights and controls are placed in this car.

Meanwhile, the engineers would be working in the hull and in the engine cars 'fitting and testing engines, petrol systems, oil systems and so on, whilst the controls for all the various items throughout the ship are being joined up and passed down to the control car, where they are arranged in groups as most convenient for the use of the commander'.

By then the outer covers had been stretched across the exterior of the hull in panels between the frames. 'They are laced together, as tautly as possible,' Wallace writes 'and the opening or gap covered with a sealing strip, thus presenting to the eye a completely smooth uniform surface. This, of course, is essential for a more important reason than appearance, viz., the resistance to the air during flight.'

Stretched over the aluminium girders, the outer cover consisted of thousands of square yards of finely woven Belfast linen, heavily waterproofed and painted with silvery-blue aluminium paint to reflect the sun's rays (to reduce the overheating which would expand the gas). It seems that the linen cover was so attractive that the fiancée of Captain Geoffrey Greenland, second officer on the R34, had her wedding trousseau made from some spare airship cover.

Charles V. Wallace concludes his piece with a description of the care taken with the completed airship as it floated above the ground inside its shed:

A careful watch is maintained during all the twenty-four hours that the ship does not become light or heavy. Additional precautions are taken to avoid any mishap owing to either of these conditions' occurring by lashing the ship both to the floor and roof of her building shed. In these lashings spring balances are introduced, so that the tendency to rise or fall may be remarked at once.

In the same issue of *Beardmore News* the editor offers this amiable if slightly sardonic comment on Charles Wallace's contribution: 'If anyone cannot construct another R34 out of a box of Meccano and a pair of silk stockings, then he must have failed to digest the learned treatise on Airship Construction by Mr Wallace.'

Wallace makes no mention of the R34's power plants, but it's known that Beardmore's had wanted Rolls Royce engines (probably V12 'Eagles') for the R34. However, none was available and the best they could get were five 250-horsepower 'Maori' aero engines built by the Sunbeam Motor Car Co. Ltd of Wolverhampton. Designed by the French engineer Louis Coatalen, the 'Maori' had 12 water-cooled cylinders arranged on a 'V' block with overhead valves. These engines were to prove unreliable and prone to breakdown. They were also underpowered. Their maximum speed of 2100 rpm proved to be theoretical rather than practical.

But the Sunbeams were not without merit. They were controlled through a reduction gear box which allowed them to be warmed up without turning the airship's two-bladed timber propellers, which was a big improvement for the safety of ground crews. The gearing also allowed the engines to be rested in flight and the two wing-car engines (one on the port side and one on the starboard side) had reversing gears which helped brake the ship in the air.

Beardmore's Contract No. 575, having been transformed into His Majesty's Airship R34, was 'walked out' of her shed at Inchinnan in December 1918. The Admiralty's 'contract price' for the build was £242,100. Beardmore's did the work for £215,950, a clear profit to the firm of £29,150. And as the keel was laid down in December 1917, she had taken just over a year to build.

In many ways the R34 was the German naval Zeppelin L33 reborn. It might be seen as a tribute to a brilliant if defeated enemy. The dimensions are impressive: 643 feet long, 92 feet high and the capacity to hold almost 2 million cubic feet of hydrogen. The R34 was almost three times the length of a Boeing 747 'jumbo' jet and much higher. The generation of airships to which the R34 belonged was far bigger than any aircraft flying in the twenty-first century.

The streamlined shape of the hull was almost identical to that of its German predecessor, although the cruciform tail section was very different from the box-like tail of the Zeppelin. Where the Zeppelin had six engines, the R34 had five. The engines were contained in separate semi-streamlined 'cars', one forward (just behind the control car), one on each wing and two engines aft, which drove a single propeller. As the R34 had been built for service in war there were defensive machine-gun positions both on top of the hull and at the stern, and the interior was fitted with storage racks for bombs.

The R34 first took to the air on Friday, 20 December 1918. The man at the controls was Major George Herbert Scott of the Royal Naval Air Service (RNAS), a stocky, balding 30-year-old who was to skipper the R34 in her days of glory. Scott was a marine engineer turned aviator who held one of the first airship licences issued by the RNAS. He'd spent most of the war patrolling the North Sea and the eastern Atlantic scouting in various rigid and non-rigid airships for German submarines and warships. The R34's first – and very short – flight was successful enough, although it was followed by a few weeks of teething troubles.

In February 1918, two months after the R34 first flew, Scott married 20-year-old Jessie Campbell, the daughter of Archie Campbell, the supervisor of Beardmore's airship interests, and one of the most skilled engineers in Scotland. The couple were married at the United Free Church in Clydebank. There's a story that when the new Mrs Scott was asked whether she was worried about the plan to fly the R34 across the Atlantic she replied with some aplomb: 'Why should I worry? My father built the ship and my husband commands it.'

George Scott and Archie Campbell had a lot in common.

Although they hailed from different ends of Britain (Catford and Clydebank respectively), both men had trained as marine engineers and both had worked for the shipbuilding firm of Sociedad Española De Construcción at Ferrol in northern Spain. Indeed, prior to joining Beardmore's (in 1912), Archie Campbell had been one of the Spanish firm's directors. And before that he'd worked in shipyards in Bilbao and Cadiz, where he'd supervised the building of the cruiser *Estremadura*. For his efforts Campbell was awarded the 'Cruz De Merito Naval' by the king of Spain.

The next time the R34 left the ground was on Friday, 14 March 1919. It was a fairly public event, with the Scottish press and some heavyweight officials in attendance, among them the Beardmore's director, Colonel J. Smith Park, the manager of the Inchinnan works, Jack Loudon, and Scott's father-in-law, Archie Campbell. The *Glasgow Herald* account of that day talks of 'the bow and the forward gondola glistening in the bright sunshine'. Once again Major George Herbert Scott was at the controls. His second-in-command was Captain Geoffrey Greenland, one-time skipper of the Royal Navy sloop *Bluebell*.

That bright spring day the R34 stayed in the air for more than five hours, flying down the Clyde as far as the rock known as Ailsa Craig and watched all the way down and back by thousands of excited Glaswegians and Clydesiders who had turned out to marvel at the biggest aircraft any of them had ever seen, or were ever likely to see again. The weather remained fine all day and Scott cautiously took the R34 up to 2,000 feet to see how she would perform. She performed handsomely.

Ten days later, on Monday, 24 March, the R34 was in the air for the third time, but on a much more ambitious flight. After taking off from Inchinnan at around 17.00 in an evening of miserable weather, Scott turned the R34's nose south-east and flew down to Newcastle, turned south-west again to Liverpool, then flew directly west across the Irish Sea to Dublin, by which time it was late in the evening.

The R34 seems to have loitered over the city for some hours because the correspondent for *The Times* reported that one of his contacts had seen the airship over south Dublin at 22.00 and that he himself had witnessed the huge shape cruising around the sky in the early hours of Tuesday, 25 March. *The Times* man went on to speculate that the airship might have been waiting for the weather to improve before heading northeast back to Scotland.

Whether or not that was the case, it was to prove a bad return journey. On the way back to Inchinnan over the island of Arran the ship's port elevator jammed, sending the R34 soaring up to an estimated 8,000 feet (a height that was off the ship's altimeter). As the ship climbed the engines stopped, some fuel tanks in the keel broke away from the 'slings' that held them in place and they toppled down through the outer cover into the sea. The R34 wasn't brought back under control until Corporal Bob Burgess, one of the ship's riggers, climbed outside and kicked the jammed elevator free.

But R34's problems did not end there. As she headed northeast she ran into some seriously cold weather which iced up the water in the ballast bags. When Scott tried to land at Inchinnan he found that he couldn't dump enough water to lighten the ship and, as a result, the R34 came down too fast and landed too heavily. The impact sent the control car crashing into the hull, snapping girders and wires, tearing the outer fabric and snapping the propellors on the wing engine cars. The damage was extensive and serious. It would be weeks before the R34 was in condition to take to the air again. The 24-hour, 600-mile testing flight had been a bit of a disaster.

It was bad luck and a major setback. The accident happened just as the race to be first to fly the Atlantic was becoming serious. Contestant after contestant was announcing plans to try for the £10,000 on offer from the *Daily Mail*. For the R34's transatlantic project the timing could hardly have been worse.

The landing accident at Inchinnan prompted one sad little ceremony. Before the R34 was 'walked out' in December 1918

some of the women who had worked on the construction of
the airship had pinned a soft toy in the shape of a black cat to
the R34's control car. It was intended to be the ship's lucky
mascot. On the evening of the unhappy landing Corporal Bob
Burgess quietly removed and burned the toy cat.

2

Atlantic Dreaming

Long before any flight across the Atlantic could ever have been realised, it was being imagined. And vividly, in the case of the American writer Edgar Allan Poe. In April 1844 Poe pulled off one of the great hoaxes in newspaper history when he persuaded the New York *Sun* to run a long story about a specially built balloon, the *Victoria*, manned by an eight-strong coterie of British gentlefolk, which had crossed the Atlantic from North Wales to Sullivan's Island in South Carolina.

Poe's impish genius was to make the leader of his imaginary expedition a real adventurer, the Irish balloonist (and virtuoso flautist) Thomas Monck Mason. In 1836 Monck Mason, along with Charles Green and Robert Hollond (later MP for Hastings) had impressed the world by flying a hot-air balloon from Vauxhall Gardens in London to Weilburg in Germany, a distance of almost 500 miles. Two years later, in 1838, Monck Mason wrote an account of the flight grandly entitled *Aeronautica*.

In Poe's tale – told as the diary of one of the imaginary aeronauts – the expedition had set out to fly from North Wales to Paris when their craft was gripped by an easterly gale and sent scudding out over the Atlantic. Monck Mason and his aeronauts decided not to struggle back to Europe but to surf the wind all the way to America. As they flew they passed over dozens of ships and 'many of the vessels fired signal guns; and in all we were saluted by loud cheers (which we heard with surprising distinctness) and the waving of caps and handkerchiefs'. Flying in an open basket at 25,000 feet was, it seems, no problem when one was well wrapped up in sensible tweed and woollens.

After a mere 75 hours in the air Poe had the intrepid

aeronauts touch down safely in North Carolina. 'The great problem is accomplished,' Poe's imaginary diarist writes. 'We have crossed the Atlantic – fairly and easily crossed it in a balloon! God be praised! Who shall say that anything is impossible hereafter?' The imaginary diary was then rushed by imaginary courier to New York where a gullible (or perhaps cynical) newspaper editor ran Poe's fable word for word. In fact, it was splashed all over the front page as 'The Atlantic Crossed in Three Days! Signal Triumph of Mr Monck Mason's Flying Machine!'

New Yorkers just couldn't get enough of the story. Crowds thronged the street outside the offices of the *Sun*. Newspaper vendors sold out in minutes. Copies started changing hands at inflated prices. Alarmed by the gullibility of New Yorkers and a bit scared by what he'd started, Edgar Allan Poe stood on the steps of the newspaper office shouting that the story was a hoax and he was the perpetrator. He was ignored. Nobody believed him. New Yorkers *wanted* to believe that the Atlantic Ocean had been flown. They preferred to believe that a bunch of air-going British toffs had conquered the mighty sea.

But eight years after Poe penned his fantasy a real, powered and steerable airship took to the air. It was the creation of the Frenchman Henri Giffard, who had made money by improving the safety of steam engines. In 1852 Giffard put together an airship which was held aloft by a bag filled with 88,000 cubic feet of hydrogen under which was slung a platform holding a 3-horsepower steam engine that drove a propeller. Steering was by a canvas sail. In this unlikely but genuinely historic device Giffard flew 17 miles from a Paris racecourse to Élancourt near Trappes at the stately pace of 6 miles per hour. There was no return flight because the wind was too strong.

Giffard's short, slow flight ushered in the airship era. It's an era that owes a lot to the ingenuity of the French. In 1878 another Frenchman, one Charles Ritchel, devised a small, hand-powered airship of which he managed to sell five copies. In 1883 yet another Frenchman, one Gaston Tissandier, a one-time army balloon pilot, took to the air in a lighter-than-air craft driven by a small electric motor.

A year later the French army engineer called Charles Renard produced an airship named *La France* which travelled more than 2 miles powered by an 8-horsepower electric motor designed by Arthur Constantin Krebs. In 1900 the baton passed to the Germans when the first Zeppelin left the ground. They were significant developments, every one, but none remotely capable of an Atlantic crossing. That remained the province of dreamers and fiction-writers.

One of these was one of the English-speaking world's favourite authors, Rudyard Kipling. In 1905 Kipling wrote a short story entitled 'With the Night Mail' in which he imagines the year 2000, when the skies over the Atlantic are criss-crossed by dozens of speedy airships. They are powered by 'HT&T assisted vacuo Fleury turbines' at the core of which is 'the vacuum where Fleury's Ray dances in violet-green bands and whirled turbillons of flame'. Fleury's Ray seems to be a *fin de siècle* equivalent of the 'warp drive' beloved by the creators of *Star Trek*.

In Kipling's tale (written in the present tense) the narrator is a journalist aboard one of the General Post Office's overnight mail-carriers to Quebec. The airship – 'Postal Packet 162' – is a veteran of the Atlantic run. The airships are kept on track through the skies by a system of ground-based but powerful marker lights, a bit like multi-coloured lighthouses, all regulated by the Aerial Board of Control. ' "Our planet's over-lighted, if anything" says Captain Hodgson [the ship's engineer], longing for the days when he could wander about the sky getting lost. "Now it's like driving down Piccadilly." '

In places, the writing is remarkable for a man who'd never flown. At one point in the story Kipling might be describing any night flight out of Heathrow when the central character talks of watching '. . . over-lighted London slide eastward as the gale grabs us. Then the first of the low winter clouds cuts off the view and darkens Middlesex. On the south edge of it I

see a postal packet's light ploughing through the white fleece
. . . "The Bombay Mail," says Captain Hodgson, and looks at
his watch. "She's forty minutes late." '

Two years after Kipling wrote his amiable opus, a much
darker imagining emerged from the pen of H.G. Wells in *The
War in the Air*, one of the early twentieth century's more
chilling works of science fiction. In it Wells imagines a fleet of
Imperial German airships flying more than 3,000 miles across
the Atlantic to strafe and bomb New York and massacre New
Yorkers. 'Down through the twilight sank five attacking airships,' Wells writes, 'one to the Navy Yard on East River, one
to City Hall, two over the great business buildings of Wall
Street and Lower Broadway, one to the Brooklyn Bridge . . .'

In Wells' story the New Yorkers were stunned by the
assault. 'People sat in darkness, sought counsel from telephones that were dumb. Then into the expectant hush came
a great crash and uproar, the breaking down of the Brooklyn
Bridge, the rifle fire from the Navy Yard, and the bursting of
bombs in Wall Street and the City Hall. New York as a whole
could do nothing, could understand nothing . . . In this manner the massacre of New York began. She was the first of the
great cities of the Scientific Age to suffer by the enormous
powers and grotesque limitations of aerial warfare.'

What made Wells' fiction all the more scary was that an
ambitious and expansionist Imperial Germany was already
working to develop the kind of airships that Wells so vividly
described. They were Zeppelins, named after Count Ferdinand
von Zeppelin, the aristocratic south German cavalry officer
whose brainchild they were. The advent of the Zeppelin had
taken lighter-than-air technology a serious step forward. They
were to be the blueprint and template for every successful
dirigible that was ever built, German, French, British or
American.

And while the first Zeppelin took to the air in July 1900, it
had been more than a quarter of a century in the making. In his
diary of 25 March 1874, Zeppelin had written: 'Basic idea:

large ship with rigid frames with longitudinals and rings divided into 18 separate compartments for accommodation of gas bags. Covered on outside with material. Form to simulate bird. Envisaging dynamic flight. Engine installation under the ship.' Which is the classic description of every rigid airship (or dirigible).

Aviation historians are still arguing over where Zeppelin got his idea. Some say that it came from the writing of English aviation theorist Sir George Caley (1773–1857). Others say that Zeppelin was inspired by a balloon jaunt he made in the USA in 1863, when he was the kaiser's observer of the American Civil War. Yet more say that he lifted the notion from a paper published in January 1874 by Heinrich von Stephan, the founder of the World Postal Union. Stephan's paper was entitled *World Postal Services and Airship Travel* (which may also have been the source of Rudyard Kipling's fable of 1905).

But wherever the idea of the rigid airship came from, it obsessed Ferdinand von Zeppelin and he worked tirelessly towards its realisation. He knew that it represented a large step forward for lighter-than-air aviation. By the year 1900 Zeppelin had managed to get a dirigible into the air and had built a factory at Friedrichshafen on the bank of the Bodensee (Lake Constance) near the border with Austria. From there Zeppelin's company, Luftschiffbau Zeppelin, turned out a string of experimental airships.

After many teething problems and some very nasty accidents, the Zeppelin company was put on a solid footing when the German military began ordering airships for the Kaiser's army and navy. By 1910 four civilian Zeppelins of the airline Deutsche Luftschiffahrts-Aktiengesellschaft (DELAG) were flying paying passengers around Germany, and without incident. Ferdinand von Zeppelin's great dream, it is said, was to build an airship big enough and powerful enough to fly passengers across the Atlantic.

By then, others were dreaming. One of them was Walter

Wellman, an American and a newspaper owner and journalist by trade, and an airborne adventurer by inclination. In his book *The Aerial Age* Wellman describes himself as 'Journalist, Explorer, Aeronaut', which is a fair enough description for a man who, in 1907 and again in 1909, set out to fly by balloon from Spitzbergen to the North Pole and back (a distance of about 2,000 miles). He failed, but remained undeterred.

In 1910 Wellman turned his mind to flying the Atlantic, having won backing for the venture from the *Chicago Record and Herald*, the *New York Times* and, oddly, the London *Daily Telegraph*. In a huge shed in Atlantic City, New Jersey, Wellman and his colourful photographer-turned-engineer Chester Melvin Vaniman put together a 228-foot long 'pressure' balloon (i.e. non-rigid) able to hold 345,000 cubic feet of hydrogen. Slung under the giant gas bag was a 'gondola' big enough to accommodate 1,500 gallons of petrol and a crew of six. In a patriotic moment Wellman named the craft *America*.

There's a grand Edwardian ring to Wellman's description of his creation:

> The airship *America* was a strange, a marvellous craft. To people who saw her for the first time she seemed mysterious, inexplicable, a nondescript, indeed, unlike anything else that was known for sailing upon the seas or running upon the land . . . Imagine a huge balloon-like reservoir 228 feet long – nearly a city block in New York – sharp pointed at one end, rounded at the other, 52 feet thick in all the central part . . . Massive, huge, still she is as graceful as a yacht under sail.

He goes on:

> This great reservoir is composed of cotton, silk and rubber. Where the diameter is greatest (and the upward push of the gas within most powerful) the fabric is three-ply, with three emulsions of rubber cementing the cloth together. The silk

and cotton give great strength to resist the outward pressure of the gas; the rubber emulsions hold the gas but with a small percentage of leakage . . . Splendidly tailored is this huge gas bag, all seams being wide lapped, sewn and gummed, and extra strips glued over to cover the needle holes and prevent the escape of the precious hydrogen.

Under his airship Wellman had slung what he called an 'equilibrator', some steel tanks at the end of the rope. Wellman's hope was that this odd apparatus trailing in the sea behind the ship would give it stability without slowing it down too much. At least one aviation pundit – Charles C. Turner – thought this a very bad idea. 'Unless the sea was calm as a millpond,' he wrote in the London *Observer* before the flight, 'the passage of the equilibrator through the water would be a succession of violent jerks calculated to play havoc with the machinery in the car.'

But Wellman was realist enough to know that the Atlantic presented some daunting problems. He must have voiced his misgivings to the *New York Times*, because in a piece published the week before the *America* set out the newspaper wrote that 'Neither Mr Wellman the Director nor Mr Vaniman the engineer expresses any great degree of confidence. The most they are willing to say is that in their opinion they have a reasonable chance of success, enough to warrant the effort.'

Walter Wellman and his crew began their attempt on the morning of Saturday, 15 October 1910, when they took off from the New Jersey shore. By 11 a.m. the following morning they'd flown over the Nantucket lightship, a distance of around 300 miles, and signalled back that all was well. A few hours later all stopped being well. The equilibrator had done its worst. By Sunday evening the *America* was sending radio messages that she was lost in the fog and had no idea where she was. By Monday the *America* was in the grip of a strong northerly wind and was drifting at a rate of knots towards the Caribbean.

Wellman's attempt on the Atlantic crossing came to an end on Tuesday, 18 October 1910, when the *America* ditched in the sea some 250 miles north-west of Bermuda. By sheer good luck the Royal Mail Steamer *Trent* happened to be in the area and, with some difficulty, rescued Wellman and his crew along with their cat 'Kiddo' from disaster. Once relieved of the weight of the crew and most of the petrol the *America* shot into the air and drifted off to the south, never to be seen again.

But Walter Wellman and his crew had travelled almost 1,000 miles (albeit in the wrong direction) and spent 69 hours in the air, a world record for the time. It was a good effort and much appreciated by the American public. When the RMS *Trent* berthed in New York a few days later the aviators received a heroes' welcome from a crowd of thousands. The balloon's grey tabby was installed in a gilt cage and exhibited in the window of Gimbel's department store for a while before finding a home with Walter Wellman's daughter.

The Atlantic may have defeated Walter Wellman but not Melvin Vaniman, who was even more intrepid than Wellman. Until he took to the air, Vaniman was renowned as the 'acrobatic photographer' who would take hair-raising risks to get the picture he wanted. He roamed all over the Pacific, from Hawaii to New Zealand, taking photographs with a panoramic camera he had designed himself. He caught the aviation bug while taking photographs of Sydney and the surrounding area from a hot-air balloon that he'd imported from the USA. Most of Vaniman's pictures are now in the collection of the State Library of New South Wales.

In 1912 Vaniman persuaded financier Frank Siberling and the Goodyear Tires & Rubber Co. to finance and build a new pressure balloon for another assault on the Atlantic. On Tuesday, 2 July 1912, Vaniman's new airship, the *Akron* (called after the town in which she was built), rose into the air over Atlantic City watched by a crowd of thousands. On board were Vaniman and a crew of four. As the airship reached a height of just under 2,000 feet the hydrogen in

the *Akron*'s envelope exploded into flames and the ship
crashed down to Brigantine Beach ('like a blazing meteor'
in the words of one local newspaper). All five men on board
were killed.

Vaniman may have been too ingenious by half. He had
devised a fuel system whereby, at the pull of a lever, the engines
could switch from consuming petrol to burning hydrogen from
the gas bag (a technique that the German designers were to
perfect 20 years later). But the two engines on the *Akron* were
not fitted with the safety device later known as a 'backfire
flame arrester' and the result was explosion – and the first
known fatalities of transatlantic aviation. They were Melvin
Vaniman, his younger brother Calvin, Fred Elmer, George
Boultin and Walter Gest.

But by then the conviction that the Atlantic could be crossed
by air had taken hold. There was kudos to be won and,
perhaps, money to be made. In September 1913 a committee
assembled in London chaired by Lord Montagu of Beaulieu.
Its aim was to fund a giant airship to be called *Britannia* which
would tackle the Atlantic. Typically for the time, the committee was stuffed with the aristocracy and gentry: Lord Pembroke, Lord Ruthven, Sir Albert Hime, Sir Thomas Holdich,
with letters of support from the Duke of Connaught, Lord
Roberts and the Duke of Argyll. The secretary was Captain
Hawtrey Cox, late of the 6th (Inniskilling) Dragoons.

His Majesty's Government, however, was not at all keen on
the design being proposed by the Britannia Airship Committee.
As airships were the province of the Admiralty, it was the
Admiralty which gave the *Britannia* project the thumbs down.
Which prompted Lord Montagu to resign in a huff and set
about generating a wave of indignation in high places. In
November 1913 the Admiralty backed down slightly and said
they would 'accept' the airship but only if their experts
approved the design and if the airship had any 'actual naval
value' (a get-out clause if ever there was one).

In the end it came to nothing. The Britannia Airship Committee found it impossible to raise enough money. Having set out to raise a starter fund of £15,000, by February 1914, all they could muster was a paltry £1,900, nearly half of which came from the wireless manufacturer Marconi. British industry and finance, it seemed, were just not interested in the idea of funding an airship that might close the gap between North America and Britain. By August that year most of Europe was at war and the whole project was forgotten.

It's an old saw but it's true: there's nothing like war for improving technology. In the four years between August 1914 and November 1918, aviation – both the lighter-than-air and heavier-than-air varieties – improved in leaps and bounds. This is especially true of aeroplanes. What had been a small industry producing tiny structures of timber and canvas powered by lightweight, underpowered motors, by the year 1918 was producing big four-engined biplanes and triplanes that were bombing one another's cities and killing and scaring one another's citizens.

The British were quick to spot the threat posed by the Zeppelin. One of the Royal Flying Corps' earliest aerial attacks was in October 1914 against the airship sheds at Düsseldorf and Cologne. At Cologne they scored a direct hit on a Zeppelin and the flames shot 500 feet into the sky. In November 1914 the RFC struck again when three small Avro bombers made an extraordinarily daring 125-mile flight from Belmont in central France across southern Germany to make a low-level attack on the Zeppelin company's factory, workshops and headquarters at Friedrichshafen. One of the aircraft (piloted by squadron commander E.F. Briggs) was shot down by small-arms fire.

The damage to the Freidrichshafen works was soon repaired, but it forced the Germans to throw a serious number of resources at defending the Zeppelin factory and workshops. Which prompted the author of the official account of the war in the air to write, 'All the men and material required for these additional defences were kept out of the war by the four hours' adventure of three British pilots'. The Swiss later complained that the British aircraft had violated Swiss airspace.

But while British (and French) aeroplanes proved more than equal to their German counterparts, the Allies could never rival the quality of the airships that were being produced by the Zeppelin company and its smaller rival, Schütte-Lanz. Most were built for the German navy's Airship Division, commanded by Korvetten Kapitän Peter Strasser, an advocate of air power as a way of demoralising an enemy. A slim, intense-looking man with a neat goatee beard, Strasser never wavered in his belief that airships could do what the kaiser's armies couldn't – bring the Allies to their knees. Maybe he was familiar with Wells's fable of an aerial assault by Imperial Germany on the USA.

On 10 August 1916 Strasser wrote to Vizeadmiral Reinhard Scheer, the commander of the German High Seas Fleet, 'The performance of the big airships has reinforced my conviction that England can be overcome by means of airships inasmuch as the country will be deprived of the means of existence through increasingly extensive destruction of cities, factory complexes, dockyards, harbour works with war and merchant ships lying therein, railroads etc. . . . '

He then went on to plead for more and bigger airships for the German navy. To an extent, Strasser got his way, and the Germans spent huge amounts of money on airships (far too much, in the opinion of the German army). By 1916 the German navy's 'super Zeppelins', 600 feet long and carrying crews of 20 or more, were raiding along the east coast of Britain from the Firth of Forth down to the Channel. Their bombs did (relatively) little damage and caused (relatively) few casualties but their sheer size and apparent invulnerability did generate serious unease among the British public.

But in fact, the German airships were far from invulnerable. The Zeppelins were slow and hard to manoeuvre, and their enormous bulk made them easy targets for nimble British aeroplanes. Once British pilots began arming their machine

guns with a regulation mixture of tracer, explosive and incendiary bullets the Zeppelins became airborne death traps.
All that was required to reduce a Zeppelin to a mass of flaming
hydrogen was for a couple of incendiary rounds to pierce one
of the gas bags. By late 1915 the British air defences were
taking their toll of the kaiser's airships.

One German airship skipper later described the explosive/
incendiary mixture in British machine guns as 'an invention of
the devil'. Another German airshipman declared: 'Had we
caught the man who invented that bullet during the war we
should gladly have burned him on the great flying ground at
Ahlhorn in a stream of blazing hydrogen.' The British, of
course, took another view. After the war Messrs Brock,
Pomeroy and Buckingham, the men who devised the bullets
that plagued the kaiser's airships, were rewarded (with cash)
by a grateful government. But by then Commander Frank
Arthur Brock was dead, killed in April 1918 during the Royal
Navy's assault on the harbour at Zeebrugge.

The vulnerability of airships was one of the reasons why the
British never used theirs on combat missions. Their job was
reconnaissance, patrolling out over the North Sea and the
Atlantic scouting for German warships and submarines. They
would attack a ship with bombs if the opportunity ever arose
(although only one British airship – the R29 – was ever
credited with sinking a submarine), but usually an airship's
task was to find enemy ships and warn the fleet. Britain's
modest collection of airships, rigid and non-rigid, was seen as
part of the Home Fleet and was manned by men from the
Royal Naval Air Service (RNAS).

There was, however, one thing that the airship could do that
no aeroplane could, and that was stay in the air for days at a
time. The airship's potential for long-range flight was vividly
demonstrated (to the German military, at least) in November
1917 when Zeppelin L59 made an epic flight from central
Europe down to Khartoum and back again, non-stop. It was a

vain attempt to re-arm and re-equip the small German force
that was facing a much bigger British force in Africa. In fact,
the German commander, General Paul von Lettow-Vorbeck,
didn't need much help: he was leading the floundering British
army in East Africa a merry dance.

But communications were poor and the German high command was seriously worried. The airship chosen for the job
was one of the German giants. The L59 was 743 feet long, with
a gas capacity of more than 2 million cubic feet and powered
by five Maybach engines which could produce an average
speed of 64 mph. On paper, at least, the L59 had a range of
around 9,000 miles. At the beginning of November 1917 the
L59 was ferried down to Yamboli in Bulgaria, where she was
tested then loaded up with fuel and ordnance. On Wednesday,
21 November 1917, under the command of Kapitänleutnant
Ludwig Bockholt, the L59 set out on her mission to aid the
German troops in Africa.

In a way, it was a suicide mission, at least so far as the
airship itself was concerned. The L59 was not expected to
return. Not only was the ship's cargo of weapons and ammunition to be deployed by the German troops, but also the ship
herself. The L59 was to be cannibalised, her outer cover to be
used as tents, her aluminium girders to make field hospitals
and radio masts and what was left of the petrol to fuel the
trucks. Even the keel of the ship had been clad with leather to
be used for making new boots or repairing old ones. Ludwig
Bockholt and his crew of naval aviators were to join their
countrymen in their hit-and-run jungle war.

By the standards of the day, the L59's flight was remarkable.
On the way over the Mediterranean electric storms put the
airship's radio out of action and the next day she had to dump
some of her cargo over the side to maintain height. But the L59
flew on and by Friday, 23 November 1917, was over the
Sudan when her radio came back to life – only to receive the
order to abort the flight and return to Bulgaria. When the
order came the L59 was 200 or so miles west of Khartoum and

within striking distance of where the German troops were thought to be.

But by that time the German high command had received word from their own Colonial Office that General von Lettow-Vorbeck's force had been overrun by the British (a story that may have been put about by British intelligence). There was no point in risking the airship. Without stopping for fuel, gas or water, the L59 flew back to Bulgaria over Syria and Turkey and landed in Yamboli on Sunday, 25 November 1917, having travelled around 4,200 miles and been in the air for more than four days. It was a feat of aviation that has been obscured by the smoke of war. The L59 came to grief a few months later when she was shot down near Malta, probably by 'friendly fire' from a German U-boat.

The British took the Zeppelin threat seriously right to the end. In July 1918 a task force of warships, led by the aircraft carrier HMS *Furious*, sailed out of the Firth of Forth and steamed across the North Sea to attack the airship base at Tondern in Schleswig-Holstein on the border with Denmark. When the group's seven Sopwith Camels swooped on the Tondern base they destroyed Zeppelins L54 and L60 along with the huge shed in which they were being serviced.

The German navy's airship assault on Britain came to a Wagnerian end on Monday, 5 August 1918, when Korvettenkapitän Peter Strasser himself, in Zeppelin L70, led a fleet of 12 airships across the North Sea in an effort to do what damage they could. It was probably something of a final charge against the enemy. Strasser was an intelligent and well-connected officer. He must have known that his Zeppelin campaign had failed and that Germany's defeat was not far off.

The L70 crossed the Norfolk coast just after 22.00, flying at a height of around 20,000 feet, which, the Germans knew, was too high for most British interceptors. And it was, but not for the twin-seat DH4 fighter bomber that attacked the L70 at

22.20 that summer night. The DH4 was piloted by Edgar Cadbury (of the famous chocolate family) and a Scots-Canadian gunner called Robert Leckie. As the DH4 closed with the L70 Leckie raked the hull of the airship with his Lewis gun using the now-standard mixture of explosive and incendiary bullets. Within minutes the L70 was ablaze from end to end and spiralling down to the sea.

Sixty years later, in his book *Airship Wreck*, the British writer Len Deighton tried to imagine the ruin of the L70. 'In the gathering darkness, other British aviators, far below and still climbing, were awestruck by the disintegrating tangle of gaseous flames that fell past them through the cloud layers, to make great pools of yellow sky.' Edgar Cadbury who flew the DH4 that did the damage was more prosaic. 'The loss of the L70 must have been a great shock and should have clearly demonstrated the hopelessness of sending Zeppelins to attack England.'

Cadbury was right. The loss of the L70 sent a shock through the German navy. Peter Strasser had been the driving force behind the Zeppelin assault on Britain. To make matters worse for the German navy, Strasser's body was recovered from the sea with secret documents in the pockets of his uniform. The other Zeppelins on that raid that night were harassed by British fighters and anti-aircraft fire and did little damage before returning to Germany. It was the last Zeppelin raid on Britain. The cost had become too high.

When the war in Europe came to an end in November 1918 the Zeppelin company was down, but far from out. By then the firm was being run by Dr Hugo Eckener, who took over when Count Zeppelin died in 1917. As Eckener saw it, he had two great assets in the L72 and the L73 (sister ships of the one that Peter Strasser had gone down with). Both airships had been built to fly very long range, with a view to mounting a possible bombing raid on New York. In Eckener's opinion there was no finer way to begin recovering Germany's prestige in the eyes of the post-war world than to use L72 and L73 to make the first-ever flights across the Atlantic.

In the early months of 1919 a strategy was hatched at Zeppelin headquarters whereby the two German airships would set out together across the Atlantic. The plan was for the L72 to make its way to New York, circle the city without landing and then fly back to Germany while the L73 would fly across the United States, preferably from city to city, and come down somewhere on the Pacific coast. Whether the L73 would ever return to Germany didn't matter. The publicity and the prestige were the point of the exercise.

However, when Eckener sought the go-ahead from the German government in Berlin he was turned down. Most historians believe that the scheme fell foul of the British General Edward Masterman, head of the aviation arm of the Inter-Allied Control Commission. Masterman was not about to allow the defeated Germans to pull off a transatlantic stunt ahead of the victorious British. That was certainly the opinion of Hans von Schiller, the L72's executive officer. Years later Schiller claimed that the British stopped the Zeppelins from flying the Atlantic '. . . ostensibly because they posed a military threat, but in reality because they feared Germany might win the peace with a global airline service operated with Zeppelins'.

3

1919: The Year of Flying Dangerously

The year 1919 might deserve the title 'the year of flying dangerously'. It was certainly the year that hundreds of people – pilots, engineers, mechanics, aircraft builders, newspapers – decided that the time had come to fly the Atlantic. The war was over, there were aeroplanes all over Europe and North America looking for something to do and the London *Daily Mail* was still offering £10,000 to the crew of the first aeroplane to fly non-stop from America to Europe (or vice versa). The prize had stood since 1910 but in the years of worldwide bloodletting the Atlantic had gone unchallenged and the prize money untouched.

And while £10,000 was a formidable sum in 1919 it was not, perhaps, the real prize. The real prize was the fame, prestige, worldwide publicity and possible new business that would attach to the winner. Which is why just about every serious aircraft manufacturer in Britain – Sopwith, the Short Brothers, Handley-Page, Martynside, Vickers – were all eager to find and fund pilots and navigators who were prepared to risk their necks trying to fly aeroplanes from one continent to another. Interestingly, the only really serious American contenders were the US Navy and the company run by Glen Curtiss (The Curtiss Aeroplane and Motor Company).

In its way, the transatlantic air race of 1919 was a bit like twenty-first-century Formula One motor racing, whereby the cars are supported by the big automobile makers. The sport is rich in prize money, certainly, but that's not why companies like Ferrari and Renault spend vast sums on unlikely looking machines that go round and round a track at high speed. Their reward is seeing their brand names appearing on television and in newspapers worldwide. And in learning from the fast-track technology in order to improve the performance of cars for the mass market.

At one point it seemed that the coveted Atlantic prize money might be won by a woman. Towards the end of December 1918 a story appeared in the American press that the famous American aviatrix Katherine Stinson was to make an attempt to fly back to the USA from Europe, where she had been serving as a Red Cross ambulance driver (having been turned down as a combat pilot). How serious Stinson's proposal was, and who was backing her, is far from clear from the reports.

Stinson was an interesting figure. A skilled pilot, she was the fourth woman in the USA to hold a licence, the first woman to loop the loop and the first woman trusted by the US postal service to fly mail around the country. Stinson was as brave and as competent as any of her male counterparts. But early in 1919 she was struck down in the great post-war influenza epidemic, then developed the tuberculosis that put an end to her flying career. (She later became an architect and the wife of a judge. She died in 1977.)

By the time Stinson was out of the game a reasonably serious transatlantic project had been worked out by the Swedish-born aviator Hugo Sundstedt, with his own design for a huge, twin-winged, twin-engined sea plane designed to hold a crew of two pilots and two mechanics. The project – known as *Sunrise* – was backed by the Norwegian financier Christopher Hannevig.

The plan was for Sundstedt and his co-pilot Paul Micelli to fly the aircraft from New Jersey up to St John's in Newfoundland, refuel and then fly from St John's to Ireland. Or, if conditions allowed, all the way to London, there to pick up the £10,000 promised by the *Daily Mail*. In the event the money was safe for another few months. Sundstedt's seaplane was damaged at its berth in New Jersey and never flew. The Nordic challenge was over. Hugo Sundstedt – only the second Swede to fly – died in New York in 1966.

Then in May 1919 a much more serious contender entered

the field – the US Navy. They took up the Atlantic challenge with the non-rigid airship C5, built by the Goodyear Tires & Rubber Co. at Akron in Ohio. The Americans had high hopes for the C5, although by German and British standards she was small and almost certainly underpowered. Just over 190 feet long, the C5 floated on 180,000 cubic feet of hydrogen and was powered by two 125-horsepower Hispano-Suiza engines.

The crew of four sat in a 40-foot-long control car in open cockpits, one behind the other. The ship was captained by Lieutenant Commander E.W. Coil. The plan was for the C5 to take the shortest route from the east coast of Newfoundland to the west coast of Ireland. Supporting the C5 was the USS *Chicago*, a 20-year-old, 4,500-ton cruiser (once captained by Alfred Mahan, the renowned naval strategist).

The C5 took to the air from the naval air station at Montauk Point at the eastern tip of Long Island on the morning of Tuesday, 14 May 1919, and 25 hours later landed at Quidi Vidi near St John's, Newfoundland, on the strip of land that had previously been one of the town's cricket pitches. The Americans were welcomed by the governor, Sir Alexander Harris, and a large crowd of locals. The C5 had flown 1,177 miles with no problems except for the slight bother of finding St John's in the fog. Everything looked set for the C5 to make a successful Atlantic crossing.

But, as was so often the case with airships, the wind had other ideas. The day after landing, the C5 was sitting on Quidi Vidi Lake when a fierce squall wrenched the airship from her moorings and sent her soaring into the air. There was nothing the ground crew could do to hold her down. The only injury was to Lieutenant Charles Little, the ship's executive officer, who broke his leg when he fell out of a cockpit as the C5 took off. The crew could only watch as the C5 disappeared over the horizon. The wreckage of the airship was eventually picked up 85 miles out to sea.

But the US Navy was not to be defeated. Heavier-than-air technology had already taken up the Atlantic challenge. It was in the shape of a trio of five-man Navy Curtiss NC flying boats (known affectionately as 'Nancies'). They were NC-1, NC-3 and NC-4 and they were crewed by a mixture of US Navy and US Naval Reserve airmen plus one man from the US Coastguard. There had been an NC-2 but she had been damaged by fire so was cannabalised for spare parts before the flight.

The three Nancies were never in the competition for the *Daily Mail*'s £10,000. That prize was strictly for a non-stop flight. The strategy of the Nancies was to cross the Atlantic in a series of five hops: New York to Halifax, Nova Scotia; Halifax to Trepassey Bay, Newfoundland; Trepassey Bay to Horta in the Azores; Horta to Lisbon, Portugal; Lisbon to Southampton, England. The distance between Newfoundland and the Azores may have been 700 miles less than the distance from Newfoundland to Ireland, but it was still a long and dangerous flight.

Designed by the company of Glen Curtiss (the aviator most feared by the Wright brothers), the NC was a surprisingly modern-looking machine. A biplane with 126-foot wings that sat on the top of the fuselage, it was powered by four Liberty 200-horsepower engines, one pushing and three pulling. There were three two-man cockpits: one at the very front of the fuselage for the navigator: one in front of the engines for the pilot and co-pilot; one behind the engines for the engineer and the radio operator. Behind them the tail section of the aeroplane was an elaborate box-like assembly of struts, wires and planes that held the rudder.

In fact, the Nancies had made their move before the airship C5 took to the air. The three aircraft took off from their base at Rockaway naval station on Queens, New York City on Friday, 8 May 1919, heading for Halifax. Before they reached Cape Cod the NC-4, commanded by its navigator Lieutenant-Commander Albert 'Putty' Read, began to suffer engine trouble and was forced to put in to Chatham, Massachusetts.

The NC-1 and NC-3 flew on and arrived at Halifax without incident. On Sunday, 10 May, NC-1 and NC-3 continued on their journey to Trepassey Bay in Newfoundland where they waited for Read and the NC-4, who did not arrive until Thursday, 14 May (one of the NC-4's engines had had to be replaced). It had taken the three Nancies the best part of a week to fly from New York to Newfoundland.

Two days later, on Saturday,16 May 1919, the three flying boats prepared for the longest and most arduous part of their trek. In the evening of Sunday, 17 May, they lifted off from Trepassey Bay and headed south-east towards the Azores. The three commanders were Patrick Bellinger (NC-1), Albert Read (NC-4) and John Towers (NC-3). Towers was also the overall commander of the transatlantic mission. A few years previously Towers had been the US naval attaché in London.

The US Navy's commitment was prodigious. No expense was spared. To ensure the three flying boats had a decent chance of getting across the Atlantic the navy had strung no fewer than 21 warships, most of them destroyers, in a long line about 50 miles apart from Newfoundland to the Azores. They were to act as safety ships, radio posts and navigational aids to the flyers. The uss *Greer* sat just off Mistaken Point at the north end of the line while the uss *Waters* lay south of the Azorean island of Corvo.

Everything went well enough until just before dawn on the Monday, 18 May, when the three aircraft flew into banks of heavy fog. The NC-3 ran a long way off course when the navigator mistook an American cruiser making her way back from Europe as one of the guide ships. The mistake cost the NC-3 a great deal of fuel, forcing the aircraft down onto the heavy sea where the impact of landing collapsed the struts supporting the centre engines. Unable to lift off, with no safety ship in sight, and the sea running high, John Towers and his crew were in a dangerous situation.

Much the same problem struck the NC-1, forcing Patrick Bellinger and his crew down into a sea racked by 12-foot high waves. Having landed safely, the NC-1 found the weather worsening and take-off impossible. The downed flyers spent a few nasty hours being hammered by wind and waves until, by sheer luck, they were spotted by the Greek steamer *Ionia* and rescued. The Greek seamen and the American airmen did their best to salvage the battered NC-1 but found the task beyond them and were forced to abandon the aircraft to the Atlantic.

Meanwhile Albert Read in the NC-4 was struggling to find a direction in fog that was so thick that it obscured one end of the aircraft from the other. Eventually the NC-4's radio operator picked up a signal from one of the guide ships which assured him that the aircraft was nearing the Azores. A lucky break in the fog revealed the island of Flores, which gave Read the bearing he needed to find his way to the harbour at Horta, on which the NC-4 landed around noon. The NC-4 was no sooner down than the fog descended to cover Horta completely.

By then the American authorities knew that the crew of the NC-1 were safe aboard the *Ionia* but no one had any idea what had happened to John Towers and the men of the NC-3. Towers had dumped his radio transmitter in an attempt to reduce weight, which meant that the NC-3 could receive messages but not transmit. But Towers reckoned that if the NC-3 could just stay afloat, the Atlantic currents would take them near enough the Azores for them to 'taxi' the rest of the way. Which is exactly what happened, and on Wednesday, 19 May, the NC-3 sailed into Ponta Delgada on the Azorean island of San Miguel. All three crews were safe.

At which point the Americans began to squabble. It seems that John Towers, the mission commander, wanted to climb aboard the NC-4 for the final two laps from the Azores to Portugal and from Portugal to England. Which meant that one of the NC-4's crew would have had to be bumped off the flight. The US admiral in the Azores approved Towers' suggestion but Navy Secretary Josephus Daniels turned it down on the grounds that 'Commander Read would necessarily be deprived of the chief honours if Commander Towers accompanied him'. So the crew of the NC-4 were allowed to proceed intact.

After a week on the Azores, on Tuesday, 27 May, the NC-4 roared across the harbour of Ponta Delgada and headed east over the line of American warships that were now strung out between the Azores and Lisbon. The flight was uneventful and at 20.00 that evening the NC-4 touched down on the Tagus estuary at Lisbon. Lieutenant-Commander Albert 'Putty' Read and the crew of the NC-4 had become the first men to fly from North America to Europe, albeit in five stages. They had won the transatlantic race but had no claim on the £10,000 offered by the *Daily Mail*. That was for the first non-stop flight. The money was still there to be won. And the first non-stop flight had still to be achieved.

After two days of being wined, dined and bemedalled by the Portuguese the NC-4 was off again first to Ferrol in Spain (to make a few repairs) and then across the Bay of Biscay and the English Channel to Plymouth on the south coast of England, from where the Pilgrim Fathers had embarked for America in September 1620. The NC-4 landed in the waters of Plymouth Sound in the early evening of Saturday, 31 May, escorted in by three flying boats from the fledgling Royal Air Force.

When they stepped ashore the bemused Americans found themselves the heroes of the hour. They were met by cheering crowds, a brass band and a speech from the Mayor of Plymouth followed by lunch. A week or so later they were treated to a much grander meal at the House of Commons, with an assortment of British dignitaries including Edward, the Prince of Wales. The US government and press were delighted by the rousing reception the American flyers received in Britain.

Britain's aviators may have been pipped at the post, but the game was still on. The £10,000 on offer from the *Daily Mail* was still to be won. And there were a number of teams determined to win it. One was equipped with a flying boat designed and built by Short Brothers and crewed by Major J.C.P. Wood (pilot) and Captain C.C. Wylie (navigator). The Wood/Wylie team decided to make the crossing from east to west. Their plan was to fly from London across to the west coast of Ireland, refuel, and then make the attempt from there, convinced that their biplane, with its three Rolls Royce engines, had the power and the range to do the business.

In the event, they never got across the Irish Sea. On 20 April the Wood and Wylie flying boat took off from Eastchurch in Kent, made its way across the south of England and the south of Wales and then came unstuck over the Irish Sea when their engines cut out. Wood managed to turn the aeroplane round and glide back towards land and ditch in the sea a short distance from the Anglesey coast. Wood and Wylie were rescued by launch and their flying boat was later towed ashore. But their transatlantic attempt was over.

A much more promising attempt was made the following month by the Australian test pilot Harry Hawker and his Scots navigator, Lieutenant-Commander Mackenzie Grieve RN. Hawker and Grieve had known each other since the war, when they had carried out experiments landing aeroplanes on the decks of ships. In 1919 Hawker was working as a pilot for Sopwith, and it was in an adapted Sopwith B1 biplane, suitably named *Atlantic*, that Hawker and Grieve took off from an airfield near St John's, Newfoundland at 15.48 on the afternoon of Sunday, 18 May 1919.

Getting to that point had been a fairly major operation. After being put together (and fitted with a safety boat in the rear section of the fuselage) the Sopwith had been taken apart, crated up, then shipped across the Atlantic in the hold of the ss *Digby*. The crates were put ashore at Placentia Bay at the end of March, transferred to a railway train which stopped short of St John's and then hauled by horse wagons along muddy roads to St John's. There the Sopwith was reassembled in a big barn under the eyes of Hawker and Grieve.

Also in St John's in the spring of 1919 was a team led by an old rival of Hawker's, one Freddie Raynham. But the two flyers were friendly enough and agreed to give one another two hours' notice of when the other was taking off. They also agreed that what was at stake was the 'prestige of British aviation' and that neither of them was to take silly risks. Both would wait until the weather looked favourable for the trans-atlantic attempt. As Hawker told Raynham, his plan was to 'fly the Atlantic, not fall into it'.

But Newfoundland is not known for its balmy weather, and April and May of 1919 proved particularly nasty, beset with days of fog, high winds, rain and snow. Both Hawker and Raynham managed to get in one or two test flights but every time it looked as if there might be a chance to go for the crossing the weather would close in and delay things even further.

Hawker took the opportunity to make a few changes to the Sopwith. The four-bladed propeller was changed for a lighter, two-bladed model, and skid rails were fitted under the fuselage to compensate for the landing gear, which Hawker planned to jettison as soon as he took off. He argued that the big wheels on the undercarriage would create wind resistance that would both slow the aircraft down and use up fuel. Finally, on the afternoon of Sunday, 18 May, Hawker sent the word to Raynham that he and Mackenzie Grieve had decided to go.

Shortly after taking to the air from the Mount Pearl airfield 5 miles west of St John's, Hawker released the Sopwith's undercarriage into the sea (it was later recovered) and headed east over the Atlantic. For hours the weather held good. In Hawker's own words 'we were comfortably jogging along at about 10,000 feet with nothing much in the way of cloud between us and the vault of heaven'. That changed steadily through the night and by 06.00 on Monday, 19 May, the flyers found themselves 'confronted with a bank of black clouds as solid as a range of mountains, and rearing themselves up in fantastic menacing formations'.

To make matters very much worse, their Rolls Royce 'Eagle' engine began to falter as the engine temperature soared. Desperately Hawker and Grieve tried to find a way round the clouds ahead, knowing that their Sopwith didn't have the power to climb over them. After a few hours' searching in vain they decided they would have to ditch into the sea, if possible somewhere near a ship. After another two hours, and by a stroke of extraordinary luck, they spotted the Danish cargo steamer *Mary* steaming east towards Europe. Hawker circled the ship firing flares until he was sure that the crew had seen them and then crash-landed in the sea about a mile ahead.

Once down, and kept fairly dry in their rubberised safety suits, the airmen broke out the safety-boat section of the fuselage, climbed into it and waited for the crew of the *Mary*. It took the ship's longboat almost two hours to reach the downed aircraft and rescue the fliers. Once on board the *Mary* they discussed with Captain Duhn, the Danish skipper, whether or not the Sopwith could be hauled aboard. In the end they decided it was impossible and abandoned the *Atlantic* to the Atlantic. (Remarkably, the aeroplane stayed afloat and a few days later it was salvaged by an American steamer which put the wreckage ashore at Falmouth in Cornwall.)

But by then Hawker and Grieve had lost all contact with the world and the *Mary* had no radio. Within a few days everyone in Britain believed that the men had perished. On Saturday, 24 May, five days after the Sopwith had crashed, Hawker's wife Muriel received a telegram from King George V. It read: 'The King, fearing the worst must now be realised regarding the fate of your husband, wishes to express his deep sympathy and that of the Queen in your sudden and tragic sorrow. His Majesty feels the nation lost one of its most able and daring pilots who sacrificed his life for the fame and honour of British flying.'

It wasn't until the *Mary* was off the Butt of Lewis in the Hebrides that Captain Duhn was able to signal by way of flags that Hawker and Grieve were alive and well. The information was duly radioed to the authorities and at the mouth of Loch Erribol on the north coast of Scotland the two aviators were transferred to the destroyer HMS *Woolston*, which whisked them up to HMS *Revenge* in Scapa Flow. From there they were shipped down to Thurso in Caithness to a civic welcome, lunch with Sir John Sinclair, and the start of the long train journey to

London, a heroes' welcome and a £5,000 consolation prize from the *Daily Mail*.

Bizarrely, the battered remains of the Sopwith *Atlantic* were transported from Falmouth to London, where they were hoisted onto the roof of Selfridges department store in Oxford Street for the citizenry to admire. Photographs of the time show a heap of tangled wreckage perched perilously close to the edge of the roof and held in place by a system of metal cables. It was a very odd flourish of publicity for a brave but failed venture.

Meanwhile Muriel Hawker had received the good news of her husband's survival via a telephone call from the *Daily Mirror*, which was followed by a second telegram from the king stating that 'The king rejoices with you, and the Nation, on the happy rescue of your gallant husband. He trusts that he may be long spared to you.' (He wasn't: Harry Hawker was killed in July 1921 when he unaccountably crashed his Nieuport Goshawk on his way to an aeroplane derby.)

An hour after Hawker and Mackenzie Grieve had taken off from St John's they were followed into the air by Freddie Raynham and his navigator in their specially built Martinsyde biplane. But Raynham managed to rise only 200 feet into the air from the Quidi Vidi airfield when the Martinsyde suddenly lost height, hit a piece of soft ground and flipped over. Raynham and Captain C.W.F. Morgan walked away from the crash with nothing but cuts and bruises, but in the words of one correspondent 'Their disappointment is inexpressible'. Raynham was to try again at the beginning of July, only to crash on take-off for the second time, making him the unluckiest of all the heavier-than-air contestants.

Meanwhile, St John's had seen the arrival of two new teams of British fliers and their crates of aircraft parts. The contents of one set of crates were reassembled into a Handley-Page V/1500 'Berlin Bomber' commanded by Vice-Admiral Mark Kerr, who planned to navigate the aeroplane. It would be piloted by Major Herbert Brackley, late of the Royal Flying

Corps. The other team, which arrived slightly later, was that of Captain John Alcock (pilot) and Lieutenant Arthur Whitten Brown (navigator), who were making their attempt in an adapted Vickers Vimy bomber. Both Alcock and Brown had been prisoners of war, Alcock in Turkey, Brown in Germany.

It's possible that Mark Kerr's aircraft had been broken down into too many pieces in order to ship it across the Atlantic. It arrived in no fewer than 150 crates and the task of assembling it, testing it and sorting out the snags took so long that Alcock and Brown got into the air first. The pair flew out of Lester's Field near St John's at 16.13 on Saturday, 14 June 1919, having just managed to clear some trees. It was the start of a desperately dangerous flight through fog and turbulence in which one of their engines almost caught fire, the batteries that heated their flying suits failed and they twice almost flew headlong into the sea.

'We scarcely saw the sun, or the moon, or the stars,' Alcock wrote later. 'For hours we saw none of them. The fog was very dense and at times we had to descend to within 300 feet of the sea. For four hours the machine was covered in a sheet of ice, caused by frozen sleet; at another time the sleet was so dense that my speed indicator did not work.' Four times Whitten Brown climbed out onto the wing to hack ice away from the air inlets and the fuel inspection windows.

Their hair-raising venture came to an end at 08.40 on Sunday, 15 June, when their Vickers Vimy crash-landed in a bog called Derrygimla Moor near the town of Clifden in County Galway on the west coast of Ireland. The first non-stop flight across the Atlantic had been achieved. Alcock and Whitten Brown had flown 1,890 miles between Newfoundland and Ireland in 16 hours 12 minutes. The *Daily Mail* prize of £10,000 – which had stood since 1910 – had been won. John Alcock and Arthur Whitten Brown were the toast of Britain.

Within weeks, both men had been created Knights Commander of the British Empire. And within months, John

Alcock was dead. He was killed in northern France on Thursday, 18 December 1919, while ferrying a Vickers Viking aircraft to the Paris air show. It's believed that after John Alcock's death Arthur Whitten Brown never flew again, although he lived till 1948.

The success of Alcock and Brown was a blow to Mark Kerr and Herbert Brackley, who were still sitting in Newfoundland. There seemed little point in their Handley Page coming third in the west–east race after Albert Read's NC-4 and Alcock and Brown's Vickers Vimy. Kerr and Brackley decided to attempt an overland record by flying non-stop from Newfoundland to Atlantic City in New Jersey. They got as far as Parrsboro in Nova Scotia before they were forced down for repairs. Their Handley Page V/1500 was later hopelessly damaged while landing on the racecourse at Cleveland, Ohio, on its way to Chicago.

There were no more attempts in 1919 to fly the Atlantic from North America to Europe. It had been done twice, via a stopover in the Azores by the US Navy and non-stop by Alcock and Brown. The challenge now was the longer and much harder one of an east–west flight from Europe to America, against the prevailing wind and the endlessly shifty Atlantic weather. There was only one aircraft ready for that challenge and that was the R34.

4

Enter the Men from the Ministry

Just who thought it might be a good idea to send an airship across the Atlantic is not at all clear. The archive suggests that the notion came from somewhere within the Admiralty – probably from the Royal Naval Air Service – at the end of December 1918. Having spent around £242,000 building the R34, and having run out of war for it to fight, it made sense to find something useful for the airship to do. If that something could also demonstrate the money-making potential of airships while at the same time boosting Britain's prestige in the post-war world, then so much the better.

That appears to have been the Admiralty's thinking. In a brief summary of the R34 transatlantic project (written in March 1919) Brigadier-General Robert Marsland Groves, then Deputy Chief of the Air Staff (DCAS), claimed that the Admiralty wrote to the newly-formed Air Ministry on 30 December 1918 offering 'certain airships and stations' for the purposes of 'commercial demonstration'. Groves goes on 'The Admiralty offer included specifically the loan of Rigid Airship R34 for a flight to America'.

It was an interesting offer, and one that the Air Ministry could not refuse out of hand. It came at a time when the British government (or parts of it anyway) was anxious to promote the country's post-war aviation industry. It was also a time when aviation experts across that world were arguing about aviation's future. Did it lie with small, fast, heavier-than-air aeroplanes? Or did it lie with the huge lighter-than-air craft like the R34 and its German ancestors? Airships or aeroplanes? Which was the future? No one was quite sure.

The answer may seem obvious now, but it was a genuine dilemma then. Aeroplanes may have been faster but they were small, cramped and had nothing like the range of an airship. No aeroplane in 1919 could possibly have carried a useful number of passengers across the Atlantic. On the other hand, airships were slow, cumbersome, vulnerable to wind and weather, hard to land and were held aloft by huge quantities of explosive hydrogen. Both technologies had their limitations. The solution, according to some, was to put together a system that used airships for long-haul flights and aeroplanes for short-haul work.

One of the most vocal advocates of an aeroplane/airship system was George Holt Thomas, now largely forgotten but one of the most influential aircraft manufacturers of his day (and the man who is said to have inspired Viscount Rothermere's *Daily Mail* to promote aviation). 'The airship is dependent for its short-stage connections on the aeroplane,' Holt Thomas wrote in his book *Aerial Transport*, 'therefore what you want . . . is an additional, or rather complementary scheme of aeroplane transport, which would "feed" the main airship lines . . . London to New York by air will certainly become a commercial proposition . . .'

Holt Thomas' opinions carried some weight with the military. During the hostilities his factories turned out hundreds of aeroplanes for the Royal Flying Corps (RFC) and the Royal Naval Air Service (RNAS). It's estimated that around 30 per cent of the British fighters flown in World War I were designed by Holt Thomas' brilliant chief designer Geoffrey De Havilland. It's entirely possible that George Holt Thomas may have been whispering in the First Sea Lord's ear.

Or it may have been the men from Vickers, the Admiralty's favourite airship builder. In February 1919 *Flight* magazine carried three long articles written by Vickers and entitled 'The Possibilities of Airship Transport Services'. The articles were illustrated by drawings of an 800-foot-long airship designed to accommodate 80 passengers in a long cabin on the top of the hull. The ship would float on 3.5 million cubic feet of hydrogen and be powered across the sky by six engines, whose

3,500-horsepower would give her a cruising speed of 60 mph. On paper the Vickers ship would be capable of making London to New York in 60 hours.

Passengers would enter by the bow from a mooring tower, then take an interior lift to passenger quarters which were divided into twenty four-berth cabins. They would dine at long tables in a saloon, relax in a fire-proofed smoking lounge (for 'fervent worshippers of Lady Nicotine') and stroll in the open air on sheltered decks where 'the air currents are carried away over the heads of the passengers by the stream-lined shape of the aft portion of the cabin'. There would be an observation car slung below the hull. All the passenger quarters were to be heated by electric radiators.

But such a project wouldn't come cheap. Vickers made it clear that any such airship service would need the help of the British taxpayer, who would be expected to let the airship companies use the existing military airship bases free of charge, supply all the aircrews and the ground-based handling parties, and stump up for all the insurance costs, which were calculated £110,000 a year. This, the men from Vickers argued, was how the pre-war German government helped make a success of the early Zeppelin services.

But whether it was Holt Thomas, Vickers, or the Admiralty who was behind the idea of using a military airship for 'commercial demonstration', the idea took root. On Thursday, 6 March 1919, a special conference was called at the Air Ministry chaired by Winston Churchill, then Secretary of State for War and Air. It was attended by, among others, men from Beardmore's, Armstrong Whitworth, the Cunard shipping line, the Holt Thomas interests and, interestingly, the General Post Office. The GPO saw a promising market in flying mail and newspapers between Britain and North America – an idea that had been explored by Rudyard Kipling in his 1905 airship tale 'With the Night Mail'.

Churchill seems to have told the companies that if they wanted the R34 to venture across the Atlantic to test the commercial potential of airships they would have to carry some of the cost. Not only of manning, equipping and fuelling the flight itself, but also the cost of the advance party that would need to travel to the USA to make ready the landing site. Initial costs were calculated at £2,000, later bumped up to £3,000. The final cost was, without doubt, much more.

After another few weeks of discussion it was decided to go ahead with the attempt on the Atlantic some time in June or early July that year. There was even a vague plan (or at least a hope) that a landing on US soil might be accomplished on Friday, 4 July, America's independence day, which would be a spectacular tribute by the British Empire to its one-time colony and war-time ally, the United States.

Having issued the go-ahead, the R34 team then had to finalise the arrangements with the Americans. This proved an awkward business. An invitation for a British airship to fly to the USA had come from the Aero Club of America, who had the use of an airfield at Atlantic City in New Jersey. But the Aero Club of America was a civilian organisation whose vice president was Henry Woodhouse. And Woodhouse was a serious irritant to the US military, which Groves, a strong advocate of the project, could not afford to alienate. At the same time, he didn't want to snub the enterprising aviators of the Aero Club and risk a storm of hostile American publicity.

This dilemma was outlined in a confidential minute from Brigadier-General Lionel Charlton, the recently appointed air attaché at the British Embassy in Washington. Charlton wrote: 'I have been made aware that the Aero Club of America commanded no sympathy with the Army and Navy Air Service, nor with the Manufacturers' Aircraft Association, and that this was on account of the personality of Mr Henry Woodhouse, a Vice-President, the active brain of the organisation, and the editor and proprietor of two or three aeronautical magazines.'

The US military were right to be wary of Henry Woodhouse. His real name was Mario Casalengo, an Italian immigrant who had spent four years in jail for killing a man in a restaurant brawl. Ambitious, devious and bright, Woodhouse/Casalengo was a classic hustler. He began writing about aviation, founded a number of flying magazines and joined the Aero Club of America, which he gradually took over. In 1918 Woodhouse's past came back to haunt him when his enemies inside the club accused him of being a murderer and a fraud. The row did not go unnoticed by America's straitlaced officer class, who set their faces against him.

That particular problem was settled at the end of May 1919 when John W. Davis, the US ambassador in London, informed the Marquess of Curzon, the Foreign Secretary, that while the US War Department had 'no objection to the landing of the British dirigible at Atlantic City, it is of the opinion that it would be preferable for the landing to be made at one of the Government fields, in order to afford more efficient assistance and facilities for security by the United States Government'. After which Groves had to tell Woodhouse/Casalengo and the Aero Club of America that, regrettably, their airfield in Atlantic City was not up to scratch.

But there was also the problem of the inter-service rivalry between the US Navy and the US Army. Both services were anxious to host the very first airship ever to visit the United States and were jockeying for position vis-à-vis the British project. This is also confirmed by Brigadier-General Charlton's minute. 'At different times I have been approached by both Army and Navy Air Service officials with offers of help and suggesting Army and Navy Air Service Stations as the terminus of the voyage of the R34.'

Various 'termini' were on offer. The US Navy was suggesting its air station at Montauk on the eastern tip of Long Island. The base was reasonably well equipped but was a long way from the engines of publicity in New York City. The US Army was offering the army airbase on Roosevelt Field in Mineola, also on Long Island but just a short drive (around 25 miles) from Manhattan. Other alternatives were the army's Langley Field in Virginia and the navy's base at Cape May at the bottom end of New Jersey. The front runner, so far as the British were concerned, was the airfield at Mineola, Long Island.

Eventually a solution was worked out which seemed to satisfy all parties. The R34 would make its landfall on the US Army's field at Mineola carrying an observer from the US Navy on the flight from Britain to the USA. But the American observer on the return journey from the USA to the UK would be an officer of the US Army. That way both US services could claim that one of their men was the first American to fly non-stop across the Atlantic, one east–west, the other west–east. It was a deal that the Americans were happy to accept.

The two Americans chosen for the R34 flights were Lieu-tenant-Commander Zachary Lansdowne of the US Navy, and Lieutenant-Colonel William Hensley of the US Army. Both men had fairly colourful military histories and both had some experience of lighter-than-air craft, Lansdowne with airships and balloons in wartime Europe and Hensley as commander of the US Army's balloon school. Both were products of small-town USA: Lansdowne hailed from the western edge of Ohio and Hensley was born and raised in Nebraska.

Winston Churchill may have been unenthusiastic, but the R34 transatlantic project had influential backers in General John Seely MP, then Under-Secretary of State for Air and Deputy Chief of the Air Staff, Robert Marsland Groves. John Seely (like many senior officers of the time) was a veteran of the Boer War as well as the war in Europe. Groves was a Royal Navy officer turned aviator who had done sterling work as a Wing Commander with the Royal Naval Air Service in France and had won a DSO for his pains. Both men were energetic advocates of aviation and air power.

For the next few months, Seely and Groves steered the R34 transatlantic project through the tangled thickets of party politics and inter-departmental rivalries. By then more than one politician (and notably Winston Churchill) and some senior civil servants had come to believe that the hydrogen-filled airship was a dead-end technology and that pursuing it was a waste of money. Seely and Groves were determined men, and heavily committed to the R34.

But if any one man can be regarded as the force behind the R34 and its trek across the Atlantic it has to be the strange figure of Brigadier-General Edward Maitland Maitland. At every stage in the R34's life Maitland was there, guarding it when it was no more than an idea lurking in the ruin of a Zeppelin, consulting on the design, keeping an eye on the building in Scotland, watching over its trial flights, defending the project against hostile forces in Whitehall, coaxing the media to take a friendly interest and finally keeping an hour-by-hour 'log' of the R34's journey, which he later published as a book.

It's hard not to read about Maitland without seeing another strange warrior from that time, Thomas Edward Lawrence, Lawrence of Arabia. The parallels are striking. Both were born in the 1880s and educated at public school and Oxbridge. Both were small men, and both probably homosexual. Both earned their spurs under fire in distant parts (Lawrence in the Middle East, Maitland in South Africa). Both were brave to the point of recklessness, and had a strong feeling for poetry. Maitland, like Lawrence, seems to have been able to withstand just about any hardship without complaint. Both represented a species of imperial British warrior that has long since disappeared.

Like Lawrence, Maitland seems to have sought out danger just in order to confront it. He was a brave infantry officer, an early and daring aeroplane pilot, an experimental parachutist, an intrepid balloonist and a skilled airship captain. One of the shrewder aviation correspondents of the period, H. Massac Buist of the *Morning Post*, once described Maitland and his career as 'That brilliant little officer, Brigadier-General E.M. Maitland, who has had more adventures and mishaps in the air than it is given most men to survive'.

Pictures of Edward Maitland show a dark-haired, dandyish

man sporting the upturned military moustache favoured by so many Edwardian military gents. The elder son of Cambridgeshire barrister Arthur Gee (who assumed his wife's surname in 1903), Edward Maitland was born in London in 1880 and educated at Haileybury boarding school and Trinity College Cambridge. He abandoned his studies in 1901 to volunteer for the Boer War in South Africa, in which he served as a junior officer with the Essex Regiment in the heat and dust of the Orange River colony, and with enough distinction to win the Queen's Medal and four clasps.

Some time in the early 1900s Maitland became infected by the flying bug, which he never shook off. Although he held an aeroplane pilot's licence, and bought a Howard-Wright aircraft (in which he crashed, damaging both his legs) he developed a passion for lighter-than-air flight that was to stay with him for the rest of his life. Balloons and airships were, he averred, the best way to fly.

In November 1908 Maitland, along with aviation journalist Charles Turner and the French aviator Auguste Gaudron, made an attempt on the world long-distance ballooning record by flying from London to Matek Derevni in what was then Russia and is now Latvia. It was a bitterly cold and hazardous journey of 1,117 miles on which their balloon almost came down in the North Sea, nearly crashed in Germany, was shot at by a Russian border guard and soared in the dark to a perilous 17,000 feet. The flight ended in a crash landing on a frozen lake in a blizzard.

In his account of the adventure Charles Turner has nothing but praise for Edward Maitland. He describes him as 'The most uncomplaining, imperturbable man I ever met. He never counted danger, and when he met it he never showed a sign.' Turner particularly admired Maitland's 'quiet endurance and his indifference to discomfort, cold or wet or when on "short commons", or the victim of an indifferent cook or the clumsy servant, he would smile good humouredly or make some philosophical remark'. The two men were to remain good friends.

In the years between 1910 and 1919 Maitland moved from service to service. He left the Essex Regiment for an attachment to the Royal Engineers balloon school at Farnborough, then became commander of No. 1 Company of the Air Battalion (renamed as No. 1 Squadron, Royal Flying Corps). When airships were made the responsibility of the Admiralty he moved with them to the Royal Naval Air Service (RNAS) as a wing commander. Maitland was lucky not to be trapped in Germany when war broke out in 1914. He'd been in Bittenfeld, north-east of Stuttgart, to assess a 'Parseval' airship the Admiralty had ordered from the Germans. He returned to Britain just days before war was declared.

In September 1914 Maitland was posted to Belgium, where he was impressed by the usefulness of the Belgian and French 'kite-balloons' which were used for observation and artillery spotting. They were small, tethered balloons under which was slung a platform manned by two men equipped with maps, binoculars and range-finding instruments. They sat at an altitude of around 1,500 to 2,000 feet and communicated with the ground by telephone cable. In Maitland's opinion kite balloons were superior to anything possessed by Britain and he urged that British versions should be built. The authorities agreed, and Maitland was given the job of setting up and running the kite-balloon training school at Roehampton.

After that he moved to the airship school at Wormwood Scrubs, where he developed a taste for high-level parachuting. In 1915 Maitland made his most famous paradrop when he jumped from a balloon at 10,800 feet in a standard service parachute. He fell at the rate of 12 feet per second 'a rapid transition from low pressure to high pressure' that caused 'some discomfort' after he landed. According to his friend Charles Turner the jump would have killed Maitland if one of the balloon pilots hadn't noticed 'in the nick of time a fault in the attachment of the parachute'.

In July 1916 Maitland was awarded a Distinguished Service Order (DSO) for 'extremely valuable and gallant work in connection with airships and parachutes'. According to the citation in the *London Gazette* he 'carried out experiments at his own personal risk, and has made some descents under enemy fire'.

Maitland never married, which led to speculation that he was homosexual. He may have been, but he certainly had loyal women friends, among them Kathleen, Countess of Drogheda and Lady Sybil Grant.

The latter is an interesting figure, the raffish daughter of the Earl of Rosebery and the wife of General Sir Charles Grant, and a handsome woman with a look of the Pre-Raphaelite about her. She was also energetic, hard-working and a moderately talented novelist and poet. The best of her poems was probably the one she wrote in memory of her brother, Neil Primrose (an MP turned soldier), who was killed fighting in Palestine. In later life Grant grew eccentric, lived in a caravan, had a hawker's licence, cultivated gypsies and set aside a slice of the Rosebery family estate near Epsom for the use of gypsies and their horses.

There's a brief impression of Sybil as an old lady by the writer James Lees-Milne. He wrote to his diary 'On her head was an orange bonnet draped with an orange scarf. She had orange hair, her lips were the vividest orange I have ever beheld. She took me into the orangery, where she lives all the time.' Sybil's younger brother Harry, the sixth Earl of Rosebery, was a short-lived Secretary of State for Scotland in 1945.

In her collection of poems entitled *The End of the Day*, Sybil includes six poems dedicated to lighter-than-air craft: the non-rigid kite-balloon, the non-rigid NS1 and the rigids R24, R33, R34 and R36. The worst, unfortunately, is the one entitled *Pro Patria Volans*, dedicated to the flight of the R34. It's an overblown, pompous piece of work that grates. None of Sybil's poems can be regarded as great poetry, but what does shine through is her love of flying and her admiration for the machines and the men who fly them. In her poem *Above the Clouds* (dedicated to the R34's sister ship the R33) she writes:

> Each pilot through the air ascending
> Crosses the intervening stages
> A votary: goes humbly questing:
> Through these same degrees.
>
> Language: forsaken on the earth world,
> Then music, from a thousand song-birds,
> Abandoned when – the ship ascending –
> Meets visions manifest.
>
> Visions for waking eyes – cloud visions –
> Bright veils close-drawn in preparation
> For those last speechless wonder spaces,
> Brooding above the world.

It's easy to see why Edward Maitland would find a woman with such a passion for aviation – his kind of aviation – attractive. At the very least, the two were good friends. To the end of his life Maitland never lost contact with Lady Sybil Grant.

In his excellent history of the rigid airship Douglas H. Robinson describes Maitland as the 'guiding genius' behind the R34 project and 'a much beloved leader possessed of great personal charm, an army airship officer from the pre-war days, and a dedicated believer in the future of the rigid airship'. There's similar praise in Walter Raleigh's official account *The War in the Air*, which characterises Maitland as 'one of the earliest of the aeronautical pioneers who, almost alone, preferred the airship to the aeroplane'.

Which may be something of an exaggeration, but it's certainly true that no one lobbied harder than Edward Maitland. He was utterly convinced that airships like the R34 were the way ahead for British aviation, especially civil aviation. He shared the (widely-held) belief that the system which was bound to develop was one in which aeroplanes would do the short-haul flying while a new generation of airships would dominate the long-haul, inter-continental routes. And he saw a successful transatlantic flight by the R34 as evidence that this dream was about to be realised.

5

(East) Fortune Favours the Brave

The R34, with Maitland aboard, lifted off from its Inchinnan birthplace for the last time on Wednesday, 28 May 1919. After circling the field and dipping her bow in salute to the men and women who had created her, she turned east to head across central Scotland to the Royal Naval Air Service base at East Fortune, east of Edinburgh. She took with her a stray tabby kitten which had been rescued from the streets of Renfrew by engineer George Graham and which, for regrettable reasons, had been named 'Whoopsie'. The ship's crew had also settled on a nickname for the R34, the biggest airship in the British fleet, and that was 'Tiny'.

And what should have been a short hop across the narrow waist of Scotland between the Clyde and the Forth became a long, hard slog. Thick fog on the Firth of Forth and the North Sea meant the airship had to spend the night loitering over the sea waiting for a glimpse of the airship base at East Fortune. That glimpse was to be a long time coming. In fact the ship wandered as far south as Yorkshire. It was a tired, thirsty and hungry crew of aviators that finally climbed out of the airship after 21 hours in the air.

In 1919 the RNAS base at East Fortune comprised around 400 acres of farmland commandeered by the Admiralty from a local landowner. Lying on a coastal plain bounded on the south by the Lammermuir hills and on the north by the Firth of Forth, the salient features of the landscape are the two ancient volcanic 'plugs' known as Berwick Law and Traprain Law. The whale-backed hill of Traprain was once the site of a settlement of the powerful tribe of Britons known to the Romans as the Votadinii and to themselves as the Gododdin.

Their epic poem Y *Gododdin* contains the first ever mention of the legendary Celtic hero Arthur.

The name East Fortune has nothing to do with luck. It's a corruption of the name 'fort-toun', or 'fort-town' and possibly refers to the farms which supplied victuals to a nearby fortress. By the end of the eighteenth century most of the land around East Fortune was owned by the Kinloch family who built the neo-classical Gilmerton House which stands just south of the airfield. The Kinlochs were reputed to be 'enlightened' proprietors; they also happened to live in a particularly fertile area, and their patch of East Lothian became one of Scotland's bread baskets.

The World War I air station at East Fortune (motto 'Fortune Favours the Brave') was set up to protect the naval base and dockyard at Rosyth, some 30 miles west on the north bank of the Firth of Forth, and also to offer some protection to the City of Edinburgh. It was one of two such bases on the east coast of Scotland, the other being at Longside, near Peterhead. Unusually, East Fortune housed both aeroplanes and airships. From East Fortune coastal non-rigid airships (and later dirigibles) patrolled the North Sea in search of German submarines and warships.

The airship part of the base was at the north end and comprised three big airship sheds, the biggest of which was built for dirigibles like the R34 and the other two for the smaller, non-rigid coastal airships. The main dirigible shed at East Fortune was modelled on No. 2 shed at Pulham in Norfolk: 700 feet long, 180 feet wide, 110 feet high, made from 300 tons of steel clad in corrugated iron and painted in green/brown camouflage pattern with strategically placed high wind breaks around the sheds.

To the north of the airship sheds, near the perimeter of the base, lay a collection of low buildings which were the barracks, workshops, coal stores, hydrogen plants, boiler house, fuel stores, canteens and an infirmary. As the air base lay close to the main east-coast railway line, a stretch of railway track ran from East Fortune station into the airship base. In 1919 East Fortune was commanded by Colonel Roland Hunt, whose quarters were in the old farmhouse of East Fortoun.

Hunt had known since the middle of April 1919 that his base had been earmarked to house the R34. It was not a prospect he welcomed. In fact, on 18 April he had written to the Secretary of the Admiralty claiming that East Fortune 'is not in a position to receive this ship, due to lack of men and gas'. He pointed out that his main shed was already occupied by R29, which was having new gas bags fitted and that his entire force (military and civilian) consisted of 156 men, far short of the 500 needed to handle a ship the size of the R34.

To compound the problem, Hunt said, the R34 'cannot be maintained until the Gas Plant is put in order, and even then it is estimated that tubes of hydrogen will be required to be supplied from outside sources. For this a considerable number of men are required, to make the gas and discharge the tubes into the holder.'

But orders were orders, work on the R29 was speeded up and by the beginning of June the R34 and her crew had settled into East Fortune. With her trials behind her, she was in good condition. Seely, Groves and Maitland were confident that the R34 had the power to see her across the Atlantic even against the prevailing westerly wind. The damage had been repaired, the ship had been tested, the Americans had been squared. All that was needed now was for His Majesty's Government to give the final go-ahead.

There was, however, the question of how the British and American press should be handled. That was left to one of the project's more unlikely participants, Brigadier-General Ernest Swinton, the (short-lived) Controller of Information at the Air Ministry. Another decorated Boer War veteran and one-time engineer, Swinton had served as an 'official' war correspondent on the Western Front. He was also arguably the man who invented the battle tank (a claim that he officially made in 1920). He later became Chichele Professor of Military History at Oxford, a Fellow of All Souls and Colonel Commandant of the Royal Tank Corps.

Between them, Swinton and Maitland hammered out the press and public relations strategy for the R34's voyage. Swinton had wanted one of his own men on the flight, but when Maitland told him that was impractical it was agreed that Maitland himself would write a 'narrative', a day-by-day log, copies of which would be handed over to America's five biggest press agencies and British reporters in the USA. It was left to Maitland to decide who should give interviews to the press but it was 'suggested' that he 'should warn his officers of the subjects to which they should refer'. Swinton was an old-fashioned military man who believed that information to the public was best tightly controlled.

It was also decided that one of the R34's crew should be equipped with a camera and act as the R34's photographer (a job that was given to the Admiralty's observer, Major Jack Pritchard) but that 'these photographs should be official and the property of the government'. No other cameras were to be allowed on board. All pictures were to be sent to 'C. of I., Air Ministry', that is, Swinton himself. The weak spot in Swinton's campaign was the USA. In one of his memos he acknowledged that photographs 'of every type' would be taken in the USA and regretted that 'it will not be possible to control these in any way'.

While Seely, Groves, Maitland and Swinton were putting everything in place for the R34's voyage, His Majesty's Government was holding back. Ministers were waiting for the Germans to accept the terms of the peace treaty being hammered out at Versailles. But these terms were so harsh and so humiliating that they generated all kinds of political turbulence in Germany, which caused the German delegation to refuse to accept them. They disputed the treaty article by article, line by line, until, in the spring of 1919, there was a real chance that the Germans would walk out and war would erupt all over again. It would be a war into which the R34 – Britain's biggest and most powerful airship – would certainly be pitched.

The French and the British were plainly still stinging from attacks by German aviators, particularly the Zeppelin bombing raids. This can be seen in the 'Military, Naval and Aviation Clauses' of the treaty. Article 198, for example, specifies that 'The armed forces of Germany must not include any military or naval air forces', the only aircraft that were to be allowed were 100 flying boats to be used for seeking out mines and 'No dirigible shall be kept'.

Article 202 was particularly draconian. All 'military and naval aeronautical material' was to be handed over to the Allies including 'dirigibles able to take the air, being manufactured, repaired or assembled; plant for the manufacture of hydrogen; dirigible shed and shelters of every kind for aircraft. Pending their delivery, dirigibles will, at the expense of Germany, be maintained inflated with hydrogen . . .'

There's no doubt that the prospect of renewed war delayed the R34's great adventure. That is confirmed by a number of letters and memoranda between the Air Ministry and the Admiralty in the first few months of 1919. As late as the middle of June 1919 the Admiralty were warning that they might have to pull the plug on the whole transatlantic venture if the Germans didn't sign. On 14 June the Secretary of the Admiralty wrote to the Secretary of the Air Ministry stating:

> I am commanded by My Lord Commissioners of the Admiralty to inform you, for the information of the Air Council, that in the event of necessity for enforcing the blockade of Germany, it is regretted that the proposed flight of R.34 will have to be abandoned, as this ship, together with R.33, will be required for operations with the Commander in Chief, Atlantic and Home Fleets.

Interestingly, when Groves passed this information on to Under-Secretary of State Seely he was told to press on regardless. 'Brigadier-General Seely himself was of the opinion that it is most desirable that we should cross to America,' Groves recorded in his diary, 'and indeed he felt that it would impress Germany and the rest of the world just as much if we sent her to the US as if we used her only in the North Sea'.

Groves and Seely knew that the R34 was far too valuable to be risked in some futile skirmish over the German coast. 'We all agreed with the Admiralty opinion that it would be inadvisable to send her into the Baltic or the vicinity of Germany if the Germans declined to sign the Peace Terms, as she could be so easily destroyed by a single enthusiast.' (Which, for such keen advocates of lighter-than-air aviation, was a frank admission of the vulnerability of all hydrogen-filled airships.)

By then, however, the R34 was cruising over the Baltic coast of Germany, fully armed, in a display of British air power. In the preface to his handwritten account of the R34's flight, Edward Maitland was very clear that the purpose of the flight was to remind the Germans just who had won. The transatlantic flight had been originally planned for the beginning of June, Maitland wrote, 'but owing to the uncertainty of the Germans signing the peace terms the British Admiralty decided to retain her for an extended cruise up the Baltic and along the German coastline'.

The R34 left East Fortune at 06.00 on Tuesday, 17 June, carrying no bombs but with Lewis machine guns mounted in the cars and on the upper platforms. She tracked south-east across the North Sea to fly over the massive fortifications on the island of Heligoland, then over Wilhelmshaven, Friedrichshafen, Hamburg, the Kiel Canal and along Germany's stretch of the Baltic coast. At one point the guns were manned when the R34 was buzzed by a German aeroplane, but the encounter came to nothing. Having shown herself to the Germans, the R34 then turned north-west and returned to Scotland via Scandinavia.

After 56 hours in the air R34 came down at East Fortune on Friday, 20 June. A few days later Scott was in London reporting the Baltic flight to Seely and Groves in London. Scott told them that the ship had flown 2,400 nautical miles, usually against the wind, and had burned 2,700 gallons of petrol. By and large, he said, the ship had performed well and the crew had learned a great deal about flying in 'stormy weather conditions'. The only real problem had been that one of the Sunbeam engines had failed and had to be closed down.

At that meeting Seely was anxious to know when the R34 would be ready to start across the Atlantic, although he assured Scott that the decision was his and that he was under no pressure. Scott told him that his best estimate was 'about the evening of the 1st July', to which Seely replied that it would be 'most fortunate' if the R34 could make it across by 4 July. Seely then decided that the R34's flight should not be announced until the airship was under way.

It was to be another three days, Saturday, 28 June, before two German officials, Dr Hermann Müller and Dr Johannes Bell, finally put their signatures to the Treaty of Versailles. It is well known that German naval officers at Scapa Flow in the Orkneys responded to the treaty terms by scuppering 70 ships of their High Seas Fleet. But it is usually forgotten that aviators at the airship bases at Nordholz and Wittmundhafen destroyed six of their finest Zeppelins (L14, L42, L63, L65, L52 and L56). This was done partly to thwart the Allies but also to prevent them falling into the hands of the Communists who were threatening to take over the country.

On the day that the Treaty of Versailles was signed the R34 was issued with her 'flying orders', which began 'Being in all respects ready for the air, and subject to the C.O., East Fortune, acquiescing in your departure from the Station, you will proceed on the first favourable opportunity, after receiving permission from the Air Ministry'. That permission would depend on the weather being favourable. The objects of the venture were described as:

    i   An extended test of the ship's behaviour under service
        conditions in the Atlantic.
    ii An extended long-distance navigation trial.
    iii To visit the United States of America.

The airship's course, speed and navigation were left to the crew, but if possible they were to pass over Halifax, Nova Scotia, to drop a message.

> If, after consuming half of the fuel carried on leaving, you feel any reasonable doubt of being able to reach New York with 1,000 gallons in reserve, you are to turn back if the weather conditions are favourable for doing so. You are to be prepared, as a last resort, to proceed to either of the cruisers to be taken in tow.

There was a stern instruction on how the crew of the R34 should behave in New York. 'You are not to remain at the landing ground longer than is necessary to re-fuel and re-gas. Nevertheless, if your officers and crew are exhausted, you may remain for a few hours longer, provided the safety of the ship is not endangered thereby. None of your officers and crew are to leave the immediate vicinity of the ship.' (If ever a flying order was to be ignored it was that one.)

The warships assigned to help the R34 across the Atlantic were the battle cruisers HMS *Tiger* and HMS *Renown*. Fittingly, both ships were built in Clydeside shipyards, the *Tiger* at John Brown's in 1914 and the *Renown* at Fairfield's in 1916. Both were heavyweights, between 27,000 and 28,000 tons, between 700 and 800 feet long and capable of speeds of 30 knots. The *Tiger* was the more battle-scarred of the two, being a veteran of the naval engagements at Dogger Bank in 1915, Jutland in 1916 (where she took 16 hits) and Heligoland in 1917. They were part of the Home Fleet based at Rosyth on the Firth of Forth and Scapa Flow in the Orkneys.

Their role in what the Admiralty codenamed 'Operation BR' was to provide some security to the R34 in the case of the airship having to ditch in the sea, but mainly to supply her with information about the weather. To that end two RAF meteorological officers were attached to each ship. There were also 'a complete set of meteorological instruments for each battle-cruiser'.

Tiger and the *Renown* were assigned positions on either side of the R34's course, *Tiger* to the south, *Renown* to the north. The *Tiger* was instructed to reach position latitude 55° north, longitude 40° west by 12.00 on Wednesday, 2 July. The *Renown* was ordered to take up position on latitude 60° north, longitude 25° west by midnight on Tuesday, 1 July. Both ships were instructed to be economical with their fuel and 'when on their stations may remain stopped if the weather conditions admit'.

On 30 June, Groves informed Churchill and Seely that the R34 would be 'ready for the air by tomorrow morning, July 1st', and while the weather prospects looked good, they would be at their best on the night of 2–3 July. The ship was to be skippered by Major George Herbert Scott, with Brigadier-General Maitland being sent by the Air Ministry 'to report on the behaviour of the ship and other kindred matters'. Any messages for the USA had to be on the 22.00 hours train from King's Cross to Edinburgh on 1 July and 'It is suggested that HM The King be informed of her [R34's] departure'.

On Tuesday, 1 July, the Air Ministry circulated editors of the British press with details of the publicity arrangements. They were informed that during the day a press officer would be on duty in room 545, India House, Kingsway in Holborn and during the night one could be found at Room 226 in the huge and splendid Hotel Cecil on the Embankment. They were assured that 'any messages which may be received from the airship during the course of her flight will be passed immediately to the Press through the News Agencies'.

With the exception of Zachary Lansdowne, US Navy, the crew selected for the transatlantic journey had been with the R34 since she'd first taken to the air. Although in the process of becoming members of the new Royal Air Force, most had learned their trade with the Royal Naval Air Service and were veterans of the long, cold U-Boat spotting flights over the North Sea. The R34's captain, Major George Scott, had joined the RNAS at the outbreak of war in 1914, had skippered Britain's first rigid airship (No. 9) and then commanded the (German-built) non-rigid Parseval P4.

Under Scott were his second officer, Captain Geoffrey Greenland, third officer Lieutenant Harold Luck, engineering officer Lieutenant John Shotter, navigating officer Major Gilbert Cooke, radio officer Lieutenant Ronald Durrant, and the meteorological officer Lieutenant Guy Harris. Also on board were Brigadier-General Edward Maitland (observer for the Air Ministry), Major Jack Pritchard (observer for the Admiralty) and Lieutenant-Commander Zachary Lansdowne (observer for the United States Navy). Non-commissioned officers and other ranks comprised three coxswains, two wireless operators, eleven engineers (two for each engine and one specialising in petrol supply) and four riggers.

At East Fortune the last few days were spent readying the airship for the Atlantic crossing. Every square inch of fabric on the outer cover and the gas bags was checked and rechecked. The Sunbeam engines were overhauled and 24 additional petrol tanks were installed in the keel, bringing the ship's capacity up to 6,000 gallons. The crew space in the keel was lengthened from just over 28 feet to almost 33 feet and was fitted with fold-down tables, tanks of drinking water and wash-hand basins, and bomb racks were replaced by food lockers.

The supplies that were loaded onto the R34 for her journey were brand names that would have been familiar to any Edwardian explorer. Among the pounds of bread, cooked beef, cold hams, meat pies, stewed beef, potatoes, eggs, tea, sugar and cheese were household brands: Horlicks, Oxo meat extract, Nestlé's condensed milk and Bovril, plus 24 loaves of Veda bread (a long-lasting malted bread devised in Scotland and still baked in Northern Ireland) and '14 2-pound tins of assorted jams'. There were also eight boxes of toffee and 36 pounds of chocolate (enough for 4 ounces per man per day).

Fruit and vegetables were few and far between. The only items that fit that bill were 55 pounds of potatoes ('cooked in their skins') and the '45 one-pound boxes of Fruitarian cake', a heavy, fruit-laden treat beloved of the tea-houses of Edwardian Britain. There was also a store of chewing gum to help the R34's smokers (most of the crew) through the journey. Everything was carefully weighed and it all added up to 545.5 pounds. The fact that all cooking had to be done on a plate welded to one of the engine exhausts kept meals simple (and often cold).

Medical supplies were modest: bandages for burns, triangular bandages, cotton wool, plasters, ointment, iodine, castor oil capsules, a flask of ammonia spirits, safety pins, a clinical thermometer, dissecting forceps and a pair of scissors. Among the items in the 'tablet case' were aspirin, quinine sulphate, potassium permanganate, vegetable laxatives, potassium chlorate, cough tinctures and mustard leaves. The role of the R34's doctor was assigned to the young third officer, Lieutenant Harold Luck.

Also on board the R34 were 112 pounds of mail and parcels, including a film of the Paris Peace Conference and letters to their opposite numbers in the USA from King George V, Prime Minister Lloyd George, the President of the Board of Trade, the Chairman of Customs and Excise and the Postmaster General. There was also a small quantity of platinum from the London jewellers Derby & Co. for a New York bullion dealer. Derby & Co. paid 30 guineas to RAF charities for the privilege of having the metal dispatched across the Atlantic by air.

By modern standards the R34's navigation and flight instruments were primitive. There were two naval sextants, one in the control car and another on the roof of the ship, a bubble sextant and a Beck's bomb-sight designed to measure ground speed and drift. There was a 'standard' British compass fitted at the top of the hull and a better American compass in the control car, along with three chronometer watches and a star globe. The R34 had no reliable altimeter, something that was to prove a serious problem.

The airship did, however, carry a library of useful texts, mainly nautical tables, sun and star tables, lists of lights and their time signals plus a set of charts of the British and US coasts. By way of lighter reading there was a copy of that late nineteenth-century masterpiece of popular science, *Cloud Studies,* by Arthur W. Clayden, a man who loved clouds and enthused over their 'delicacy of detail and texture, richness of contrast, beauty of form and light and colour'. And Edward Maitland confessed to carrying a copy of Kipling's optimistic airship yarn 'With the Night Mail' and a volume of Emerson's poetry.

By then the R34's route across the Atlantic had been plotted. The idea (or at least the hope) was to ride the wind. It's true that the prevailing wind over the Atlantic is westerly, but it's also true that in the northern hemisphere depressions ('cyclones') rotate anti-clockwise. So if the R34 could catch the northern arc of an incoming cyclone the anti-clockwise, that is, east–west wind would help it across the Atlantic. This would save time and, more importantly, large quantities of fuel. And if the cyclone was in the right place over the Atlantic, that arc would take the airship on – or close to – the Atlantic's busy shipping lanes.

On the evening of Tuesday, 1 July, Colonel Roland Hunt, the commanding officer at East Fortune, hosted a dinner in the officers' mess for the crew of the R34 (or at least most of them). According to the *Scotsman* it was 'a merry send-off'. The toast of 'Good luck to the R34' was 'pledged with all cordiality'. Maitland replied, saying that the venture was of 'the very greatest importance', which he believed would bring the UK and the USA closer together. 'And when Britain and America were all one and pulled together,' Maitland declared 'it did not matter much what the rest of the world thought or did.'

Standing in for Scott (who, for some reason, was absent), Major Gilbert Cooke, the navigating officer, thanked East Fortune for the 'hearty send-off' and said 'The whole of us are absolutely confident we can pull this stunt off successfully, and we are proud to have the head of the airship service as a member of the crew with us'. Zachary Lansdowne made what the *Scotsman* called a 'humorous reply' in which he suspected that, prohibition notwithstanding, 'there would still be one or two bottles left in America for the benefit of the R34'.

One of the guests at that pre-flight dinner was Maitland's friend, Kathleen Pelham Burn, the Countess of Drogheda. Like Sybil Grant, the countess was an admirer of aeroplanes, airships and airmen, and throughout the war had worked for aviation charities. And like Sybil Grant, she was a sprig of the Scots gentry, the daughter of Charles Pelham Burn of Prestonfield in Midlothian. (A few years later the countess was at the centre of a society divorce case after being abandoned by her husband in, of all places, North Berwick.)

While the R34's officers and their guests were enjoying the wine and food at their 'merry send-off', at precisely 22.00 the huge doors of the brightly-lit airship shed were slid open. This was done to allow the R34 a few hours to 'acclimatise' herself to the temperature and the humidity of the air before setting off on her epic journey.

6

Day One: Wednesday, 2 July 1919

Buried in the manuscript department of the National Library of Scotland in Edinburgh there's a document that aviation historians and scholars seem to have largely overlooked. It's a buff-coloured, foolscap-sized notebook with a stiff cover on which is printed 'SO Duplicate Manifold Book Folio' (SO presumably being Stationery Office). The title, which is type-written on a yellowed, peeling label, describes the work inside: *Original Narrative of R34's Flight to America and Back July3rd–13th, 1919*.

On the flyleaf there's a typed inscription which reads 'To Lady Sybil Grant as a slight token of gratitude for the very valuable assistance she has rendered to the Airship Service, not only on this particular flight, but throughout the war'. The inscription is signed in blue ink 'E.M. Maitland, Brigadier-General, RAF'.

What the big notebook contains is Brigadier-General Edward Maitland's hand-written log of the first-ever non-stop flight across the Atlantic from east to west by His Majesty's Airship R34 in July 1919. Hand-written in pencil (some of which is now fading), it is a first-hand account of an extra-ordinary journey by what was then Britain's biggest and most advanced airship.

In the months that followed the flight Maitland used his log, together with the technical reports of his fellow officers and his own recollections to write, and then publish, an hour-by-hour, sometimes minute-by-minute, voyage across the Atlantic and back. The book is not particularly well-written, as Maitland himself wryly admitted. In places the grammar and the punctuation are rocky. But as the writer pointed out, 'R34 is not a literary effort, neither, therefore, am I an author'.

Perhaps not, but these fading pages are a valuable record of an important piece of aviation history. They contain the highs and lows, scares and exhilaration, boredom and discomfort, disappointments and triumphs of the long and often dangerous flight. And it's told by an intelligent and sensitive man who loved flying, knew airships and aviation and who also enjoyed lying in his hammock absorbed in the fables of Rudyard Kipling and the transcendental poetry of the American philosopher/poet Ralph Waldo Emerson.

Maitland's is the best account we have of that flight. The officers' reports (there are seven of them) are what they should be – straightforward, factual accounts and observations of how the big airship behaved during the long flight. They focus on the problems that emerged – navigation, weather, engineering, supplies etc. – along with suggestions as to how they could be corrected. They were written for official eyes: Maitland's was written for the world's media.

When Maitland signed a publishing deal with Hodder & Stoughton to produce an extended version of his log, he wrote to his literary hero Rudyard Kipling, author of the airship fable 'With the Night Mail', asking for the great man's blessing. In November 1920 Kipling wrote back promising to 'look out for the R34's log most keenly, and the more since, in my own mind, I have always fancied the dirigible against the aeroplane for the overhead haulage of the years to come'.

Kipling went on to draw an odd, if interesting, parallel. 'It's curious to think that R34's work has been, relatively, no more than young James Watt's brooding over the kettle on his mother's hob. Watt, I expect, didn't realise the steam-loco (indeed, I believe he objected to it) but you, and everyone aboard R34, must have felt that you stood at the opening verse of an opening chapter of endless possibilities, and I know what my own interest and pride were in seeing a dream shape itself and come true.'

Maitland is exaggerating when he claims that 'Every word of this diary was written on board the Airship during the journey . . . the writer perched in odd corners, and amid continuous interruptions and ever-changing surroundings, to the silent accompaniment of the wireless, like ghostly whispers across lonely space', but he has captured the essence of the long flight. 'Every incident, important or trifling, was recorded at the actual time of happening. Even to stop to focus or to pigeon-hole these would have been to destroy actuality.'

That actuality is certainly there. But so too is Maitland's sense of wonder at the landscapes and cloudscapes over which and through which the R34 was travelling. Some of the descriptive passages of sky, cloud and weather are written by a man who plainly relished the grandeur of it all. It is an account laced with vivid, well-written passages. For example: 'There is a cloudless and deep blue sky overhead, and now occasionally we get glimpses of vivid blue sea through gaps in the cloud beneath . . . We feel in a world of our own up here amidst this dazzling array of snow-white clouds.' But he's just as often – more often, in fact – prosaic and to the point.

It would be impossible to paint a picture of the R34's flight to the USA and back without using the resources of Edward Maitland's book. The men who had ventured out over the Atlantic before him – Harry Hawker, Mackenzie Grieve, John Alcock, Arthur Whitten Brown – had done it in tiny, cramped aeroplanes in which writing was the last thing on their minds. Maitland had the time and (relative) luxury of recording the flight of the R34 as it happened, hour by hour, day by day. Which makes his log a unique and genuinely historic document.

Here's how Maitland described the R34's departure in the early hours of Wednesday, 2 July 1919:

Midnight on a wet and windy night in July, and the big Airship Station at East Fortune is all agog with bustle and excitement. The moment eagerly anticipated for weeks past has at last arrived, and R34, Britain's largest and most efficient Rigid Airship – is about to start upon her 3,000 miles journey across the Atlantic, bound for Long Island, New York.

In the ordinary course of events the Airship Station at this hour would be peacefully asleep; but now there are lights everywhere, orders are sharply given and promptly obeyed, and final arrangements hurriedly carried out. At 1 a.m. the crew of eight officers and twenty-two men climb aboard, dressed in their flying clothes, having had an excellent dinner to fortify them for their long journey.

The crew's 'flying clothes' were bulky, one-piece flying suits with fur collars and built-in inflatable life-saving collars and integral parachute harnesses. Under these cumbersome suits they wore specially-designed silk underwear. It was an outfit about which most of the crew complained and shrugged off whenever they could. Many of the men carried good-luck tokens. George Herbert Scott's was a little gold 'thumbs-up' charm from a charm bracelet; John Shotter, the ship's engineering officer, wore one of his wife's silk stockings round his neck.

Once aboard the R34 the 30-strong crew scattered all over the airship to man their take-off and landing positions: on the steering wheel, at the height elevators, in the radio cabin, in the four engine rooms, at the water ballast tanks, on the pumps to the petrol tanks, on the mooring platform to handle the guy ropes. One man (Lance Corporal Forteath) was stationed at the top of the ladder that ran from the control car to the keel 'for general transmission of orders in the event of breakdown'. Scott, Maitland and most of the officers and senior NCOs remained in the control car.

That control car was the heart of the ship. Surviving drawings show an extraordinary piece of engineering. Fifty feet long and constructed of the same lightweight aluminium girders as the rest of the ship, it was slung under the front of the hull to which it was connected by a covered ladder. Eleven large windows of toughened glass (some of which opened) offered good visibility on three sides. Just behind the control room was the radio room, and beyond that an engine car housing the forward engine. The engine car was separated slightly from the control car to help cut down the vibration that might impair radio transmission and reception.

The controls were more like those of a ship, a submarine perhaps, than of any aeroplane. The nautical steering wheel and the elevators were attached by a system of wires and cables to the cruciform fins – rudder and stabilisers – at the stern. The five engines were controlled by a telegraph system almost identical to that used on ships. The skipper literally 'rang down' to the engine rooms when he wanted to stop, slow down or speed up. Telephones and voice pipes in the control car were connected to the engine cars and to strategic points along the keel.

By way of instrumentation there was a bubble statascope (which acted as a not very accurate altimeter), an inclinometer, a thermometer, a speed indicator, a clock, a rise-and-fall indicator and a pressure gauge which measured the hydrogen in the gas bags. In the event of the car's electric lights failing, all the instruments had been heavily 'radiumised' with a mixture of radium and zinc sulphide so that they glowed green in the dark (the carcinogenic hazards of radium were unknown in 1919).

The control car also contained an array of electrical apparatus: a telephone control board; telephone battery; distributing board; bomb release control board; bomb release battery; Dean horn signalling keys; Aldis signalling lamp; Aldis lamp fuses; chart table lamp. There were also two low-level cabinets containing six 'Guardian Angel' parachutes. Other parachutes were distributed along the keel.

The 'first watch' in the control car for the start of the Atlantic journey were Sergeant Murray Watson (helmsman), Sergeant Walter Mayes (elevators), Major Gilbert Cooke (navigator), Lieutenant Guy Harris (meteorologist), Major Jack Pritchard (special duties), Captain Geoffrey Greenland

(first officer), Major George Scott (R34's captain) and Brigadier-General Edward Maitland (special duties).

At 01.23, with the crew safely aboard and at their assigned
posts, the R34 was 'walked out' of her shed, stern first, by a
'handling party' of 400 airmen, 80 women and 150 soldiers
from the Black Watch. There were more than 500 men and
women hanging onto the ropes and cables that connected the
huge dirigible to the earth. Lilliputians to the airship's Gulliver.
As soon as the ship's stern was clear of the wind screen the R34
was swung round 180° to face the north-easterly wind. As
Maitland recorded in his log:

> At first sight the weather looks far from suitable. It is very
> dark, rain is falling slightly – the clouds appear to be very
> low, and the wind whistles mournfully around the big
> Airship shed. The weather reports, however, in mid-Atlan-
> tic, are more or less favourable . . . The wind in the West of
> Scotland and North of Ireland is from the north-east, and
> may prove of assistance to us until we are well out into the
> Atlantic. Major Scott, therefore, decides, despite the bad
> local weather conditions, to get away as soon as possible.

Scott's eagerness to get under way was shared by his meteorological officer, Lieutenant Guy Harris. 'Moderate north to
north-easterly winds prevailed over Scotland and the North of
Ireland,' Harris wrote in his post-flight report. 'At this time
quiet weather existed over the whole of the North Atlantic
Ocean. An unusual occurrence. It is believed that a more
favourable occasion would not have existed for a considerable
period.'

At 01.39 the R34's five Sunbeam 'Maori' engines coughed
and then roared into life; three minutes later, at 01.42, George
Scott gave the signal for the bugler to sound the 'let go'. Within
seconds the R34 had slipped out of the hands of the handling
party and climbed slowly into the night sky to disappear into a
bank of low cloud. 'Rousing cheers reach us through the

clouds,' Maitland wrote, 'and hearten us for the task we have in front of us.'

Maitland made a rather strange observation on first leaving the ground. He seems to have been trying to catch the mood of the men in the control car. 'When flying at night, possibly on account of the darkness, there is always a feeling of utter loneliness directly one loses sight of the ground. We feel this loneliness very much tonight; possibly owing to the fact that we are bound for a totally unknown destination across the wide Atlantic.'

But it didn't last. 'Such a feeling is only momentary, however, and is soon dispelled by the immediate need for action. Scott rings down 600 revolutions on all five engines, and each engine room in turn acknowledges the signal on the dial in the foremost car. Cooke, our navigator, sets a course NW for Rosyth and the Clyde.'

George Scott's version of the take-off from East Fortune is more prosaic. 'The ship left the ground with bags 99 per cent full. At 200 feet 0.25 tons of water were released in order to clear shed, she was taken up at once to 1,500 feet in an endeavour to get above the clouds, but at this height there was still a thin layer of cloud above, with occasional breaks. Ship flying about 1 ton heavy.'

Maitland recorded the crew's feelings:

Great satisfaction in getting away on scheduled time. A week previously it had been announced that R34 would leave for USA at 2 a.m. on Wednesday, July 2nd, therefore she actually commenced her journey a few minutes before scheduled time.

It is interesting to remember that when an Airship sets out for a long-distance voyage carrying her maximum allowance of petrol, she can only rise to a limited height at the outset of her journey without throwing some of it overboard as ballast. As she proceeds on her voyage she can, if so desired, gradually increase her height as the petrol is consumed by the engines.

For this reason the next few hours will form one of the most anxious periods during our journey as Scott, with 4,900 gallons of petrol on board, weighing 15.8 tons, has to keep his ship as low as possible, and at the same time pass over a part of Scotland in the darkness where, at some points, the hills rise to a height of over 3,000 feet.

Half an hour later the R34 was flying along the coast of the Firth of Forth, and heading towards the naval base at Rosyth, where much of the Home Fleet lay at anchor. Maitland continued:

All is now more or less plain sailing, as we can make out the Firth of Forth. Passing over Forth Bridge and Rosyth, which shows up clearly – a blaze of lights. Train underneath plainly visible, not only from glowing funnel but also white smoke. Height 1,500 feet. Rosyth is a beautiful sight – a fairyland of lights. Ships in docks and ships moored in Firth plainly visible. Scott reduces height to 1,200 feet.

At 02.25 the 'good luck' signals began coming in to the R34. 'Wireless signal from General Groves, Deputy Chief of Staff, Air Ministry: "To General Maitland, Major Scott, Officers and Crew of R34; All success to your flight and good luck to all on board, – R. M. Groves" . . . Wireless signal from HMS *Furious*; "All good wishes from Captain and Flying Squadron".'

A few minutes later Maitland noticed that daylight was already glimmering in the east.

Getting light – very streaky and dirty-looking sky. Following Firth of Forth and Clyde Canal just south of hills in Stirlingshire, where the highest hill is 1,870 feet. Visibility good, clouds about 2,500 feet. Stratus-wind about 25 miles per hour NE by N. Clouds as we go west seem to be becoming more compact, and taking more shape. Got away

with 4,900 gallons of petrol, which should give us an
endurance of 4,000 miles at an average air speed of 37
knots, or 45 mph . . . Passing under black ominous-looking
rain cloud 1,000 feet above us. High hills on starboard
beam causing bumps and making ship pitch slightly.

After an hour's cautious flying over the centre of Scotland the
R34 found herself near her own birthplace.

Glasgow on port beam – a big blaze of light. Following
course of Clyde due west. Inchinnan on port beam about 4
miles away. (Inchinnan is of special interest to us, as it is
R34's birth-place, where she was built by Messrs Beardmore, of Dalmuir.) It is more or less light now, and high hills
to the north show up very clearly. Weather behind us
looking black as ink – we seem to be getting better weather
by going west.

But the R34 very quickly ran into the problem that was to
plague all low-flying airships – the complexity of the atmosphere.

Violent bumps off Dumbarton hills bring big strains on
ship, particularly upon her elevators and rudders. Strong
vertical currents of air. Ship alternately up by the bow and
by the stern. All movements very slow and gradual. Nothing
sufficient to cause seasickness (or should I call it 'airsick-
ness'?). Gorgeous scenery on starboard beam.

   Ship at one moment 24° up by the bow, and liquid in
inclinometer has disappeared altogether! This is the biggest
angle we have yet experienced and it becomes necessary to
hold on. Harris, our Meteorological Officer, says that an
Airship travelling at 6,000 feet would be quite above all
these disturbances; but we cannot afford to go to that level
at the commencement of a long voyage like this, as we don't
want to lose any gas from expansion.

These 'bumps' are, without doubt, caused by the high hills to the north, and are mainly katabatic in origin. Great masses of air piling up against the hills are forced upwards, become cooled, and descend on the other side, displacing the warmer air at the foot of the hills, thus causing squalls, 'bumps', and generally unstable conditions. They will be met with nearly always in this region . . .

Which was a shrewd analysis. Katabatic winds (also known as downslope winds or gravity winds) are a well-known and often dangerous condition of mountainous areas. In the Rockies they are known as the 'chinook', in the Alps as the 'föhn'.

Over Greenock – following Clyde at 1,500 feet – and picking our way through the hills. We carefully avoid going over 1,500 feet, and so save losing gas. Average speed over ground during last hour 60 miles per hour, which is good considering the bumpiness of the air. Wonderful panorama of mountains over Loch Lomond, gradually getting salmon-pink as the sun begins to appear in the east – pink sky silhouetted near mouth of the Clyde, which, at this point, is about a mile wide. Heading in southerly direction down Clyde with wind now astern and the Isle of Arran ahead – a very mountainous island. 'Bumps' again troublesome.

Passing over oil steamer going up the Clyde – the crew wave us a greeting. Sunrise over lowest point of Bute. Very big storm over mainland on port beam and very dirty-looking weather ahead; we steer slightly to the west to avoid it. Wind estimated to be 15 miles per hour from NE.

Major Pritchard begins to get active with camera. Discovered comfortable perch on top of fresh-water tank in forward car – glad to sit down. Passing over small island called Holy Island, 1,000 feet high with sheer precipice on both east and west sides. Average speed making good 58 knots. Altered course 260°. Meteorological Officer climbs to roof of Airship 100 feet above us to gaze upon the sky, and returns, somewhat breathless from his exertions, with a generally favourable report.

In the summer dawn the R34 headed south-west around the island of Arran and then north-west along the North Channel between the Mull of Kintyre and the north-east coast of Ireland. 'Had fifteen minutes sleep in forward car sitting on fresh-water tank,' Maitland wrote. By then the airship was flying off Rathlin Head and heading towards Rathlin Island, which Maitland describes:

A green little island with very fine precipitous cliffs – half-moon shape. There is a lighthouse built at the west point of this island, and the whole cliff appears to have been strengthened with concrete.

One last word with Meteorological Officer, who says weather conditions and prospects extremely good, and so to bed, with a comfortable feeling of confidence. Hammock berth No. 11 has been allotted to me: a nice deep, roomy hammock – but slung very high. Had to get passing member of the crew to give me a leg up – mentally resolved I must be more agile next time. Getting in is quite an acrobatic feat, and falling out is better avoided in a service airship like R34, because there is only a thin outer cover of fabric on the underside of the keel on either side of the narrow walking way, and the luckless individual who tips out of his hammock would, in all probability, break through this fabric cover and soon find himself in the Atlantic.

With the ship flying at around 1,500 feet Scott shut down the forward engine, ran the remaining four engines at 1,600 rpm, and with a north-easterly wind behind him managed a respectable enough speed over the sea of 57 mph. He knew that he needed to save fuel when he could. Although in theory there was more than enough fuel in the R34's tanks to see her across to New York, the margin was not great. A day of strong headwinds could easily reduce that margin to something very slender. At 05.42 Scott radioed the Air Ministry in London: 'Off Rathlin Island, NE coast of Ireland, heading for Atlantic – all well.'

How much sleep Maitland managed to snatch that first morning he doesn't say. But it couldn't have been much because at 06.00 he was recording:

Large banks of white fleecy cloud now come rolling in from the Atlantic, gradually blotting out all view of the sea. At first we are above these clouds, but gradually they rise higher, and we plough our way into the middle of them. On leaving East Fortune a depression was centred over the southern part of the North Sea, with the result that it would be bound to extend as far as the west coasts of Scotland and Ireland; and so cloud and rain must be expected till we get well away into the Atlantic.

Plugging away steadily into the fog – nothing visible or audible, not even the sea. Ship now becomes very heavy, due to rain and cooling down after superheating. Scott keeps her 12° up by the bow in order to maintain a steady height. This kind of weather in particular makes one realise the essential importance of navigation in all its forms, as we cannot see a yard ahead of us. Suddenly we catch a glimpse of the sea through a hole in the clouds, and notice we have a slight drift to the south, already estimated by both Scott and Cooke.

As rain becomes heavier Scott tries to get down below the clouds, but these prove to be too low, and it is discovered that these clouds are drier low down than up top. This was later found to be the general rule, the wettest part of the cloud being the top, and should be of great interest to pilots flying through rain when it is impossible to climb high enough to get above the clouds.

It is now breakfast time and we sit down to this meal in

two watches – fifteen in each watch. In the officers' living room the first watch for breakfast includes Scott, Cooke, Pritchard (Air Ministry Technical Observer), Lansdowne (United States Naval Airship Service), Shotter (Engineer Officer) and Harris (Meteorological Officer).

We discuss R34's recent flight up the Baltic, and are all unanimous that large Rigid Airships – even in high winds – are *much* steadier over the sea than surface ships; and agree that, in the future, people who are bad sailors will prefer to make the long sea passages by Airship, if only to avoid seasickness. In the adjoining compartment the gramophone is entertaining the crew to the latest Jazz tunes, such as 'The Wild, Wild Women', etc!

Still in thick fog, cold and damp. We compare our dangers with those of surface ships. Beyond its discomfort, this fog does not worry us in the least; besides, an Airship always has the alternative of climbing above it should she wish to do so, which need not always be the case. The surface ship has the iceberg to fear, but these have no terrors for us. No iceberg over 700 feet has been seen in the North Atlantic, 200 feet being considered a high one. High icebergs have been known in the Southern Hemisphere up to 1,100 feet.

At 07.48 the R34 received a message from HMS *Tiger*, one of the two supporting heavy cruisers, via the radio station at Ponta del Garda on the Azores. The message gave the cruiser's position and a weather report: 'Barometer 30.33, falling slowly; wind SSW, under 5 mph. Thick fog bank. Visibility nil. Sea moderate.'

Which was much the same as the outlook from the R34, as Maitland recorded:

Nothing but fog, estimated by Harris to go down to within 150 feet of the water. Five minutes later we find ourselves right out above the fog – height still 1,500 feet – and beneath a cloudy sky with clouds at about 8,000 feet. We are therefore in between two layers of clouds; a condition in which Alcock and Brown found themselves on more than one occasion during their recent Atlantic crossing from west to east. An excellent cloud horizon now presents itself on all sides, of which Cooke, our Navigating Officer, at once takes advantage.

In 1919 aerial navigation was, to say the least, in its infancy. Cooke had to fix (or try to fix) his position using a naval sextant not too different from the kind his great namesake found his way round the globe with in the eighteenth century. Using a sextant depends on being able to fix the angle between the horizon and the sun or the stars. Having no sea horizon to use, Cooke's only alternative was to find the horizon of a cloud layer. These 'cloud horizons' were better than nothing but far from perfect, as Maitland pointed out:

Cooke reckons it is easy to make as much as a 50-mile error in locating one's position when using a cloud horizon as a substitute for a sea horizon. Sky above clearing, and large patches of blue sky appearing. Temperature has risen to 60° Fahrenheit. Passing through this thick cloud the ship has collected a considerable quantity of electricity, with the result that the wireless operators report unpleasant electric shocks. Airship is probably negative and the cloud is positive, causing slight discharge from the cloud to the ship.

Scott brings ship down to 1,300 feet, level into the cloud bank, as she is beginning to heat up and the gas bags are full. This will have the effect of keeping her temperature down, and so avoid losing gas. Even clouds have their uses! Cooke has three independent and specially constructed chronometer watches, which he carefully checks one against the other, and with which he will keep dead accurate Greenwich time with us throughout the voyage. This is essential to assist him in plotting his exact position.

Scott is able by skilful handling to keep the ship in these thick clouds to avoid superheating. At the same time he judges it so nicely that Cooke, standing on the top of the ship, is able to get observations with sextant on sun and cloud horizon – his eye being practically on a level with the cloud horizon, the only thing peeping up above the top of the cloud-bank being the top of his head, which is functioning in the same way as a submarine periscope! What a strange sight it would have been to another passing aircraft to see a man's head skimming along the top of a cloud-bank at forty knots!

One method we use for calculating drift is to look down vertically through a bomb-sight having previously set the instrument to the course the ship is steering. Then, by getting the top of a wave moving parallel to the lines in the bomb-sight, one can read off on the dial the actual course made good. Subtract from this the course steered and one gets the angle of the drift.

Stopped forward and two aft engines, and now running on only the two wing engines at 1,600 revolutions. Air speed 30 knots or 36 mph, which is the most economical speed for this type of Airship, as she only consumes 25 gallons of petrol per hour on the two wing engines. Wind is east, 7 miles per hour, so we are making a good 40 miles per hour, with three engines resting. Fog still thick, and visibility nil. Water dripping in through roof. Temperature 54° F. Cold and damp.

At 11.15 Maitland noted that the R34 was

. . . 400 miles from East Fortune and 200 miles into the Atlantic from Bloody Foreland. There is practically no wind and we are making quite good air speed with our two engines only. Pitot tube gets filled up with fog and rain, and needs hauling in and blowing out occasionally, to get true readings. WT [wireless telegraph] arrangements are that we communicate with East Fortune as long as possible and then – when they fade out – we shall still have Pembroke, then Ponta del Garda (Azores) and finally Glace Bay.

Fog thicker and thicker, and we can see nothing, so think lunch would be a good idea. Excellent beef stew and potatoes. Caley's chocolate. Cold water to drink. We compare our views on the distribution of air pressure on the western side of the Atlantic, the winds we are likely to meet with, the fog we are likely to run into, the advantages of Directional Wireless for navigational purposes, cloud horizons etc. Scott, Cooke and Harris in comparing their experiences and expounding their theories are most interesting.

During meal-times ship is inclined to get an angle slightly down by the bow, owing to officers' and crew's dining quarters being situated too far forward. This must be corrected in future designs. Necessary to send some of the crew aft to correct trim. I notice they don't forget to take their food with them.

At midday Maitland decided to try to catch a few hours' sleep.

The sleeping arrangements consist of a hammock for each man off watch, suspended from the main girder of the triangular internal keel, which runs from end to end of the ship. Decide to turn in and get some sleep. It is quite hot in the keel so sleep in underclothing only – outside sleeping bag – too hot inside. Slept soundly till 2.45 p.m., and feel much rested.

Maitland woke to a surprise.

Scott comes to my hammock and tells me that there is a stowaway on board. Just before starting it had been decided that one of the members of the crew (AC2 W.W. Ballantyne) must be left behind, the numbers being limited of necessity to 30. Ballantyne, on his own confession, hid himself in the darkness high up above the keel, on one of the longitudinal girders between the gas bags, and has just emerged from his hiding place.

He says he could not bear the thought of being left behind. Cannot help sympathising with his motive, but it is bad from a disciplinary point of view, to say nothing of risking the success of the flight. Without his weight we could have carried 200 lbs more petrol, and of course he has been allotted neither food nor hammock. Had there been land beneath us instead of ocean we would have put him off at once in a parachute: but as we are now out in the Atlantic, there is nothing for it but to take him across and make the best use of his services. Necessary disciplinary action will be deferred until we arrive in America.

The R34's stowaway was Aircraftman second class William 'Billy' Ballantyne, an irrepressible 22-year old from Tyneside. He had been assigned to the R34's flight crew until late in the day when he was 'bumped' off to make way for the American observer, Zachary Lansdowne. But Ballantyne was having none of it. The R34 was not about to fly the Atlantic without him, even if it meant risking a court martial. It is likely that some of his fellow airmen helped smuggle him aboard.

Ballantyne had inserted himself onto a girder between two of the ship's gas bags. But after 12 hours' breathing in small quantities of hydrogen he became violently sick and his retching gave him away. He was hauled down to the control car, given a dressing-down by Scott and Maitland, and then spent a few hours in one of the hammocks dosed with quinine. Ballantyne spent the rest of the trip peeling potatoes and manning the petrol pumps. But as late as 1979, when he was in his 80s, Ballantyne was telling people that he had 'no regrets' about stowing away.

At 15.30 Maitland wrote

Durrant, our Wireless Officer, reports he has just spoken to St John's Newfoundland, who, though very faint, proceed to send us weather report. As we are still in touch with East Fortune and Clifden and have been exchanging signals with the Azores since reaching the Irish coast, our communications are, so far, admirable.

Very beautiful rainbow effect on the clouds: one complete rainbow encircles the ship, and another smaller one encircles our shadow on the water; both are very vivid in their colouring. Colours in sequence from centre of circle: white, yellow, pink, dark blue, green, yellow, pink, yellow, pink, green. This rainbow or 'glory' seems to be only evident when the clouds are thin, and sea can be almost discerned through them.

Teatime. Bread and butter, greengage jam and two cups of scalding hot tea, which has been boiled over the exhaust pipe 'cooker' fitted to the forward engine. 'Fruitarian' cake is also tried for the first time. It has rather a sickly taste, but is very sustaining; the whole assisted by Miss Lee White on the gramophone! Greenland, the First Officer of the ship, is vainly trying to discover the culprit who used his toothbrush for stirring the mustard at lunch!

And then, another stowaway:

Found a tabby kitten in the forepart of the keel, and recognised it as the one that was with us on our 21-hour flight from Inchinnan to East Fortune. There are also two carrier pigeons on board, and it is rather a question as to what use they can ever be, and what we had better do with them. Pigeons only fly overseas in the direction in which they have been trained, and, as these have been trained in the North Sea to fly west, they would presumably fly towards America directly we let them go, regardless of whether they could do the distance or not.

We decide to keep them on board and – if not necessary to

use them on outward journey – to release them in sight of
Ireland on return journey to see if they would (a) fly towards
land if they could see it, (b) get on from Ireland to England.
Anyway, if not released at all, they can claim to be the first
pigeons to fly (?) the Atlantic.

By the end of that first afternoon the R34 was flying westwards
at a height of 2,000 feet.

At this height we find ourselves well over the clouds, and the
view is enchanting – as far as the eye can see a vast ocean of
white fleecy clouds, ending in the most perfect of cloud
horizons. There is a cloudless and deep blue sky overhead,
and now occasionally we get glimpses of vivid blue sea
through gaps in the clouds beneath. Our navigator does not
miss this opportunity, and at once gets busy taking observations with sextant of the sun and cloud horizon.

We feel in a world of our own up here amidst this dazzling
display of snow-white clouds. No words can express the
wonder, the grandeur, or the loneliness of it all; one must
experience these joys for oneself before one can even begin
to realise them. Two particularly fine specimens of 'windy
cirrus' cloud now appear on our port beam, and are clearly
silhouetted at an enormous height against the azure sky.
These cirrus clouds (officially known as 'Cirrus Ventosus')
are very distinctive – little curly clouds like a black-cock's
tail feathers.

Specimens of 'Flocculent Cirro Stratus', rather resembling
a diamond tiara, high in the centre and sloping away on
both sides, also begin to appear away to the south. The
appearance of these two types of cloud is interpreted by
Harris as a first and infallible indication of a depression
coming up from the south. We think that this depression
may help us, provided we have crossed its path in advance.
It is interesting to note that, as yet, we have received no
notice of any depression coming out of the south in any

weather reports. Scott thinks we are making better headway up here above the clouds than we were when inside the clouds: though he cannot yet, of course, be certain of this.

Alcock and Brown finished their flight of 1,800 miles in 16 hours. We have now taken 17 hours for 610 miles, so that their speed made good is three times as fast as ours. They, of course, were flying from west to east with a following wind behind them, while we are flying in the reverse direction with the prevailing wind against us. It will be noticed that our speed is distinctly low, but we have been running for a large part of the time on only three engines, with two engines resting.

It must be remembered that Scott has to nurse his engines for the return journey, and had it not been for this, our speed for this outward journey could have been a third as fast again. At this rate, and if all goes well, and if that depression in the south does not interfere, we should see St John's, if not shrouded in fog (as it usually is) about midnight tomorrow, July 3rd.

At 19.00 the R34 received word from the Marconi radio station at Clifden that a depression was creeping up the Atlantic from the south. 'This confirms Harris's previous forecast at 5.40 p.m. on seeing the cirrus clouds,' Maitland wrote, 'and is admirable proof of the accuracy and value of cloud forecasting. We are all quite excited about this approaching depression, as it is exactly the weather conditions we were hoping to get.'

On the face of it a cyclone bringing wind and rain would seem bad news. But, as mentioned earlier, in the northern hemisphere air moves around cyclones in an anti-clockwise direction, so if the airship could get to the top of the cyclone it might ride the wind westwards. As Maitland explained: 'With any luck we should be benefited by the helping easterly wind on the north side of it, and, as we get further towards the Newfoundland coast, it should become more northerly, and blow us down towards New York. Weather situation has therefore become extremely interesting, and it now remains to be seen whether our hopes and forecasts will be realised.'

Meanwhile there were 31 men to be fed and watered, no easy matter on an airship.

> Our cooking arrangements are too primitive. Impossible to boil water slowly – can only boil fast. No frying facilities, which would be a boon – particularly for breakfast. No fresh vegetables on board. We must remember to get these, also fruit for the return journey, and generally arrange for more complete cooking arrangements on our next long-distance flight. Cup of hot cocoa. Lay down for half an hour before evening meal, and read Emerson's poems. Noticeable leakage from petrol tanks when ship takes up big angle by bow or stern, causing unpleasant smell of petrol vapour in keel. This must be remedied in future.

> We are just on top of the clouds now – alternately in the sun, and then plunging through thick banks of cloud, The sun is low down on the western horizon, and we are steering straight for it, making Pritchard at the elevators curse himself for having forgotten to bring tinted glasses.

But on that first evening the navigating officer, Gilbert Cooke, discovered that at least one of his instruments was inaccurate enough to be dangerous. Cooke later reported that 'Between 18.42 GMT and 21.09 GMT three sets of observations on Sun and Moon were taken with a Bubble Sextant. These sights were so unreliable, and the altitudes obtained were so doubtful, that this Sextant was not again used. This instrument was one of about a dozen which were made for experimental purposes about three years ago.'

While Cooke was fretting about the accuracy of the R34's instruments, Maitland was admiring the cloudscape. At 20.55 he wrote:

Sun is now setting, and gradually disappears below the lower cloud horizon, throwing a wonderful pink glow on the white clouds in every direction: a very beautiful sunset, and very cold. Turned in – feeling very tired and sleepy. Owing to early start have many hours of sleep to make up. Thought out splendid scheme for getting into hammock: get good grip on main keel girder, pull up on arms and then lower down into hammock from above – very quick and quite easy. It is cold up here in the keel at night, but we feel very warm and snug in our sleeping bags.

All through this first night in the Atlantic the ordinary Airship routine, viz., navigating, steering, working the elevators, attending to the engines etc., is continued, watch by watch, as in the daytime. The night is very dark, but the airship is lit by electric throughout, a much enlarged car lighting system having been fitted. There is a light to every instrument, which can be switched on as required, and, in the case of failure of the lighting system, all figures and indicators are radiumised. This radium paint is so luminous that, in most cases, the lighting installation is unnecessary.

Up to date on the whole of journey Scott estimates we have used on average 1.24 gallons of petrol per nautical mile made good. This, if it continues, should give us 1,100 gallons of petrol, over and above, on our arrival in New York. This, so far as we have gone, is an extremely good consumption figure, especially when one remembers how much we changed course to clear the high hills of Scotland. Hope we shall be able to maintain this average; but have presentiment that we won't.

7

Day Two: Thursday, 3 July 1919

Through the early hours of Thursday, 3 July, the R34 ploughed her westerly course. At 02.45 the ship received the last message from her base at East Fortune, which was now slipping out of range. At 04.20 Gilbert Cooke climbed to the top of the hull and took sextant observations from the cloud horizon on the stars Polaris, Capella and the constellation Andromeda. His readings gave the R34 a position of 52° 40′ north, 30° 15′ west. An hour later the R34 made radio contact with the steamer *Hellig Olav* bound for Copenhagen. 'Wish we could see her instead of only talking to her,' Maitland noted in his log.

Oddly for a man well used to flying, Maitland seems to have been genuinely taken aback by the sheer size and desolation of the Atlantic. Although the R34 was tracking along one of the world's busiest shipping routes and was frequently in radio contact with ships heading both east and west, none of the crew had laid eyes on a ship since they had left the Clyde. Time after time Maitland remarked on this fact.

At 09.20 Maitland wrote:

Clock put back another hour. Making good 30 knots. We are now over the Westbound Steamship route from the Clyde to Cape Race, and momentarily crossing the Eastbound route from Belle Isle to Plymouth. We are well over halfway between Ireland and Newfoundland, and are back again on the Great Circle route, having been slightly to the south of it, owing to the drift effect of a northerly wind.

If visible we should see Cape Race, Newfoundland, 24 hours from now – distance 750 nautical miles. Put this cheerful information up on notice board in dining room.

Lieut. Shotter, Engineer Officer, who, through many causes, has been prevented from getting his fair share of sleep, is beginning to feel rather exhausted, and is dosed with aspirin by Luck, who is our amateur doctor for the voyage in addition to his duties as Third Officer.

Harris informs me that in his experience it either blows hard in the western Atlantic or there is fog. This may be regarded as an almost infallible rule. Got quite a nice view of Atlantic during short gap in clouds for about three minutes – sea a deep blue colour. Big swell. Visibility on surface of sea probably very good, but overcast. Estimated drift, 10°. Height 900 feet. Running on forward and after engines only. Wind estimated to be SE, about 10 knots. Air speed 33½ knots.

Scott reckons we are making good 38 knots and using roughly 38 gallons of petrol an hour, which is quite a good state of affairs. Scott's method of estimating wind on surface of sea is to watch a wave breaking, when foam is left on the surface, and the wave goes down wind. The foam then appears to move up wind, and the resultant effect gives you more or less reliable direction of wind on surface of sea.

The *Aquitania* is, according to Marconi's Telegraph Communication Chart for July, now between Long. 30° and 20° W, or two thirds of the way across to Ireland. We should be hearing her soon, though we can only speak her on a relay as our WT spark range is limited to 120 miles. This same chart tells that the following steamers should also be within range of our WT spark set: ss *Sardinian, Canada, Michigan, Mesava, Mattwa, Orduna, Vestris, Manhattan, Rochambeau*. In addition, if in distress, we could probably get the ss *Sunderland* on our spark set, as she should be just within range. We are in touch with Glace Bay for the first time.

Glace Bay (from the French *Baie de Glace* – Bay of Ice) was the coal-mining town on Cape Breton on northern Nova Scotia, where Gugliemo Marconi had set up the first commercial transatlantic wireless transmitting station in 1907. Its European counterpart was the Marconi station at Clifden in County Galway, on the west coast of Ireland. Both stations transmitted on a long wave (short wave transmission did not emerge until 1926) and had their own electricity generating stations. The Glace Bay station was powered by coal, Clifden's by peat.

One of the early problems was that radio reception at the Marconi stations kept being interrupted or suppressed by the powerful transmitters. When the transmitters were working reception was almost impossible. Marconi solved this in 1913 by erecting a 'duplex' system whereby the company's transmitters and receivers were kept miles apart. Thus the receiving station on Cape Breton was near the town of Louisborough well to the south of Glace Bay. The Marconi receiver in Ireland was at Letterfrack, a good 35 miles from Clifden. The Clifden transmitter was shut down in 1922 after being irreparably damaged during the Irish Civil War.

As the British military were one of the firm's important customers, the Marconi Wireless, Telegraph and Signal Company was only too willing to help the R34 across the Atlantic. The stations on the Marconi radio network, which was then probably the best in the world, were instructed to give the airship every assistance and the Marconi offices in the west end of London installed a large window display which charted the progress of the R34. It was a good deal: a useful service for the R34 and excellent publicity for Marconi.

At 09.35 Maitland wrote:

Scott alters course a little to the north so as to be in position to use the easterly wind on the north side of the approaching depression as much as possible. Weather report from St John's: 'Barometer 1010.2. Steady; temperature 44° F. Fog. Visibility about half mile, fog seaward, wind westerly, very light.' This is all right.

Turned in for an hour but unable to sleep. Become

absorbed in Kipling's story of 'The Night Mail' in *Actions and Reactions*. Think I must have read this story 50 times! Every time I read it the more impressed I become with the reality of its prophecies, which give one that very same 'atmosphere' of Aerial Liner travel that we are actually experiencing during every moment of this journey.

Maitland's fascination with Rudyard Kipling's yarn is interesting. He seemed to see in the story the future of aviation. Although it was described by Arnold Bennett as a 'glittering essay in the sham-technical' the story is still well-regarded by science-fiction buffs. Kipling spiced it with whimsical 'advertisements' and 'official' notices from an all-powerful global bureaucracy known as the 'Aerial Board of Control'. But he also predicted a great deal that later (much later) transpired: air traffic control systems, organised flight paths, an elaborate network of radio stations that supplied aircraft with instructions, crucial hazard warnings and weather reports.

At noon Maitland wrote:

Midday meal – cold roast beef with one cold potato each. We are short of potatoes, having apparently eaten too many yesterday! Bread and butter, cheese, chocolate and a cup of tea. Wind SE to SE by S. Strength 15 to 20 knots. Clouds near surface of sea have cleared away, and we now have a visibility of about 40 or 50 miles in all directions. Sky overcast with thin cloud. This is really the first time we have had an all-round view of the Atlantic since we started. Sea is very blue, a biggish swell and many white horses. Hope that, with this good visibility, we may at last see a passing ship. One of crew (a rigger) is ill. Temperature 102. Confined to hammock and dosed with quinine and salts.

Running on forward and after engines only, resting both wing engines. Height 1,100 feet. We cannot tell our height above sea accurately, as we don't know what the barometer is reading. Our aneroid shows a height of 1,200 feet. Scott thought it more likely to be 1,500 feet, as one cannot well assume that the barometer here on the surface of the water is the same as the barometer was when we left the ground at East Fortune.

We now try the experiment of lowering an instrument known as a sea-level aneroid, and specially designed to record atmospheric pressure readings, down to the surface of the water. The ship is not slowed down for the purpose in any way, and as this has not been tried before success is problematical. Result is no good, as the instrument shows exactly the same reading on reaching the car again as it had before starting. It had undoubtedly recorded the reading on surface, but got jerked (being a very sensitive instrument) on the quick haul-up.

Until we know our exact height above the sea we cannot plot our exact position, so until we speak to a ship in our vicinity and get her barometer reading we still lack means for such a calculation. Some suitable method of getting this information must be perfected before we do any more long overseas flights.

The airship is throwing a very dark shadow on the surface of the sea on starboard side – almost immediately underneath the ship. By taking with a sextant the angle subtended by length of shadow, and knowing the length of the shadow to be 640 feet, he gets the true height. In this case the height works out at 2,100 feet, whilst the aneroid gives us only 1,200 feet – a variation of 900 feet.

This lack of a reliable method of calculating the height of an aircraft above the planet was serious. Over the sea it was not so critical, but over land it could be (and often was) lethal. It was to be another decade before a German-born emigrant to the USA called Paul Kollsman came up with a rugged and reliable barometric altimeter. Kollsman produced the device in 1928 and saw it tested in 1929 by the renowned US aviator and pioneer of instrument flying, Lieutenant-Colonel Jimmy

Doolittle. Modern versions of Kollsman's altimeter are now standard on most of the world's aircraft.

Durrant is speaking to ss *Canada* on our WT spark set. Another WT operator (Corporal Powell) is trying to get her on the directional wireless, so that we may know in what direction to look for her. All we know at the moment is that she is *somewhere* within 120 miles of us, and bound for Liverpool. She gives her position as follows: 'Long. 39° 42′ W, Lat. 51° 16′ N (or 60 miles SSE from us), barometer 30.8 rising. Wind and sea moderate from SE . . .

Her wireless operator tells us that great enthusiasm prevails on board, and that every one is hoping to catch sight of us. This feeling is mutual, but, although we do our best to get her on our directional wireless, besides gazing through our glasses in every direction, she remains just beyond our visibility. Scott now brings his ship down to the 1,200-foot level, to try and find a more easterly trend in the wind.

Even though the men on the R34 never did manage to lay eyes on her, the contact with the *Canada* was important.

The reading on ss *Canada*'s barometer is of the greatest value, and is exactly the information of which we are in need. We can now work out our true height above the sea, and consequently fix our exact position. Her barometer on the surface reads 30.8, whilst ours in the ship is 29.7. This shows a difference of 30.8–29.7, or 1.1 inches. Remembering the rule that for every 1,000 feet you rise the barometer falls 1 inch, we get our height as 1,000 feet, which tallies almost exactly with Scott's estimate of 900 feet inaccuracy mentioned above.

It is quite possible that Scott's calculation of 900 feet may still be dead accurate, as ss *Canada* is some 50 or 60 miles away, and the change in barometer over that distance may well work out at 100 feet. What a relief it is to remember that peace prevails and we need no longer keep sharp and constant look-out for enemy submarines.

Which is an odd remark. Submarines were never a threat to airships. The only (very uncertain) record of an airship being downed by gunfire from a submarine was a case of 'friendly fire' when a German U-boat in the Mediterranean downed Zeppelin L59, the famous *Afrika* airship that had flown from Bulgaria to the Sudan and back.

Nothing weighed more heavily on the R34's crew than the strictly enforced smoking ban. 'Not being allowed to smoke is a great privation upon long flights of this description,' Maitland declared 'and is acutely felt by all members of the crew, particularly after meals. Special arrangements to allow this will be made on future long-distance Airship journeys.' (As indeed they were: the civil airships of the 1920s and 1930s all had asbestos-lined smoke rooms.)

Harris unwisely shuts his hand on the door of WT cabin – painful, but not serious. Flow of language not audible to me, as fortunately forward engine happens to be running.

Conditions now very pleasant. Blue sky above and blue sea below – nice and warm. We remove nearly all our clothes and feel delightfully comfortable. Thank goodness there are no appearances to keep up on board our Aerial Liner: and we don't mind what we look like or who sees us! Fine cirrus clouds on starboard beam.

Sadly, Maitland doesn't go into any detail about feeling 'delightfully comfortable'. But the image of 31 semi-naked airmen (and a cat) scampering all over the keel, rigging and control car of a giant airship over the middle of the Atlantic is comic. He continued:

Very big drift, estimated at 30°. Ship practically travelling sideways. Wind is estimated to be SSE, 30 knots, and helping us considerably. Scott calculates, by measuring angles on shadow with sextant, that we are making a good 40 knots. Cooke calculates with drift calculator that we are making good 38 knots. I log accordingly our speed made good as 39 knots, and so everyone is satisfied! Durrant hears *Aquitania*, but does not speak to her. St John's reports wind easterly, which is good hearing.

That afternoon the R34 was hit with the first of the engine problems that were to plague the flights to the USA and back. Maitland reported:

Trouble with starboard amidships engine. Engine stopped. No details yet. Engine restarted. A small screw on water jacket had worked loose, and this has been made secure with a piece of copper sheeting and the entire supply of the crew's chewing gum (which was hastily chewed first by Engineer Officer and two engineers!). We will never be without a good supply of this in future, and this should be a very good and unexpected advertisement for Mr Edmondson's brand of chewing gum!

When this colourful story began going around aviation circles after the flight there was a slightly hurt response from the Sunbeam Motor Car Company. At the end of July one of the firm's executives wrote to *Flight* magazine declaring that the R34's chewing-gum drama was greatly exaggerated. 'It was used to secure a water plate on a cylinder jacket. The men fitted a small plate secured by gum. When Sunbeam examined the engine they couldn't find it and had to have it pointed out.' (Which may have said more for the tenacity of Mr Edmondson's chewing gum than for the build of the Sunbeam engine.)

The speed with which an airship could be blown off-course made navigation a constant problem, as Maitland acknowledged:

Scott and Cooke spend much time at chart table with protractors, dividers, stop-watches and many navigational text books, measuring angles of drift and calculating course made good. Whenever the surface of the sea is visible, observations are taken with Drift Indicator to check our course and speed. This is also frequently checked by timing the ship's shadow when visible in passing some defined spot, such as foam left by a breaking wave.

Aerial navigation is more complicated than navigation on the surface of the sea, owing to the existence of a third dimension: but there is no reason why, when Directional Wireless has been perfected, and when we know more about the air and its peculiarities, it should not become very accurate. Wind rising – sea beginning to get rough – visibility 1 mile.

By 16.00 Maitland was, yet again, longing to catch sight of a ship, any ship. He wrote:

We should soon be over the Canadian summer route of steamers bound for the St Lawrence via Belle Isle Strait, and may perhaps sight a ship. From our experience so far on this voyage, it seems an absolute miracle to me that Hawker should have found a ship when he did in this vast Atlantic. We are now in the vicinity of the well-known Labrador current, and there are already indications of these cold currents in the fog which is beginning to appear above the surface of the water.

The oceanography of the North Atlantic is complex. The Labrador current is an extension of a powerful current of cold water that flows from the Arctic down the east coast of Greenland (the East Greenland Current) turns northward up along the west coast (the West Greenland Current) and then turns again at the top of Baffin Bay to run down the west coast of Canada (the Baffin Island Current and the Labrador

Current). Off the south-east coast of Newfoundland the cold
water of the Labrador Current runs into the warmer water of
the Gulf Stream, with results that can be unpredictable.

> Cooke gets good observation of sun to sea horizon. Wind
> which is 45 knots and 'backing', and we are being carried
> rather far north and off the direct course we originally
> intended. Position now about due south of Greenland.
> Angle of drift about 50°. Petrol expended, 1,546 gallons.
> Petrol left, 3,354 gallons.
>
> We are gradually getting further and further into the
> shallow depression which was reported yesterday coming
> up from the South Atlantic. For the last four hours the sea
> has been rising, and now the wind is SSE, about 45 knots,
> and we are travelling sideways over the sea making good
> 25 to 30 knots. Harris thinks, when we have passed the
> centre of this depression, we should get a more easterly wind
> and clearer sky, so go right ahead into it, and are full of
> confidence.

An hour later Harris' confidence had ebbed somewhat.

> All visibility gone, and thick fog everywhere. It is unplea-
> santly cold, we are not only fully dressed, but wearing
> overcoats as well. Conditions at present are not at all nice,
> and it is an anxious time from now on, until we see how the
> weather develops. We are a little over 300 miles from the
> nearest point of Newfoundland, viz., Trinity Bay, and 350
> miles from St John's. Estimated drift 70°. In all probability
> we should get across the centre of this depression in two or
> three hours' time. It is raining very fast, which is a good sign,
> as it nearly always rains near the centre of a depression.
>
> In spite of our drift angle of 70° we are making good a
> forward course direct on Belle Isle, which is at the most
> northerly point of Newfoundland, and the entrance to the
> Gulf of St Lawrence. White horses just visible occasionally

Above. Pride of the Clyde. The R34 leaves the airship shed at Inchinnan in which she was built. The huge shed was dismantled in the early 1920s. *University of Glasgow Archives*

Left. Cathedral in the sky. A rare image of the R34's lofty interior lined with fuel tanks. The narrow 'walking way' was a constant hazard to the crew. *National Museums of Scotland*

Right. 'T.E. Lawrence with his head in the clouds'. An apt description of Brigadier-General Edward Maitland, aviator extraordinaire and a zealous supporter of lighter-than-air flight. He was the driving force behind the R34's trans-atlantic journey. *National Portrait Gallery*

Below. Afore ye go. Some of the R34's crew. Front row centre, holding his dog 'Judy', is the R34's captain, Major George Herbert Scott. On his right the American observer, Lieutenant-Commander Zachary Lansdowne, US Navy. *National Museums of Scotland*

Above. Lift off. A (somewhat romanticised) watercolour painting of the R34 taking off from East Fortune airfield in the early hours of 2nd July, 1919. She was 'walked out' of her hangar by more than 500 servicemen and women. *National Museums of Scotland*

Left. The stowaways. Aircraftsman William 'Billy' Ballantyne stowed away in the R34's rigging rather than be left off the flight. The kitten 'Whoopsie' seems to have been smuggled aboard by engineer George Graham. *National Museums of Scotland*

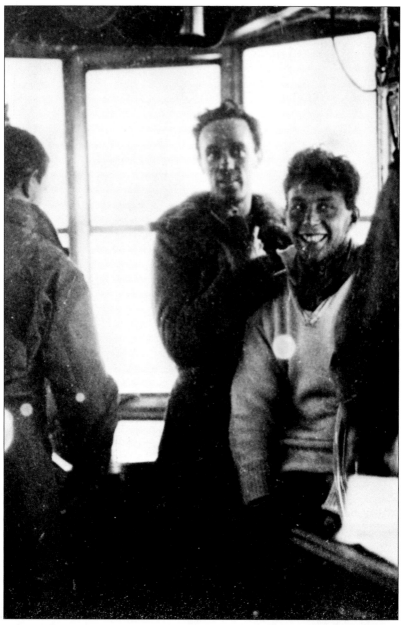

Dressing down. Ballantyne is quizzed by officers in the control car. He was told that if he'd been detected while the R34 was over land he'd have been strapped to parachute and kicked out. He was threatened with court martial but one was never held. *National Museums of Scotland*

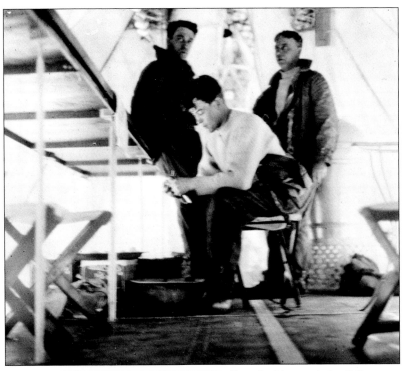

Above. Punishment duties. Ballantyne peeling spuds. He spent the remainder of the trip doing the ship's dirty work but never regretted stowing away. But he was not allowed to make the return journey. Ballantyne spent the rest of his career rising through the ranks of the RAF and was commissioned in the Second World War. *National Museums of Scotland*

Left. The engineer as hero. Lieutenant (later General) John Shotter, the R34's engineering officer. Shotter kept the R34's inadequate Sunbeam engines going, occasionally at risk to life and limb. He was awarded an Air Force Cross. *National Museums of Scotland*

New York, New York. Sunday, 6th July, 1919 and the R34 touches down at Roosevelt Field, Mineola, Long Island with the help of the US Army. The airship was met by huge crowds and the crew spent almost a week being lavishly wined and dined by their American hosts. *National Museums of Scotland*

Above. Back in Blighty. The R34's captain George Herbert Scott takes questions from the press after the R34 touched down at Pulham in Norfolk. No reason was ever given for diverting the ship to Pulham instead of East Fortune in Scotland (where the officers and crew were based). *National Museums of Scotland*

Right. The poet. Lady Sybil Grant, the beautiful if raffish daughter of the Earl of Rosebery and a close friend of Edward Maitland. Poet, journalist and film maker, she was fascinated by airships. One of her poems is dedicated to the R34's transatlantic voyage. *National Portrait Gallery*

through the fog. Sea very rough. HMS *Tiger* reports: 'Wind SE by S, 20 miles per hour, freshening. Squally sky. 2/10 Cirrus Stratus. 3/10 Stratus, misty to the SW Visibility 10 miles. Sea moderate. Position Lat. 53° 50' N, Long. 40° W Barometer 30.25 falling slowly.'

Struck by fierce squall. Heavy rain. Ship remarkably steady considering intensity of squall. Scott remarked he would not like to take a 23-class rigid into this.

Scott was referring to a previous generation of airships – which were first walked out in 1917 – which were smaller, lighter, less powerful and less streamlined than the R34. Four of them were built: His Majesty's Airships 23, 24, 25 and 26.

By then the R34 was in the thick of it. Maitland wrote:

The rain is driving through the roof of the fore car in many places, and there is a thin film of water over the chart table. The wind is roaring to such an extent that we have to shout to make ourselves heard. Time for the evening meal, but no one gives it a thought while this entertainment is going on. Scott gets his bald patch thoroughly soaked whenever he peeps out through window to watch direction of wind.

Am much struck by the steadiness of the ship in this squall, which is a very severe one. Beyond a gradual and very slow pitching, causing us to hold on and making everything slip about pretty considerably, we feel no inconvenience, and not the slightest symptom of seasickness. The sea, on the other hand, when last we saw it, was very rough, and I, for one, being the worst possible sailor, would certainly be feeling horribly ill if I were on board a surface ship! Scott has consultation with Luck, his Third Officer, and decides to try to climb right out of this depression. Nose of ship put up accordingly.

Our evening meal of bread and butter, cheese and Oxo is a simple one, and not particularly appetising. Resolve to take a personal interest in the food question for the return journey. We sit seven of us in a circle, Luck, Scott, Cooke, Lansdowne, Harris, Shotter and myself, talking about everything except Airships and storms in the Atlantic. For want of chairs Shotter and Lansdowne sit on the floor underneath the table – as good a place as any. The cat purrs contentedly in Harris's lap, with one eye always on the food!

Our height is now 3,400 feet, and we are well out of the clouds right out of the depression, exactly as foretold by Harris. The rain has ceased and we are travelling quite smoothly again. This is probably the first time that the top of the danger area of a shallow depression has been scientifically observed and photographed from above.

The lesson we learn from this is that the rain and wind usually to be expected with a 'shallow' depression only prevail up to a low level, so that on encountering such a depression, the best course is to seek a higher level and continue flying comfortably above it. With a 'deep' depression, upon the other hand, the higher you go the worse the wind and rain will undoubtedly become; and the best policy to pursue is to circumvent them and so turn them to useful advantage.

The trick, of course, is somehow to distinguish a shallow depression from a deep one. This is never easy and was very much harder in 1919 than it is now. Depressions (or cyclones) are columns of air swirling at varying speeds around an 'eye' of low pressure. North of the equator they circulate anti-clockwise; in the southern hemisphere they circulate clockwise. In height they can be anything between a few thousand feet and more than 5 miles. Maitland described the atmosphere as the R34 flew out of the depression:

To the west the clouds have lifted, and we see a most wonderful and interesting sky. Black, angry clouds above us, giving place to the clouds of a grey mouse colour, then a clear and bright salmon-pink expanse, changing lower down the horizon to darker clouds with a rich golden lining as the sun sinks below the surface. The sea is not visible, and is covered by a fluffy grey feather-bed of cloud, slightly undulating, and extending as far as the eye can reach.

The moon is just breaking through the black clouds immediately above us. To the east we see below us the black ominous depression from which we have just emerged, while away more to the south the cloud-bed over which we are passing seems to end suddenly and merge into the horizon. The lessons to be learnt from this magnificent cloudscape are difficult at present to estimate. The sunset is a very stormy one, but this is not to be wondered at when actually inside a depression.

The sky ahead looks lighter, but the cloud-bed beneath us should be 'packing' more, and not so 'fleecy' if we are to get better weather. Perhaps it will 'pack' more later on? We are collecting some valuable meteorological data on this flight without a doubt, and each fresh phenomenon as it appears is instantly explained by the ever-alert Harris, who astonishes us all with his meteorological knowledge under so many and varied conditions. He possesses plenty of 'imagination', and this seems to me to be an essential qualification for the art of reading the clouds and thoroughly appreciating their meaning.

Which would have warmed the heart of that Victorian/Edwardian naturalist and meteorologist Arthur William Clayden. His book *Cloud Studies* was one of the dozen or so texts in the R34's little library. No one knew better than Clayden how much imagination, estimation and sheer guesswork was required in understanding (or trying to understand) the clouds in the air. He wrote that:

Clouds are among the most inaccessible of terrestrial objects. Except by balloon ascents, by sending up kites bearing recording instruments, or by making observations among the mountain tops, we have no means of getting at them to study the conditions under which they exist. Temperature, pressure, humidity, have generally to be guessed at, those guesses being based on the scanty data which have been laboriously obtained by one or another of those cumbrous methods. Moreover, many clouds have such vast dimensions that it is very difficult to grasp all that goes in such a space.

As Clayden saw it, meteorology was in its infancy. But he pinned a lot of hope on the fast-improving technology of photography.

The workers are few and there is much to be done; for it is mainly to whose who will photograph the higher clouds, and so trace the stages of their growth and decay, that we must look for the data which will enable us to solve the problems they present, and so enlarge the narrow boundaries of our knowledge of some of the most beautiful things in nature.

By 21.00 that Thursday evening Maitland reported that the weather over the Atlantic seemed to be improving. 'Clouds are all the time getting lower, 15 minutes ago they were 3,200 feet above the water, now they are 2,000 feet only, and it is possible that in half an hour's time they may have cleared away altogether, and allow us a clear view of the sea.'

An hour later a minor accident had Second Officer Harold Luck reaching for the R34's medicine chest. 'One of the engineers – Sergt W.A. Scull – is reported sick. Top portion of thumbnail torn and thumb badly bruised, caught in moving part of machinery. Very painful, but not serious. Says he will be all right tomorrow.'

8

Day Three: Friday, 4 July 1919

There's always something special about something seen for the
first time. For the crew of the R34 the morning of Friday, 4
July 1919, was an exhilarating one, as Maitland's log reflects.
It was hardly surprising. It was probably the very first time that
the icebergs of the North Atlantic had been seen from the air.
And that spectacular sight came after a dawn that Maitland
logged as 'Wonderful sunrise, the different colours being the
softest imaginable, just like a wash drawing'.

Then at 07.00 Maitland recorded:

Height 1,000 feet. Bright blue sky above, thin fog partly
obscuring the sea beneath us. Sea moderate. Big swell. The
fog bank seems to end abruptly 10 miles or so away towards
the south, where the sea appears to be clear of fog, and a
very deep blue. Standing out conspicuously in this blue
patch of sea we see an enormous white iceberg. The sun
is shining brightly on its steep sides, and we estimate it as
roughly 300 yards square and about 150 feet high.

While Maitland thrilled to the sight, he recognised its menace.

As these icebergs sometimes cover an underwater area of
between seven and nine times their height above the surface,
we wonder whether it is aground, as depth of water at that
point is only 150 fathoms. Looking down upon this huge
iceberg from the open window of the forward car we can
clearly see treacherous green ice protruding under the water
in all directions. As this underwater ice could, under no
circumstances, be seen from a surface ship, it brings home to
one the hidden dangers that ocean-going vessels are liable to

meet within this portion of the Atlantic, where fogs may be expected at all times of the year.

Maitland was seeing one of the thousands of icebergs that are 'calved' every year from the glaciers that flow down the west coast of Greenland and collapse into Baffin Bay and the Davis Strait. The ice is then picked up by the Labrador Current and driven south, sometimes into the shipping lanes and very occasionally as far south as the Caribbean. Some icebergs are the size of six-storey buildings: others are no bigger than the top of a grand piano or a dining-room table. Even now the small ones (known as 'growlers') are hard for radar to spot. All of them are a danger to shipping.

Although these mountains of fresh-water ice are in the process of melting into the sea, the bigger ones can take a long time to disappear. So long as they are intact they are a threat. No one has any idea how many ships and boats have foundered in the North Atlantic after being gutted on blades of ice. The danger is at its height in a stretch of water 250 miles south-east of Newfoundland known as 'Iceberg Alley'. It was here that the RMS *Titanic* came to grief in April 1912.

The sight of the huge, spectacular crag of ice prompted Maitland into yet another paean of praise for the likely comfort and safety of the still-to-be-invented passenger airship, which he had come to call the 'airship liner' or 'aeroliner'. He was utterly convinced that the transoceanic dirigible was the future of civil aviation, and imagined some kind of air traffic control, an idea he may have picked up from Rudyard Kipling:

The Airship Liner of the future will undoubtedly have risks of collision with her sister liners of the air in the same way that ocean-going liners have with one another, but – thank goodness! – we shall always be entirely immune from any iceberg risks, or from such enemies as rocks, reefs or shoals. As a matter of fact, our chances of collision in the air should be considerably less than those of sea-going vessels, because we will have another dimension to fall back upon and, in all probability, will fly at pre-arranged levels.

For much of that Friday morning the R34 flew over a sea covered in lumps of ice.

Another big iceberg can just be seen in the dim distance. These are the only objects of any kind, sort, or description we have yet observed on this journey. Altered course for St John's. Fog still clinging to the surface of the water, which therefore must be very cold. Extraordinary crimpy wave-like appearance of clouds rolling down underneath us from the north. Harris has never seen this before. Pritchard gets photograph.

Small iceberg a point or two off our starboard beam, about 50 feet high and very close to us. Another photo-graph. Other icebergs visible in the distance away to the south. On our port beam there is a long stretch of clear blue sea sandwiched between wide expanses of fog on either side, looking just like a blue river flowing between two wide snow-covered banks. Cause – a warm current of air which prevents cloud from hanging over it. This well illustrates the rule that over cold currents of water the clouds will cling to the surface.

From a purely flying point of view we would prefer the clouds to be higher, so that we could get inside them and prevent superheating. The clouds are, however, rising. We have watched them gradually increasing in size from little wisps of vapour just above the water. They now assume definite shape, and we can be quite certain that they are rising. There is blue sky and a hot sun above, so Scott decides to try a lower level and get inside the clouds, where we are bound to cool down considerably.

We are now in touch with Cape Race, 250 miles away, on our spark transmitter set: they give us two directional

bearings. We should soon be in touch with Canso, Nova
Scotia.

Cape Race, at the southern tip of Newfoundland, and Canso,
on the east coast of Nova Scotia, were two important radio
stations, much used by transatlantic shipping. The station at
Cape Race – which had been in place since 1904 – was the first
to receive distress messages from the *Titanic* when she foundered on the ice.

Maitland went on:

> Having burnt a lot of petrol, the ship is light, so Scott has to
> force her down on the elevators to get her into the cloud
> bank. We are now over a large ice-field – masses of broken
> ice floating on the surface in every direction. Take a turn
> with Pritchard of pumping petrol, which is a laborious and
> most unpleasant proceeding, and must be avoided in future
> ships. Feel slight symptoms of toothache.

At 09.00 Maitland reported that:

> Ship down by nose 15° to get down into the clouds, which
> are now just beneath us. Height 1,500 feet. Clouds look
> rather 'switchy-backy' ahead, indicating presence of more
> icebergs. Weather report from St John's: 'Wind N, 3 miles
> per hour. Drizzling. Visibility 1 mile.'
>
> Enormous pieces of floating ice under us now; small
> icebergs in themselves. The ice is blue-green under water,
> with frozen snow on top, and the whole sea seems to be full
> of little blobs of cream in every direction – very pretty sight.
> The fog is thickening as we get nearer the coast of New-
> foundland, and only occasionally do we get a glimpse of the
> sea. We are now well inside the cloud-bank.

There's a more prosaic report of the R34's flight across the ice
in the report of Gilbert Cooke, the navigating officer. 'Three or
four icebergs were sighted in the morning and early forenoon,'

Cooke wrote. 'During the latter part of the forenoon the Ship was flying over an icefield. There was no wind to speak of, visibility was low, observations of Sun were not taken, owing to lack of horizon.'

That morning the R34 received the first of the 'well done' messages from well-wishers in North America. 'A message reaches us from the Governor of Newfoundland: "To General Maitland, officers and crew, R34; on behalf of Newfoundland I greet you as you pass on your enterprising journey. Harris, Governor."' Harris was Sir Charles Alexander Harris, a Welshman who had worked his way up through the Colonial Office until he was knighted in 1917 and appointed Governor of Newfoundland. He held the job until 1922. 'Hardly have we replied when Cape Race say : "I have radios for you." We answer: "Go ahead." First message reads as follows: "To R34 from Canadian Pacific Railway; Hearty greetings to the crew of R34 on its initial trip across the Atlantic. Can you give us any story, please? – Manager of Telegraphs."'

As the R34 neared the coast of North America the messages came in thick and fast. Enough for Maitland to write 'Similar messages come through, and it strikes one as being rather strange that messages of congratulation should be coming in and duly pinned on the noticeboard in the dining room from the countries we are struggling to reach, and long before we have even caught a glimpse of them.'

All that morning the R34 flew over the ice. At 11.50 Maitland wrote:

Still drifting over ice-field, making good headway. Scott much relieved at discovering this, as we haven't seen the sea for some hours and, for all any of us knew, we might have been making no headway at all. Our calculations now show that if we meet a stiff headwind going down the coast we may find ourselves in difficulties over petrol. We must have been consuming more than we thought. Latest check gives us 2,222 gallons.

This was the first sounding of an ominous note that was to grow louder and louder over the next two days. As the R34 began the voyage with 6,000 gallons it meant that she'd burned almost 75 per cent of her petrol supply, and she still had well over 1,000 miles to go to Long Island. And the fine weather brought its own problems.

At 12.15 Maitland noted,

Gas temperature is now 106°, and air temperature 40° – a difference of 66°. This is the biggest differentiation between gas and air temperatures that we have ever yet experienced in the Airship Service. The reason the air is so cold is because we are over the Labrador current and the sea is full of ice. The effect on the ship caused by this big differentiation in temperatures is to produce excessive superheating, and it becomes necessary therefore to increase height to 4,000 feet in order to reduce this effect.

But 35 minutes later came a brief glimpse of the prospect for which they'd all been waiting. 'Land in sight. Hooray! First spotted by Scott on starboard bow: a few small rocky islands visible for a second or two through the clouds, and instantly swallowed up again. Eventually make them out to be the north coastline of Newfoundland. This is quite the most thrilling moment of our voyage – great excitement on board.'

In his post-flight account Gilbert Cooke wrote:

At 15.50 GMT (Greenwich Mean Time), 12.50 SMT (Ship's Mean Time) a rocky headland was sighted, sticking up through the fog, 3 or 4 miles away. As the Ship's position was not known exactly, course was altered to the Southward, parallel to the coast, in hopes that a clear patch might be found. This, however, was not struck, so 40 minutes later, course was altered to the West, and coast was crossed, at about 16.30 GMT [13.30 ship's time].

Which came as a relief to Cooke. For days he hadn't seen enough of the Atlantic to take regular sun-to-sea sextant readings. He'd been climbing up and down the rope ladder to the top of the hull trying to get a fix on the ship's position from the cloud horizon, although clouds – and particularly cumulus clouds – often decline to create a horizon. But now, with land under the hull, navigating would be that much easier. Cooke reported later that 'The remainder of the Westward flight from the purely navigational point of view calls for no remarks, as the Ship was almost continually in sight of land'.

Gilbert Cooke liked to downplay his role by joking that as the coastline of America was 3,000 miles long he could 'hardly miss her', but he had done an impressive job. He had steered the big airship westward through cloud, fog, rain, headwinds, crosswinds, updraughts and downdraughts, with the most basic of instruments and with a direction-finding radio system that had proved useless. And while the R34 had been forced by wind and weather to zigzag (up and down as well as north and south), Cooke had always checked the drift. He had never allowed the ship to fly further north than 53° latitude or further south than 50° latitude.

But Maitland was exuberant at the landfall:

Whether or not we now succeed in getting through to New York, we have at any rate successfully accomplished the first stage of our adventure, and are the first to bridge the gulf from East to West by way of air. Those of us on duty in the forward car compare our method of crossing with that of Columbus over 400 years ago. How easy our task, compared to what his must have been!

Crossing the coastline – occasional glimpses of rocky cliffs and small islands through the fog. Message comes through via Cape Race: 'To R34 from Senior Naval Officer, St John's: Request to be informed if you intend passing over St John's, and if so what time?' Reply: 'Yes – probably about 4 p.m. GMT.'

At 13.05 the R34 received a (slightly anxious) message from the Air Ministry in London via the Marconi station at Clifden in County Galway. 'Report fuel expended and number of engines in use.' Fifteen minutes later the R34 radioed back, via the station at St John's, Newfoundland, 'Expended 2,900 gallons of petrol. All engines running well. Position 49° 05′ N, 50° 20′ W'.

As the flight went on, John Shotter grew increasingly anxious about the petrol supply. The Sunbeam 'Maori' engines in his charge were drinking petrol at a faster rate than had been expected. Every time the R34 ran into a westerly wind her fuel consumption shot up alarmingly. With Guy Harris, the R34's meteorologist, predicting strong winds off the American continent, Shotter had good reason to be worried.

For most of that afternoon the R34 flew over the landscape of Newfoundland which is, in fact, the northern end of the Appalachian Mountains that begin in Alabama far to the south. At 14.30 Maitland wrote:

We are passing over Newfoundland at 1500 feet, and the fog has momentarily cleared. Away to the east the country is flat: a mass of large and small lakes. The ground appears to be very rocky, with many large forests. The lakes look extraordinarily deep, and there appears to be water everywhere – goodness knows what the annual rainfall must be! The trees are thick, and one is struck by the number of dead trees both standing and lying on the ground.

To the west there are ranges of hills and big lakes, and we are travelling parallel with, and about 30 miles inland from the coast-line. No sign of habitation or civilisation anywhere; I've never seen such a bleak, barren country in all my life. After much calculation Cooke makes out we have crossed the coast of Newfoundland on the north-west side of Trinity Bay.

Which fact pleased Maitland no end.

Kipling in his story 'With the Night Mail' written as long ago as 1909, chose Trinity Bay as the point where his westward-bound aerial liner of the future first strikes land, and now we, in the first aircraft to cross the Atlantic from E to W, ten years later, first sight land at this Trinity Bay. Mr Kipling, to celebrate this coincidence, gave the writer a signed copy of his book and, in return, received the actual volume we carried on board, inscribed with the signatures of all the crew.

The ever-practical George Herbert Scott doesn't seem to have seen as much of the landscape as Maitland. He later reported:

The fog was still thick, and only occasional glimpses were obtained of the land below, which consisted of woods and lakes, one railway was crossed, but it was not until well inland that the clouds rose to a sufficient height to fly below them, and as we were then over a practically unexplored part of the country, it was still somewhat difficult to fix our exact position. This was definitely fixed when flying out over the south coast of Newfoundland down Fortune Bay.

Over the little town of Fortune the R34 carried out its first mail-man duty, as Maitland explained:

Dropped messages to Governor of Newfoundland and to Sir Robert Borden [Prime Minister of Canada] by parachute, on chance of their being picked up and delivered. Parachute messages fall into huge forest, so it is a very forlorn hope. Message from St John's: 'Can we be of any assistance? Congratulations on successful voyage. Martinsyde aeroplane will attempt to join you.' To St John's from R34: 'Tell Mr. Raynham to beware of long aerials hanging from R34 when he gets near us.'

But Freddie Raynham was to get nowhere near the R34. A second crash on take-off from Quidi Vidi near St John's put an end to his dream of being one of the first to fly the Atlantic.

'We are in thick fog again, with occasional glimpses of the country underneath,' Maitland recorded. 'Message from HMS *Sentinel* giving us her position at easterly end of Bonavista Bay, and also giving us our position.' Bonavista Bay is a long, shallow indentation on the east coast of Newfoundland to the north of the point where the R34 crossed the coast. Some of the R34's crew might have been familiar with *Sentinel*. She was a light cruiser of 2,800 tons, built by Vickers at Barrow-in-Furness, and had been part of the cruiser squadron based on the River Humber. She formed part of the 'gun line' of ships and artillery that was tasked with protecting the north of England from raiding Zeppelins.

Maitland continued:

We are making good thirty-eight to forty knots, there being no wind on the ground. Course set for Fortune Harbour. In working out our time since leaving the Irish coast at Rathlin Island on July 2nd and crossing the coast of Newfoundland on July 4th, we discover we have flown the Atlantic land to land in exactly fifty-nine hours.

Passing out of Fortune Harbour. Very picturesque – high cliff with miles upon miles of forest coming right down to the water's edge. Somebody remarks that most of these trees belong to Lord Northcliffe, and go to help produce *The Times* and *Daily Mail*. Very blue water, deep and transparent. Wonderful natural harbour and fiords – very like Norway. Little groups of hutments at each harbour with piles of cut timber, which appears to be the principal industry in the country, bar fishing.

Inhabitants gaze up at us (presumably in astonishment). They make no demonstration whatsoever. Nice little fishing village on promontory, a delightful collection of what looks like tiny pink, blue and white dolls' houses! Miles away, out at sea, looking right across the peninsula to the east, we can see a huge iceberg, with the sun gleaming on its perpendicular walls of ice. Unpleasant neuralgic toothache at intervals – presumably a sign of fatigue. Message from Lt. Col. Lucas asking when we would land New York. Replied: 'Early Sunday morning.' We have still 870 miles to go.

Little sailing ships under full sail look like toys on the Serpentine. Sea in this gigantic harbour deep blue. Flat calm – not a breath of wind. We see a Telegraph Office marked on our chart as the little town of Fortune, so we decide again to drop messages to Governor of Newfoundland and others at that spot. Threw out messages but parachute burst on opening.

The clock has been put back again. The sun is shining brightly, and the water on the S of Newfoundland is a still deeper blue. Along the coast-line the water is completely transparent and a bright green right up to the beach: a gorgeous colour – green as any emerald. The shades of green gradually darken as the water gets deeper, until they finally become the deepest of deep blue.

About 20 miles off the southern tip of Newfoundland lies a tiny remnant of the vast French empire in North America that once stretched from the Mississippi to the Atlantic coast until part of it was conquered by the British in the 1760s and the rest sold to the USA in 1803. All that remained to France were a cluster of tiny islands, the biggest of which are St Pierre and Miquelon. They are still part of France. Late in the afternoon the R34 was overflying that historical oddity, as Maitland wrote at 16.35:

We are now over the two French islands Miquelon and St Pierre, and are steering a course for Halifax, Nova Scotia. We refer to the *Newfoundland and Labrador Pilot Book*, and read with particular interest the description of the Newfoundland cod fisheries, which are probably the finest in the world. This is also the happy hunting-ground for halibut and Mother Carey's chickens. Air speed 35½ knots on forward and two wing engines. Fresh following wind of about 10 miles per hour, so we are making good 45½ knots on three engines, which is excellent.

The French flag flying over the signal station at St Pierre is smartly dipped in salute as we pass over. Being taken completely by surprise, we were unable to dip our 'White Ensign' in response. The reason is this: we fly our ensign aft, and it takes quite an appreciable time to send a man to the after end of the ship to make a signal. Smart fellow that French signaller – he certainly caught us out badly. Shotter is a bit anxious over his petrol consumption figures, and is adding them up continuously.

St Pierre and Miquelon were to become famous (notorious might be a better word) a few years after the R34's flyover for their part in the Scotch whisky industry's war against the 'noble experiment' of Prohibition. Between 1920 and 1933 millions of gallons of Scotch (and other drinks) were imported from Europe to St Pierre and Miquelon, where they were stored in French government warehouses. In 1922, for example, the islands imported 116,000 gallons of booze – more than 20 gallons for each of the 6,000 population.

Not that it was being drunk on the islands. The whisky was there to be sold to the 'rum runners' whose ships lay in a long line just a few miles off the American coast like so many floating liquor shops. From there it was sold on to New York and New Jersey gangsters, who shuttled back and forward in fast speedboats that the US Coastguard found almost impossible to catch. Despite years of American protests, the British and French governments refused to step in and halt the trade.

Message from General Seely, Under-Secretary of State for Air: 'Warmest congratulations to General Maitland and to tell all your gallant comrades. Best wishes for completion of voyage.' We are now out to sea again, passing Nova Scotia, and over tramp steamer ss *Seal*, bound for Sydney. She is the first ship we have actually set eyes on throughout the whole of this journey. Message from *Seal*: 'Good luck. God speed.'

Clear weather. Making good 27 knots on three engines, resting remaining two. Sea moderate. Wind now not so favourable. Land again in sight. Northerly point of Cape Breton Island, Nova Scotia. Lighthouse giving four flashes. We have averaged 32½ knots between Newfoundland and Nova Scotia. At this rate we should make Halifax 2.30 a.m. tomorrow. ss *Metagama* speaks to us: 'Hearty congratulations. Your progress watched with much interest – all success.'

Which was a message from one Clyde-built vessel to another. The *Metagama* was a 12,500-ton passenger liner built by Barclay, Curle & Co. of Glasgow for the transatlantic service run by the Canadian Pacific Railway. She was used during the war as a troop carrier and in July 1919 was (probably) on her way back to Canada with Canadian troops. At 20.50 the R34 radioed back 'Position 100 miles ENE Cape Breton. Thanks for wishes. Commander R34.'

Later that evening the R34 listened to a radio exchange that suggested that yet another aircrew had come to grief. 'We intercept Cape Race talking to the Handley-Page aeroplane, piloted by Major Brackley and Rear-Admiral Mark Kerr, which is now starting to fly from St John's to New York, where we all hope to foregather,' Maitland recorded at 23.00 that evening. 'The messages are as follows – from Cape Race: "How are you going on? Send V's for bearing." From Handley-Page: "Going strong – 85 mph." Handley-Page signals break off suddenly.'

But what had been a bad Friday for Kerr and Brackley had been a vivid and successful one for the men of the R34. Edward

Maitland ended his with an entry in his log which reads: 'Intercepted on wireless that Dempsey had knocked out Jess Willard in third round for heavyweight championship of the world! And so to bed.'

9

Day Four: Saturday, 5 July 1919

A few weeks before the R34 set off, *Flight* magazine carried a longish article by Major H.E. Wimperis of the RAF in which he compared the problems of navigating through the air with those of navigating across the ocean. Wimperis had no doubt as to which was the easier option. 'Aircraft are concerned with another ocean,' he wrote 'that of the air itself. Its tides are far less easy to predict than the tides in the sea, and are of a far, far higher velocity. Its tides are the winds themselves and their intensity may range to 100 miles an hour or even more. Here are no permanent tide charts to guide the would-be navigator, be his need ever so pressing.'

As Major Wimperis saw it, there was an urgent need for such aerial 'tide charts' now that more and more aircraft were taking to the air above the planet. That fact in itself, he thought, should produce the desired result. 'Meteorology, ever willing to help but sometimes lacking the means, is at last being placed in a position in which it can include in its worldwide survey the study of the winds of the upper air. Such study is absolutely essential to the future of air navigation . . .'

But no such information was available to the R34 on Saturday, 5 July 1919. She was to be battered by head winds, threatened by thunderstorms, sent reeling by bizarre shifts in air pressure and jolted by atmospheric electricity. It went on for most of the day and into the evening, forcing the crew into their parachutes and to hang on grimly to anything they could find. Although the men later played down the experience, there were times that Saturday when they feared for their lives. More than once it looked as if the R34 would meet its end over the islands of the western Atlantic.

It must have reminded Edward Maitland of a vivid passage from Kipling's 'With the Night Mail':

> She comes up nobly, but the laterals buffet the left and right like the pinions of angry angels. She is jolted off course four ways at once, and cuffed into place again, only to be swung aside and dropped into new chaos. We are never without a corposant grinning on our bows, or rolling head over heels from nose to midships, and to the crackle of electricity around and within us is added once or twice the rattle of hail.

The day began badly and then got steadily worse. In the early hours of that Saturday morning the R34 was making surprisingly slow progress down the east coast of Nova Scotia. 'Very dark,' Maitland wrote at 02.30. 'The lights of Whitehaven show up brightly on our starboard beam, and we make out the lights of a steamer passing us to the east. Two aft engines resting. Air speed 36 knots. Making good nothing. Strong head wind against us, and low cloud. Height 1,000 feet. Returned to hammock! Too depressing!'

The airship had run into the strongest wind it had encountered so far. The resistance was formidable.

> We are up against a wind barrage, which is probably peculiar to the east coast of Nova Scotia. It is typical of its kind, and Harris thinks it would be met with usually along this coast when wind is from a westerly quarter. If only we had sufficient petrol we would now change course to the westward, crossing the American coast, and so get round behind this barrage.

But there was no way the R34 could dodge the wind. She just didn't have the resources. As Guy Harris later wrote:

> As it does not extend far inland, it would be possible for airships flying, say, from Newfoundland to Nova Scotia to avoid this trouble by flying behind it and overland.

Harris, who had experienced the western Atlantic in the weather ship *Montcalm*, was plainly troubled by the battering the R34 received from the wind off the coast of Nova Scotia: 'With winds from an easterly quarter during the Summer months bumps over the coast line will probably be found severe enough to be considered dangerous.'

Despite the 'very severe' atmospherics the R34 experienced that night the ship did manage to keep in touch with the radio stations at Canso (some miles to their west) and Barrington Passage (on the southern tip of Nova Scotia). The radio log records an exchange with Canso at 02.45:

'Where are you now?'
The reply: 'Making towards New York.'
'Do you want a bearing?'
'Not yet.'
'Righto, any time.'
Then from Barrington Passage: 'I have 700 words weather for you. Can I carry on or send it at intervals?'
'Go right ahead.'
From Canso: 'Your bearing 81° E of us. Handley-Page aeroplane has crashed.'
We ask anxiously if any one is hurt, and are much relieved at getting a reassuring reply. Came down to 600-foot level to dodge wind.

As the R34 ploughed on into the wind using up large quantities of petrol and getting nowhere fast, Scott grew increasingly worried. He was now facing a dilemma. Should the R34 struggle on with all five engines running flat-out to try to make some progress but use up fuel? Or should the ship head west, inland across Nova Scotia to get out of the wind and risk the perils of that arm of the Gulf of Maine known as the Bay of Fundy? At around 07.00 that morning, when the airship was near the town of Guysborough, Scott made his decision: he turned the R34 west.

At 08.52 the R34 signalled the navy at Halifax, Nova Scotia via Canso: 'If required could you supply destroyer to tow, please? Scott, commander R34.' It was to take Halifax more than two hours to reply to the R34's question, and the answer was 'No destroyer available, only tugs here.' So the R34 flew on across the centre of Nova Scotia. Maitland described the landscape passing under the R34:

> Miles and miles of endless forest. Here and there a clearing with a hut or two, some cattle, and an acre or so of cultivated ground. Any number of small rivers and lakes – inhabitants always seem to settle near the rivers. Marguerite daisies very pretty on all cleared ground. Put the wind up a big brown eagle. The few people we see look up at us, but make no sign. Scott keeps ship down to 800 feet all over this country, to avoid the wind at the higher levels. Our nose is down 10°, and the people on the ground probably think we are out of control and about to crash into the trees.

As she flew low over the wooded interior the R34 must have presented an awesome sight. It's unlikely that many of the inhabitants – foresters, shepherds, fishermen or small farmers – had even heard of a dirigible, let alone seen one. They may have picked up tales of noisy goings-on with aeroplanes around St John's, but this was something different entirely.

It's not hard to imagine a couple of woodsmen working in a clearing, hearing a strange noise and looking up to see a huge shape blotting out the sun and then disappearing over the trees. Or to visualise a fisherman baiting his lines in some cove on the Minas Basin looking out across the water and then gaping in wonder at more than 600 feet of silvery-blue airship, and its reflection, cruising slowly towards the Bay of Fundy. As Maitland wrote:

> It is wonderful what detail we see when flying at this low level. The trees each settler cut down last winter are neatly

stacked and look like little bundles of asparagus; and we see exactly where he gets his water, the extent of his housing accommodation, and the amount of land he has cultivated. The character of the soil is clearly visible to us, the natural drainage of the country stands revealed, and we get an insight into the rainfall, the types of trees which do best, the bird life and the depth of the lakes; whilst the glorious and invigorating fragrance of these enormous pine forests come up to us as a refreshing tonic, putting new life into everyone on board.

And in a sentence redolent of the British officer class 'We all agree we must come again to Nova Scotia for shooting and fishing'.

The R34 tracked on. 'Following the St Mary's Valley over the water-shed. Course W, 21 knots. Twenty-seven knots made good. Junction of Guysborough and Colchester counties, Nova Scotia. We work out our speed over the ground to be 27 knots by measuring shadow of Airship on the trees with stopwatch. Shadow is one-tenth of a mile long.'

He doesn't say so in his report, but Scott must have known that he was about to take the R34 into the skies above one of the most unpredictable stretches of water on the planet. The Bay of Fundy runs north-west–south-east between Nova Scotia and New Brunswick. It is roughly 150 miles long and 75 miles wide at its widest, which is on the border with the US state of Maine. At its north end the bay forks into two narrow stretches of water, Chignecto Bay to the west and the Minas Basin to the east.

What makes the Bay of Fundy particularly hazardous are its tides. It has the biggest tides in the world, bar none. Every day billions of tons of Atlantic seawater flow rapidly out of the Gulf of Maine up the east side of the bay and then ebb down the west. In places there can be as much as 55 feet between a low tide and a high tide. The currents are deep, fast and treacherous, whirlpools are common and there are rapids on the St John River in New Brunswick which actually run backwards.

The tides are at their highest on the Nova Scotia side, and particularly in the Minas Basin. There they have been recorded at more than 70 feet. There are also fast-running tidal 'bores' on most of the rivers that run into the Minas Basin – the rivers St Croix, Meander, Shubenacadie, Maccan and Salmon. Nowadays they are one of Nova Scotia's tourist attractions. In 1919 they were regarded as a menace.

Canadian historians still write about the 'Saxby Gale' of October 1869, when a hurricane swept up the Gulf of Maine and into the Bay of Fundy and created a storm surge that poured inland, killing more than 100 people, destroying cattle, flooding farmland and wrecking dozens of ships and fishing boats. The storm coincided with a very high spring tide. The gale takes its name from Stephen Saxby, a British naval officer and amateur astronomer who calculated the position of the moon vis-à-vis the earth and warned of the calamity a year before it happened.

But it doesn't need a hurricane to make the Bay of Fundy dangerous. When that volume of sea is running fast between two stretches of land, it has an effect on the atmosphere. Just how it happens, no one is sure, even in the twenty-first century. In 1919 all that the meteorologists could do was guess – and warn of the perils. The *Nova Scotia and Bay of Fundy Pilot* states that 'Owing to the rapid and uncertain tidal streams, the prevalence of fogs and the difficulty of obtaining anchorage due to the depth of the water, navigation in the Bay of Fundy calls for unremitting attention.'

To compound the hazards, long stretches of the New Brunswick side of the bay are lined with sandstone cliffs off which a south-westerly wind (the most common kind) rebounds to create turbulence in the air. The height of the New Brunswick cliffs varies from 50 feet at East Red Head to more than 400 feet at Roger's Head. To compound the problem, the Bay of Fundy is also notorious as a generator of powerful electrical storms, for reasons that are still not clear. Whether Scott or anyone aboard the R34 knew quite how dangerous the Bay of Fundy was is also not clear. But they had to take the R34 out of the headwinds.

As the R34 approached the Minas Basin from the east Guy Harris noticed something very odd. 'Across the whole of the (Nova Scotian) peninsula a headwind of varying velocity but constant direction was experienced, but on reaching this portion of the coast a strong following wind was encountered. This prevailed only for about 20 miles, when the wind fell to a flat calm.' In other words, without any warning the wind suddenly reversed itself then dropped completely.

Half an hour after noon the R34 was well across the Minas Basin and about to enter the Bay of Fundy proper. Maitland and his colleagues were at lunch:

> The pine-saturated atmosphere has renewed everyone's appetite. We are just getting into Fundy Bay. The petrol supply is distinctly serious. Shotter has been totalling up our available resources with ever-increasing anxiety. We cannot now afford to run all five engines at once, as they would eat up too much petrol. We have 500 miles yet to go to New York, and if we don't get any wind or bad weather against us can do it all right on three engines, assisted occasionally by a fourth.
>
> If we get much wind against us we are done, and will have to be taken in tow by a destroyer or other surface craft during the night (humiliating thought)! – the idea being that at dawn we would cast off and fly into Long Island under our own power. Other alternatives are: (a) to come down to 300 feet, ride to our drogue [sea anchor] and take in petrol from a destroyer, or (b) to land at Boston, refuel there, and then proceed to New York. A signal was sent through to the US Naval Authorities at Washington and Boston asking them to send a destroyer to stand by to give us a tow should we need one. Hope it won't be necessary.

Afterwards we discovered that the WT Station at Bar Harbour had prefixed our message with the word 'Rush', thus creating the unfortunate impression that R34 was 'in extremis'; whereas she was merely taking the precaution of asking a destroyer to meet her *in case* she should run short of petrol. It is now raining and foggy, which is the kind of weather that will suit us – fog and rain generally means no wind. Sea dead calm in the Bay. We begin to notice distinct evidence of electrical disturbances.

The disturbances were bad enough for Lieutenant Durrant, the wireless officer, to record in his log: 'Atmospherics now terrific. Got shocks through headphones, and drew sparks off aerial.' And shortly after: 'Second pair of phones burnt out.' At 13.05 the R34 signalled to the Air Ministry (via the radio station at Barrington Passage): 'Flying across Nova Scotia. Stormy headwind. Petrol beginning to get short.'

Atmospheric electricity is still a mystery. It's estimated that something like 1,000 thunderstorms are in progress over the planet at any given time. It is also estimated that 90 per cent of clouds have a positive charge in their upper reaches and a negative charge at the bottom, which creates a positive vertical dipole. And when electrified storms do break out they usually create fierce updraughts and downdraughts – as the R34 was to discover.

Maitland did not miss the ominous signs in the atmosphere:

Though the sky has not got much worse, atmospherics have become very bad, severe thunderstorm can be seen over New Brunswick, moving south down coast. This storm looks very large, and appears to be moving rapidly. Scott turns left-handed off his course towards Nova Scotia to avoid it, but storm extends eastward. He puts on all engines to try and get away from it, and orders are given to stow away all loose valuables.

Caught in violent squall on extreme outskirts of the

storm. Ship very badly thrown about, rising 700 feet in one bump. We see these bumps or squalls passing over the water. They appear to be a line of circular squalls or 'whirls' moving line abreast at very high speed. Storm almost tropical in its violence. Our first warning was when the helmsman pointed to the compass card, which was spinning round like a top. Harris thinks that had we been caught in the centre of this storm, the bumps would have been so severe that the ship might have been damaged in the air.

But nothing prevented Maitland recording the marvels he saw in the sky:

Wonderful specimens of 'Mammato Cumulus' cloud, indicating a highly perturbed state of the atmosphere. These clouds have a festoon-like appearance, and remind one rather of bunches of grapes – they are only associated with very severe disturbances. Photo by Pritchard. It is difficult to estimate the size of these storms, but as the squalls which hit the ship were about 50 miles from the storm itself, the area covered must have been many thousands of square miles.

During the summer months these storms are frequent on this coast, and are a grave danger to all aircraft. The US Weather Bureau have made a special study of them, and are usually able to forecast them a considerable period before their breaking, as indeed they did upon this occasion.

Crossing Haute Island – very pretty little island. Huge cliffs and lighthouse. Three-quarters covered with woods. Easterly cliff white with gulls. Started up third engine – only making good fifteen knots on two. Unpleasant neuralgic toothache all down left side of face. Retired to hammock and took some aspirin. Hope not going to crock up.

Shotter happened to be lying full length alongside drogue hatch when that last squall hit us and, when ship's nose first went down, would have slid through hatch into sea if he had not hooked a girder with his foot!

> Feeling very tired, so turn in and sleep soundly, despite the
> creaking of the girders in the keel, and loud buffeting of the
> wind against the outer cover.

That afternoon, with petrol running ever lower, Scott decided
to warn the Americans that the R34 might need assistance. At
15.00 hours Zachary Lansdowne sent the following message
via the radio station at Bar Harbour in Maine: 'To Operations
(Aviation) Navy Department, Washington DC, and to Commander, 2nd Naval District, Boston, Mass.: Could destroyers
proceed if required to southern end Bay of Fundy and take
HMA R34 IN TOW? SIGNED LANSDOWNE FOR CAPTAIN, R34.'

Half an hour later the US Navy replied. 'Arrangements have
been made for destroyers to be south of Cape Cod. Arrangements are being made to temporarily land you at Montauk if it
becomes essential.' Half an hour after that the US Navy
signalled: 'Destroyers *Bancroft* and *Stevens* left Boston to your
assistance at 3.30 p.m. Signed, Commander 1st Naval District.' To which the R34 replied 'Steaming down coast of New
Brunswick and Maine. Petrol running short. Please have
destroyer meet us early as possible. Signed, Lansdowne, for
Captain, R34.'

The ships assigned to assist the R34 were both fast, newish
warships of just over 1,200 tons and capable of 35 knots. The
Bancroft was destined to become one of the lend-lease warships that the USA handed over to Britain in 1940. The *Stevens*
saw some action in the latter days of World War I escorting
convoys across the Atlantic. That summer the *Stevens* was one
of the 21 or so American warships that were strung between
Newfoundland and the Azores to help the trio of Navy Curtiss
flying boats across the Atlantic. She was involved in the search
for the two aircraft that ditched.

That exchange of radio messages between the R34 and the
US Navy was later to prove embarrassing. It was picked up by
the many radio stations that were listening in. Some of them,
quite reasonably, jumped to the conclusion that the R34 was in

serious trouble and was about to come down in the sea. Within hours rumours that the R34 was in mortal danger began circulating among American newspapers and radio stations.

There was some substance in them. The airship was in danger. At 18.00 hours Maitland reported that the ship had managed to evade 'another colossal thunderstorm. Had to haul in WT aerials, as attempts to use wireless resulted in two-inch sparks owing to highly charged atmosphere. Ship again badly thrown about – very unusual temperature bumps. Came to the conclusion that a comfortable hammock is indeed the best place on occasions like these.'

What made the pitching and tossing of the R34 over the Bay of Fundy so alarming and dangerous was the fact that some of the engines were stopping and then flaring back to life in bursts of flame. The possibility of a spark igniting a slight leakage of hydrogen, and then the petrol, was always present.

An hour later Maitland wrote:

We are well clear of Nova Scotia, and heading straight for New York. Making good 24 knots with three engines and slightly favourable wind. We again anxiously take stock of our petrol. If we don't get more than 12 miles against us from now on we can make New York on three engines, and if not more than 15 against us, we can do it on two engines. Evening meal. Very hot, and our costumes are both scanty and varied. We discuss our prospects of getting straight through to New York. If we do not have any more of these electric storms we agree we have a good sporting chance.

But the Bay of Fundy refused to let up. At 21.20 Maitland recorded,

Violent temperature 'bumps', evidently caused by rapid variation of sea temperature beneath us. Ship is first lifted 400 feet and then dropped 500 feet – measured on our aneroid. Scott, who has his head out a window in the forward car, states that he saw the tail of the ship bend under the strain, whilst her angle is so steep at one moment that Cooke, resting in his hammock in the keel, is unable to get out for a minute or two, as he is head downwards at the time.

Standing more out to sea, and running on all five engines to get further from this locality, a heartbreaking manoeuvre, as it will reduce still further our depleted petrol supply. Harris has experienced this kind before, when aboard the ss *Montcalm* in these regions. The sky was completely clear when the storm broke, wind practically calm, sea glassy, and moon brilliant. For a few seconds the warm air, which seemed pine-scented (although we were well out to sea) was suddenly succeeded by very cold air, and it is these rapidly rising warm currents which throw the ship about with such violence.

Thunderstorms by day are bad enough, but at night they are particularly unpleasant, and the ship vibrates from bow to stern. We wear our parachutes, and life-belts are all ready. Our only bottle of brandy fell out of the chart locker with a crash during one of these vertical bumps – fortunately without breaking.

The R34's famous bottle of brandy was later awarded to the base surgeon at East Fortune.

In his post-flight report Guy Harris ruminated at some length on the spasms in the atmosphere above the Bay of Fundy:

From the state of the sea it was evident that these bumps do not extend [down] to surface level . . . there are no visible phenomena to give the slightest previous warning . . . The probable explanation for these extraordinary phenomena are the existence of detributaries of the Gulf Stream extending in the colder surrounding waters, causing a steep temperature gradient which is purely local . . . [and this] opens

the large and very important question of the influence of
ocean currents on the upper air . . .

That is an 'influence' that meteorologists have been trying to
understand for hundreds of years. Ever since the English
lawyer and amateur meteorologist George Hadley published
a paper in 1735, *On the Cause of the General Trade Winds,*
weather-watchers have been struggling to understand the
interplay between the sea and the atmosphere above it. Among
the renowned mathematicians and natural philosphers that
have grappled with the problem are Colin MacLaurin, Denis
Diderot, John Dalton and Immanuel Kant.

It's a subtle and complex relationship, but no one now
doubts that ocean currents have a profound effect on the
upper air. Great reservoirs of warm water (such as the ones
generated in the Gulf of Mexico) expand out into cooler seas.
The atmosphere in contact with the sea then transmits the heat
upwards, injecting energy and humidity into the air, creating
changes in temperature and air pressure.

But even when the R34 was being tossed about like a leaf in
an autumn gale Edward Maitland never lost his faith in the
airship. His footnote to the Bay of Fundy crisis reads:

It is interesting that although these 'temperature bumps' are
the worst that any of us have yet experienced, the actual
movements of the ship were felt by all to be quite slow and
gradual; in fact, upon no single occasion has there been
sufficient motion to cause the slightest sensation of sea-
sickness. As Aerial liners undoubtedly will increase considerably in size, this immunity from sea-sickness should
prove one of their most valuable commercial assets.

All through that Saturday evening the highly-charged atmosphere over the Bay of Fundy crackled with electricity. It
played havoc with the ship's communication systems. Entry
after entry in Durrant's radio log between 18.15 and 22.30

records the problem: 'Atmospherics very bad . . . Atmospherics getting worse . . . Atmospherics render reading impossible . . . Ditto . . . Hauled in aerial, approaching storm . . . Ship swaying badly . . . Tried to let aerial out again, but it charged up quickly . . . Ship caught on edge of storm . . . Aerial out again.'

At 22.30 the R34 managed to make radio contact with the American destroyers waiting at the entrance to the Bay of Fundy. At 22.36 the USS *Bancroft* put up a flare to show her position, to which the R34 replied with a few flashes from an Aldis lamp. At 22.55 the *Bancroft* radioed 'You are directly above us', to which the R34 signalled 'OK'. From that point on the R34 never lost contact with the American warships – both of which could travel almost as fast as the airship.

With the two destroyers following hard on their heels the crew of the R34 were safer than they had been for some time. But the effort involved in battling the headwinds off the east coast of Nova Scotia and then criss-crossing the Bay of Fundy to avoid the thunderstorms had taken its toll of the R34's dwindling store of petrol. Every fuel gauge told the same bad news, and every calculation that John Shotter made was more pessimistic than the last. Petrol supplies were dropping fast.

Just before midnight on Saturday, 5 July, Edward Maitland wrote in his log 'Things now don't look at all well for getting through to New York . . .'

10

New York, New York

After her battering over the Bay of Fundy the crew of the R34 were worried men. Just after midnight Zachary Lansdowne signalled to the commanding officer of the US Navy's base at Chatham, Massachusetts: 'If through shortage of gasoline R34 wishes to land Chatham, can you supply 50,000 cubic feet hydrogen and 500 gallons gasolene?' Chatham never replied but Lansdowne's message seems to have sent the US Navy searching for suitable accommodation for the R34. Seven hours later the US Navy in Washington signalled: 'Arrangements being made to temporarily land ship Montauk if it becomes essential. Advise landing Mineola. Keep us informed.' Montauk was the US Navy's air station at the eastern tip of Long Island.

Meanwhile the R34 kept contact with the two US destroyers, *Bancroft* and *Stevens*, which were trailing the airship down the Gulf of Maine. The problem the destroyers faced was that the airship kept slipping in and out of clouds. At 03.00 one of them signalled 'Will make flares again', to which the R34 replied 'You are still beneath us.' At 04.18 the destroyer signalled 'Was our last rocket ahead or astern of you?' and the R34 replied 'Astern'. Then at 05.30 'Have you sighted Chatham?' answer: 'Not yet.'

That was the R34's last contact with her American shepherds. By then things had started going right. Over the Gulf of Maine the electricity drained out of the atmosphere, the wind dropped and then swung round to the north-east, the sea and sky went calm. As the sun rose to light up the coast of the USA the mood aboard the airship had changed. At 05.30, as the R34 passed over the resort of Martha's Vineyard in Massachusetts – then, as now, something of an upper-class playground – Maitland noted in his journal 'Two biggish watering places – big hotels and many piers – evidently a yachting resort. Looks delightful.'

What was not delightful was the petrol situation. The question in everyone's mind was, would the R34 have enough fuel to make her way to Mineola in Long Island? Or would she, as seemed likely, be forced to find landfall well short? At the US Navy's base at Chatham in Massachusetts, perhaps? Or at the US naval air base at Montauk on Long Island? Both base commanders were willing to see the airship descend, but neither of their bases was equipped to deal with a machine the size of the R34.

The R34's officers all knew that their best option was to make their way to Roosevelt Field, Mineola. The US Army had fitted the landing ground with 20-ton concrete blocks on which to moor the ship and had laid on petrol, oil and hydrogen for the return journey. They also had a 300-strong landing party of soldiers in place. In the early hours of Sunday morning John Shotter whistled up a squad of engineers and riggers equipped with cups, pots, jars and anything else that could hold liquid, to scoop every last drop of petrol from the dregs of the petrol tanks and pump it into the feed tanks to the R34's five engines.

It worked, but only just. By 07.20 the R34 was over Montauk with no need to land. By 08.00 it was clear they had enough fuel to make Mineola. Edward Maitland was elated:

As we skim over this American countryside, I confess to a delightful glow of satisfaction at gazing on American soil for the first time – from above. It brings home to me more than anything else could ever do, what a small place this world really is, what an astonishing part these great Airship Liners will play in linking together the remotest places of the earth; and what interesting years lie immediately ahead!

As the airship cruised slowly over the Long Island landscape Lansdowne played the tour guide, pointing out the local sights like President Theodore Roosevelt's house at Oyster Bay. For his part Maitland was impressed by the domestic architecture. 'Lovely bungalows,' he wrote. 'All houses look quite different to English houses – so much more modern and of a different architectural style. Every house has a verandah, and they all seem to be built of wood.'

Breakfast at 08.00 was a hurried affair, most of the officers anxious to take in the scenery of Long Island. By 09.00 Maitland was noting 'Great hustle and bustle on board! The keel is full of people struggling to close reluctant suitcases, and to improve their generally dishevelled appearances – which takes a bit of doing. Thank goodness there are no bills to pay, or waiters to tip.' By then, most of the officers had found enough hot water to have a shave in preparation for their entrance onto the American stage.

And it was to be quite an entrance. By 09.30 the crew were staring down in amazement at the crowds that were flocking towards Roosevelt Field. Maitland recorded:

It is a bright clear morning, and we can see a long line of motorcars of every sort and size streaming out from New York to see us come in. There is a large motor enclosure half a mile long, where cars are standing – already six deep. I find myself mechanically counting the rows – an enormous multitude of people are gazing up at us, and a military band is playing in front of a grandstand erected for the occasion.

There's a vivid description of the R34's arrival over Long Island by a correspondent from *The Times*:

With the band playing 'God Save the King' and thousands of spectators standing bareheaded, the R34 dipped groundwards and dropped anchor at 10 o'clock this morning after a voyage which up to late last night even experts feared might end in disaster.

It was at 8.55 that the news that the giant airship was overhead brought the thousand inhabitants of Garden City and Mineola into the streets to see the R34 slowly circling overhead as she manoeuvred herself into position for landing. The number was clearly visible on her side, and her great bulk was gleaming in the morning sunshine.

The flags may have been flying and the band may have been playing, but things on the ground had not gone to plan. When it seemed the R34 would have to land somewhere in Massachusetts, the 12-man British advance crew who had been trained to usher the airship back to earth had made a dash from Washington to Boston to be ready for the R34's descent. They were still in Massachusetts when Scott decided that he had enough fuel to see the R34 to New York. Which meant that the US Army troops at Mineola were left to secure the R34 without instruction. Keen as they were, they'd never seen an airship like the R34, let alone handled one.

So it was decided that someone from the R34 would have to parachute down to show the soldiers how to land and secure the ship. Maitland, ever an eager parachutist, wanted to make the jump himself but he was overridden by Scott, who gave the job to Jack Pritchard. Pritchard climbed out of his flying suit and into his best uniform, was helped out of one of the control car's windows, and parachuted down from the R34 to make the first airborne landing on US soil by a foreigner. The *New York Times* described Pritchard's jump as 'Parachute Brings First Air Pilgrim to American Soil'.

The 'air pilgrim' did his job, the American soldiers did theirs and at 09.54 (local time) the R34, trailing a Union flag and with the Lion Rampant of Scotland emblazoned on her nose, settled down onto Roosevelt Field. It was the triumphant conclusion of the first-ever east–west flight across the Atlantic and, at 108 hours 12 minutes, the longest any aircraft had been airborne. All the drinking water and most of the food had gone and there were only 140 gallons left in the R34's petrol tanks, roughly enough for an hour's flying. It had been touch and go, a very close-run thing.

At which point the R34's public relations machine slipped into gear. The unflappable Edward Maitland, tricked out in a natty, all-white flying suit, stepped down from the control car to shake hands with the assembled American and British dignitaries who had come to welcome the R34 to the USA. After a speech by Vice-Admiral Albert Gleaves (the wartime commander of the US transatlantic convoy system) the R34's crew were, in Maitland's words, 'persuaded to give ourselves up for about 15 minutes to the cinema operators and camera men'.

He wrote later, 'This is indeed a trying ordeal, and I shall never forget the "barrage" of cameras which confronted us! They were so numerous that the operators had to face us in two ranks – the front rank kneeling, and the rear rank standing behind!' Maitland's coy tone doesn't chime with the photographs. One published by the *New York Times* shows seven of the R34's officers standing awkwardly in line and the only one that looks like he's enjoying the attention is Maitland. In his white flying suit and with the brass on his peaked hat gleaming, he stands out among the dowdier uniforms. By contrast John Shotter, the hero of the flight, looks downright scruffy.

When the men from the R34 got round to talking to reporters, their accounts varied enormously. Maitland's enthusiasm for airships seems to have wiped out his short-term memory. In a statement that must have amazed his colleagues Maitland told the *New York Times* that 'We had cheery, comfortable quarters and were on a perfectly even keel virtually all the way over. I wish to emphasise that the object of this flight is to demonstrate the future use of the rigid dirigible machine for transatlantic work. It was in every way successful.'

The R34's skipper George Scott was more frank:

We had ticklish times with the weather on four occasions, the worst in a thunderstorm. I wouldn't say it was very danger- ous, but it was very nasty and very unpleasant. It might have been serious if it had taken the planes or the rudder. At one time in the worst storm we went through, we suddenly shot upwards about 500 feet, and had a very unsettled time.

Guy Harris was even more candid. 'It was an extremely rough trip. Knowing the weather conditions of the United States I was a great deal worried. I have been worried all through the trip about the condition of the ship when it arrived here, and about the difficulties of sizing up the weather conditions here.' Harris reminded his interviewers that almost half the journey was between Newfoundland and New York, a particularly hazardous stretch of geography. 'We got such bad bumps yesterday that I would not go through them again for a thousand pounds.'

According to the *New York Times*, one of the engineers (the paper doesn't say which but it was probably Shotter) also said the trip had been far from plain sailing. 'We were fighting headwinds all the way until early this morning, when the wind suddenly veered around at the last moment,' he said. 'Things were getting desperate.' He claimed that the R34 was so short of fuel that 'if we had been only a few minutes later we might have had a serious time of it trying to get down'.

Maitland must have cringed when he read navigating officer Gilbert Cooke's view of the voyage. Cooke is reported as saying 'The weather situation in the Atlantic must be inves- tigated thoroughly before trans-oceanic travel by air between England and America can be made safe and practicable. With the limited information we now have regarding the weather conditions, transatlantic flight is highly dangerous. I consider it almost a miracle that we completed the trip successfully after what we went through last night.'

But with their feet on the ground, the men of the R34 abandoned the 'flying orders' Scott had received from the

Air Ministry. In retrospect, the orders were ludicrous. 'You are not to remain at the landing ground longer than is necessary to re-fuel and re-gas', Scott had been told. 'Nevertheless, if your officers and crew are exhausted, you may remain for a few hours longer, provided the safety of the ship is not endangered thereby. None of your officers and crew are to leave the immediate vicinity of the ship.'

All of which was dumped overboard in the jubilation. And by then the 'well done' telegrams were coming in. One of the first was from King George V (via Sir Frank Sykes, head of the new Department of Civil Aviation): 'Your flight marks the beginning of an era in which the English-speaking peoples, already drawn together in war, will be even more closely united in peace.' There were messages from Sykes himself, from the Air Council, from Groves in his role as Deputy Chief of the Air Staff and from Sir Hugh Trenchard, Chief of the Air Staff and Britain's top airman.

There was also a telegram from Winston Churchill, Secretary of State for War and Air, and a man well-known for his suspicion of airships. 'All congratulations to Major Scott and his gallant companions on their conquest of the Atlantic,' Churchill wrote. 'Henceforward East Fortune and Long Island are signal names in the history of flying. May the return be as prosperous as the outward journey.'

American hospitality was overwhelming. Temporary showers had been built at Roosevelt field and after much-needed ablutions the crew of the R34 were whisked the short distance for lunch at the Garden City Hotel as guests of the US Navy. Maitland records that 'Vice-Admiral Gleaves, who presided, makes an excellent and amusing speech, and so does Lt-Comdr Read, pilot of the NC4 . . . Other speeches follow, and Scott, Cooke, Harris and myself each do our best in the speech-making line in so far as our oratorical talents and the cocktails would permit!'

That long and lavish lunch was followed by an equally long and lavish dinner at the officers' mess at Mitchel Field, Long

Island. The dinner menu has survived: salted almonds, cold consommé, tomato bisque, tomato and cucumber salad, roast breast of Vermont turkey with cranberry jelly, assorted layer cake, Neapolitan ice cream, coffee and iced tea. All of it a very long way from the meagre and mostly cold rations to which the men had become used.

After dinner the crew of the R34 were ferried into Manhattan, where the officers were put up in the Ritz Carlton at the south end of Central Park and the NCOs and Other Ranks to rather less salubrious quarters usually occupied by the US Navy's petty officers. By the time he got to his room in the Ritz Carlton, the exhausted and slightly injured John Shotter is said to have been in a state of near collapse.

Which was hardly surprising. Lieutenant (later Brigadier-General) John Shotter did more than anyone to keep the R34 in the air and moving along. The five unreliable Sunbeam engines had given Shotter and his men a very hard time. The engines needed constant attention, day and night. And all the engineers had complained about the noise, the constant vibration (particularly in the twin-engined aft car) the petrol fumes and the pressure to make running repairs. Without exception they had difficulty sleeping in their hammocks when off duty.

Over the next few days – and in between shifts at Roosevelt Field to tend the ship – the R34's crew were wined, dined and feted in a way that few of them had ever experienced. Every time the R34's officers set foot in a restaurant diners got to their feet and applauded. Maitland described it thus:

> The United States Navy very kindly place a suite of rooms at the Ritz Carlton at our disposal, also some motorcars, and we are overwhelmed with hospitality on every side. The dentist whom I visit in Fifth Avenue repudiates any suggestion of a fee (an autograph is accepted in lieu) and this is merely one example of the generous hospitality we receive everywhere. We thought America had 'gone dry', but are quickly undeceived upon this point!

And while Maitland doesn't mention it in the published version of his log, he found the time to send transatlantic telegrams from New York to his friend Sybil Grant, informing her that the R34 had made the crossing and that he was safe and sound. They are attached to the original copy of the R34's log now in the National Library of Scotland in Edinburgh.

The stowaways – Billy Ballantyne and Whoopsie the kitten – were particular favourites with the press. Photographs of the engaging, tousle-haired Ballantyne appeared in most of the New York papers. In one of them he has Whoopsie perched on his right shoulder. Maitland was shrewd enough to see that Ballantyne was a hit and allowed him to give a longish interview to the *New York Times* (which reproduced his Geordie accent as a bizarre version of Cockney). Ballantyne, the reporter discovered, was a bit of a boxer and a big fight fan:

> You see, I'd never been to America, had my heart placed on it, and my mind too. So I sneaks out a bit before midnight, about two hours before the R34 left Scotland. I hides in the rigging. No one saw me, and we were off . . . When we were about 60 miles out Sergeant Watson stumbles over my head and of course he takes me to the head coxswain. The officers couldn't do nothing then, and I saw one of 'em smile – so I knowed I'd see the land where they pay $100,000 for a man to get in the ring for three rounds.

Ballantyne went on to declare that he wasn't at all worried about the punishment he had in store, because 'The big thing for me is that I made that trip and here I am'.

One Broadway actress offered $1,000 for the cat, which its guardian (engineer George Graham) declined. It was a Scottish cat, he told her, and belonged in Scotland. She settled for awarding the beast a fancy gold collar. The *New York Herald* even published a painful piece of doggerel dedicated to the first cat ever to fly the Atlantic: 'I have gone where no other cat has gone/ I lick my paws and rub my ears/ Who have roamed the sky before the dawn/ As I've longed to do for years and years.'

Interestingly, some American commentators saw the arrival of the R34 as a warning to the USA. The *Brooklyn Eagle*, a serious daily paper in its time, had taken a lively interest in the advent of the R34 (and even hired a Sperry biplane to fly up and 'greet' the British airship). The day after the R34 arrived the paper ruminated at some length on the implications of long-distance aircraft. In a front-page article headlined 'Danger of Attack by Air on US is Shown by R-34: Defense Measures Needed' the paper quoted an unnamed US naval officer as saying 'The days of our splendid isolation are over. The achievement of the R-34 proves it.'

The paper goes on:

In the judgment of numerous far-seeing officers of the land and sea forces of the United States, if this country ever sees a war brought to its shores from a foreign country, the warfare will be fought chiefly from the air. A floating navy would be utterly incapable of defending the coast against attack from such craft as the R-34. Such attack could only be met from the air, or by a development of anti-aircraft guns far beyond their present efficiency.

American officers see a lesson of the utmost significance in the achievement of the British dirigible. They see the days of the old-style battleship drawing to a close. For the past two or three years there has been a growing school of naval officers which has doubted the wisdom of spending vast sums of money on dreadnoughts and super-dreadnoughts that could be sunk by bombs from the air.

Which was an interesting piece of forecasting. Two years later, in July 1921, Brigadier-General Billy Mitchell of the US Army Air Service stunned the US Navy when his flight of bombers sent the captured German battleship *Ostfriesland* to the bottom of the Atlantic off Virginia. And just to show that it wasn't a fluke, he did it again a few months later by sinking the decommissioned US battleship *Alabama*. Mitchell was among the American military brass hats that turned out to welcome the R34 to Roosevelt Field.

In a rerun of H.G. Wells' story 'The War in the Air', the *Brooklyn Eagle* writer went on to conjure up the image of a fleet of high-speed, long-range airships, loaded with bombs that could lay waste the coastal cities of the USA. The airships would be refuelled with petrol, hydrogen and helium from ships and tankers sitting well offshore. These supply vessels would be defended by a ring of enemy warships. 'There would be practically no limit to the air endurance of such craft, working from a base at sea.'

And, he claimed, as things stood there was no way that the US could effectively defend itself:

In the present state of air development, and in view of the comparatively meagre appropriations now being allowed by Congress, the United States would be well-nigh helpless in such an attempted defense.

An enemy establishing a base at sea would not only employ dirigibles, but large fleets of planes to aid in the attack and to drive off adversary planes which might attack the dirigibles. Ships of the R-34 class could post themselves 2 or 3 miles above the City of New York, adjust their position to a nicety, and unloose their bombs, operating all the time under the protection of their own planes. All the heavy shore batteries in the world would not serve to defend the city from such an attack.

Another US naval officer was quoted as saying,

With a ship properly equipped it would be just as easy to resupply the R-34 at sea as it is to resupply her at Mineola. She would swing at anchor from a ship just as well as from a land anchor. She could hoist all kinds of supplies aboard. Fuel could be pumped up to her. A new supply of gas could be pumped into her balloons. She would not be limited to a single visit to the coast but could make many.

What was required, the *Brooklyn Eagle* declared, was more money for defence of the USA.

> Next winter there will unquestionably be a powerful drive on Congress for larger air appropriations. The voyage of the R-34 has made vivid to expert minds here, and probably to everybody, what has hitherto been largely a matter of speculation. No longer is much imagination required to arrive at a point of what could have happened along the coast if a fleet of long-range dirigibles and swift naval planes operating from a seabase at sea should come on an errand of war. Military experts are hoping and praying that Congress will not permit the United States to fall much further behind.

The R34's sojourn in the USA was not all wining and dining, at least not for everyone. There was work to be done. In the four days the airship had spent over the Atlantic it had taken quite a hammering. There were rents in the outer fabric to be repaired, some minor leaks in the hydrogen bags and the troublesome Sunbeam engines had to be stripped down, overhauled and parts replaced. Shotter and the engineers were kept busy cleaning carburettors and magnetos.

The *Hempstead Sentinel*, the local paper for the Mineola area, reported that 'Since Sunday, mechanics from the dirigible have been in Hempstead in quest of certain supplies, spare machine parts etc.' Which was true enough: the R34's engineers scoured the area looking for bits and pieces to repair the battered engines. More than 60 of the ship's 120 spark plugs had to be replaced. The 20-foot-long propeller blades were encrusted with oil but those were cleaned, free of charge, by a local firm. The kudos was enough.

While the Americans did their level best for the airship, with no shed in which to shelter, the R34 was vulnerable to the weather. And the weather over Long Island was slowly deteriorating. On Monday, 7 July, the ship was struck by a violent gust which tore her from one of her mooring cables, ripping a long gash in her outer cover. It took the efforts of more than 300 men to stop the R34 from drifting off over Long Island and even then, according to the *New York Times*, some of them were swept off their feet and into the air. Luckily, the damage to the cover looked worse than it was and, as Scott assured the Americans, it was easily repaired.

Scott's own report describes the problems the R34 faced while floating on her moorings at Roosevelt Field.

July 7th. – During the night rain dried off, and the sun coming out in the morning the ship becomes so light it was difficult to haul her down. During this operation, the casting in the hull forward (where the mooring point is attached) pulled out. Fortunately the casting jammed in the shackle, or the ship would have blown away. During the day the mooring-point forward was stiffened up with timber and wire strops, and the ship once more let up in the evening. The trim of the ship was much better this time and she rode at four° down by the stern.

July 8th. – During the night she tends to become heavy; but it was found possible, with about 30 men, to haul down her tail sufficiently to allow a man to climb aboard the after car. He then proceeded up into the keel, and let go water ballast. This operation was performed twice. She was again hauled down during the day, special visitors allowed aboard. She was let up again at night.

The 'special visitors' referred to by Scott were a party of US aviation experts (from the army and navy), a member of the House Aviation Committee and President Wilson's daughters, Jessie and her younger sister Eleanor. Both were the children of Wilson's first wife Edith, who died in 1914. But even the presidential offspring had to seek permission from General

Maitland. And the American public were kept 200 yards away from the R34 by military police.

Scott went on:

> July 9th. – The weather forecasts were more suitable for the homeward journey. It was, therefore, decided to leave that night or early on the morning of the 10th. During the day, however, the wind got up considerably, and became very gusty, two very nasty squalls just missing the ship. It was, therefore, decided to leave the ground as soon as possible, and gassing operations were started as soon as the sun went down.

While the R34's gas bags were being recharged with hydrogen from the hundreds of gas cylinders that had been piled up at Mineola, and her fuel tanks being refilled with petrol, oil and water, some of the crew were sharing the platform at the Carnegie Hall with no less a personage than President Wilson himself. Wilson had just returned from the peace conference at Paris and was about to make his first major foreign policy speech since the settlement at Versailles.

According to the correspondent of the London *Morning Post*, Wilson walked on to the stage to the cheers of the crowd and the strains of 'Over There', the renowned World War ditty. 'At that moment the President saw Major Scott and crossed the stage to greet him with every sign of enthusiasm. The word quickly passed from mouth to mouth who the British officer was and the audience broke again into applause which lasted some time.'

So, after four days of the high life in New York the crew of the R34 were ready for the journey home. For the return journey Lieutenant-Commander Zachary Lansdowne of the US Navy was replaced by Colonel William Hensley of the US Army's balloon corps. Hensley was a seasoned cavalryman who had served in the Philippines and had spent the summer of 1916 chasing Emiliano Zapata around the border with

Mexico. After the flight Hensley was to take up the job as Air Attaché at the US Embassy in London.

To relieve the pressure on the engineers Scott replaced one of the radio operators with two engineers from the advance party (E.E. Turner and A.W. Angus). The stowaway Billy Ballantyne returned to the UK with the rest of the advance party in the Cunard liner RMS *Aquitania,* probably in considerably more comfort than in his east–west journey. But Whoopsie, the now famous tabby kitten, flew back to Britain with the R34.

Among the last of the ship's American visitors was the Hempstead postmaster's daughter. As the local paper explained 'To a Hempstead young lady, Miss Ida Mulgannon, daughter of Postmaster Francis J. Mulgannon, went the honor of placing the mail aboard the dirigible just before it left the ground . . . There was nearly 25lbs of mail placed on board.' And at the very last minute one enthusiastic American broke through the cordon and presented the crew with a (strictly illegal) case of rum.

By then, of course, the R34 had been restocked. By the time she was ready to lift off she was carrying 4,500 gallons of petrol, 230 gallons of engine oil, 800 gallons of water (ballast and drinking), all of which added up to 18.85 tons. The crew, their luggage and food supplies added another 4 tons while spare parts (mainly engine parts) contributed another quarter of a ton. There was also a brand new phonograph, a gift from Thomas Alva Edison, who had been much impressed by the flight of the R34. The ship's total load was just over 23 tons – well within the R34's lifting capacity.

Six minutes before midnight on Wednesday, 10 July, with the wind gusting at around 30 miles an hour, the R34 rose into the air over a large crowd of cheering Americans. Oddly, the moment of leaving the earth is something that Edward Maitland – an inveterate flyer and advocate of all things aerial – found disturbing. 'Again that strange feeling of loneliness,' he wrote, 'as sudden as it is transient. Scott has 4,500 gallons of petrol on board: this should be ample and to spare for the return journey, which we anticipate will be nothing like so difficult as our journey over.'

The R34's progress over Queens and Brooklyn towards Manhattan was described by the *Brooklyn Eagle*, which had already lavished a huge amount of ink on the R34's visit: 'She presented a beautiful picture as she floated away. Bathed in the white lights of three strong searchlights from the field and just as she moved off toward the city the moon came out from behind a bank of clouds and a few drops of rain pattered down.'

The newspaper went on 'A huge silvery cigar, she seemed, with the gondolas hung beneath but appearing little more than darker specks, hardly discernible except when a searchlight swept across them. Although there were some few clouds they did not hide her . . . she suddenly shifted course and disappeared over the Queens Borough Bridge.'

According to the paper the whole city was agog. 'Word had been flashed over telephone wires in various directions before midnight and the roofs of the big downtown Brooklyn hotels, particularly the Bossert and the St George, were crowded by midnight with watchers scanning the heavens for the ship. Other crowds lined the bridges over the East River and still smaller groups gathered on the roofs of apartments, tenement houses and private dwellings.'

Being the lively newspaper it was, the *Brooklyn Eagle* used the departure of the R34 to have another dig at the US Government. A crude little cartoon drawing shows the shape of an airship caught in a searchlight's beam over a caption which runs 'Was it high winds or high prices that forced the blimp to leave us?' And under that 'The big dirigible left in the dark – where American aviation still remains.'

The coverage of the usually staid *New York Times* was even more highly coloured. As the R34 cruised over the East River and then down the spine of Manhattan, the big ship was lit up by searchlights and watched by crowds who gathered on every rooftop. 'In the searchlight every line of the R-34 was distinctly seen by the throng gazing upward from around The Times Building,' wrote the *New York Times* reporter. 'To the great crowd, enjoying . . . one of the finest spectacles New Yorkers had ever seen, there came plainly the whirring of the propellers.'

At which point his prose became distinctly purple. 'The majestic moving vision of silvery grey, the searchlight disclosing every inch of her except the forward gondola – kept purposely dark by request of the navigator – came directly over The Times Building at 1 a.m. She hovered there almost stationary for a moment.' And then 'Gathering speed as every second ticked off, she passed out of sight on her eastward course at a speed of 60 miles an hour.' The words were accompanied by a half-page illustration of a ghostly, silvery shape caught in the searchlights being cheered on by an excited, hat-waving crowd.

Edward Maitland was entranced by the cruise over midtown Manhattan:

New York at night looks wonderful from a height of 1,000 feet. Miles and miles of tiny bright twinkling lights. We wonder if it is necessary to go higher than 1,000 feet to avoid bumping into the 'skyscrapers' so Scott puts her up to 1,500 feet to be quite sure! The searchlights at first make some very unsuccessful attempts to find us, and their beams are 'feeling' through the sky in every direction. Finally they get us fair and square over Fifth Avenue . . .

The Times Square, Broadway, is a remarkable sight – we see thousands of upturned faces in spite of the early hour, and the whole scene is lit up by the gigantic electric sky-signs, which seem to concentrate about this point. One in particular – the Overland car – is a fine example of the importance of aerial advertisement, and from a height of 2,000 feet we can see its wheels revolving, and the dust rising in clouds behind it, presumably as an illustration of its speed.

But the ship was beginning to bump and rock as the air over New York became slightly turbulent. Guy Harris reckoned this was due to a cyclone making its way down from the Great Lakes, about which the R34 had been warned by the Americans. It was time to leave the skies above the USA. At 01.10 New York time Scott turned the ship's bow east down 42nd Street and set a course for Britain. 'We head for home,' Maitland wrote in his log, 'with 3,000 miles of sea between us and our Scottish base'.

11

Return: Thursday, 10 July 1919

There's no doubt that the R34's return journey was, in the parlance of the day, 'a piece of cake' compared with the flight from Scotland to the USA. From the outset the weather was in the ship's favour – as Maitland was more than happy to record.

The wind is now well behind, and our speed made good is estimated to be 65 knots, or 78 miles an hour. The weather at time of starting is decidedly helpful from America.

There is a depression west of Newfoundland, and another larger one centred to the north of Iceland; also an anticyclone over the Eastern Atlantic and Great Britain. The inference from the above is that a strong SW or W wind will prevail over the greater part of the Atlantic, and being on the southerly side of the depression centred over Newfoundland, we should get the full benefit of the 35-knot SW wind which is blowing.

At this speed (78 miles an hour) we are travelling considerably faster than the depression itself, which is probably moving eastwards at about 35 knots, or 42 mph, and it may well be that we shall run right out of it before we reach mid-Atlantic. With any luck, by keeping rather northerly of the steamship course, we may get into touch with the still bigger depression centred to the north of Iceland, and so benefit by the westerly wind which we ought to find on its southerly side.

Our course is now 49°, and we are crossing the American coast 6 miles east of Bellport, with four of our five engines running, the fifth engine resting. Very dark night. Some hot coffee from the Thermos flask presented to us by kind

American friends is particularly nice and warming. Decide to turn in.

At 05.00, while Maitland was sleeping in his hammock, the R34 passed over the Nantucket Light on Nantucket Island, that oddly-shaped scrap of land that sits in the sea at the junction of the Nantucket Sound and the Atlantic. The R34 had put America behind her.

At 09.15 the still-cheerful Maitland wrote:

We have covered 430 miles from New York already, and are going strong. After breakfast Scott and I sort out the mails, and this takes some time, as we find we have quite a large collection of parcels and letters of all descriptions. There are letters for HH the King, the Foreign Office, Admiralty, Postmaster-General; and a large number of copies of the *Public Ledger* for the editor of *The Times*. In addition we have cinematograph films of our landing in America, President Wilson's reception in New York, the Dempsey–Willard fight, and also medals for Alcock and Brown presented by the Aero Club of America.

This journey, we hope, will prove to be the fastest newspaper delivery between New York and London yet accomplished, and we will be the forerunner of a regular interchange of mails between East and West. We are now making good 72 knots or 86 mph on four engines – forward engine stopped. Wind almost dead astern, and very little drift.

Have consultation with Scott, and we decide to make straight for London and see how long it will take to cross the Atlantic from Broadway to Piccadilly Circus; from the capital of one country to the capital of the other.

Which is an odd remark for a Cambridge graduate to make: New York had never been the capital of the USA, although Philadelphia had, at least for a few years. By noon Maitland was enjoying his lunch:

Cold Bologna sausage and pickles, stewed pineapple and a ration of rum. This latter is much appreciated, as the weather has turned much colder. We discuss at some length the problem of obtaining and recording meteorological information about the upper air in the Atlantic, and all agree that one good method of getting information at small cost would be to equip all cable repair-ships with a meteorological observer, and a suitable outfit of kites and instruments. These cable repair-ships work in all parts of the world, and are often stationary at sea for days at a time; moreover, the cable routes are nearly in every case on the shortest and most direct routes between the countries they link up.

Lunch was followed by a couple of thank-you messages to their American hosts.

We send the following messages via Bar Harbour to Admiral Commanding Naval District Mineola: 'Officers and crew R34 desire to express their sincere gratitude for the valuable and efficient assistance they have received during the mooring out of R34 at Mineola. All well – making good progress. Distance covered 630 miles in 12 hours – making for London. Scott.'

To Colonel Miller, Long Island: 'Officers and crew R34 thank you personally for trouble you have taken to help us while moored out – it is much appreciated. Going strong for London – distance covered in 12 hours, 630 miles. – Scott.'

On that first day of her homeward journey the R34 made excellent progress, as a buoyant Maitland recorded:

We have averaged 67 mph ever since leaving New York. Weather fine – visibility 15 to 20 miles – wind 40 knots, SSW – sea very rough. It is difficult to measure the height of the waves from above, but it is easy to see that, in a very heavy sea like this, a surface ship would be having an extremely bad time. Up here we are as steady as a rock, and unless we look out of the windows, it is hard to realise we are travelling at all.

The sun is high, so Cooke is able to get good idea of any barometric changes by observing the angle of the ship's shadow on the water subtends with a sextant, thus calculating the distance of the shadow from the observer, and comparing with height recorded on the altimeter. This is only possible at low altitudes, i.e. about 1,500 feet. (It sounds a bit complicated, but is quite effective!) Lt.-Col. W.N. Hensley, United States Army Aviation Department, is steering, and is taking opposition watch with Pritchard, while Luck has relieved Greenland in the forward car, and Warrant-Officer Mayes is in charge of the elevators.

Course direct for London via Queenstown and Bristol Channel. We are in wireless touch with Sable Island, and about 330 miles due south of Newfoundland. Received the following two wireless messages from New York – 'To R34: Thanks for the flight, from thousands whom the spectacle thrilled – good luck to you. – *New York Times*.' 'God speed you on return to England. Hope your voyage is the forerunner of many. – *New York Herald*.'

We report our progress as follows – 'To the Air Attaché, Washington, Air Ministry and Base, via New York. Course 90, true-speed 50 knots – going well.' US Weather Bureau warn us that weather is very bad over Newfoundland, and advise us to keep as much away to the south as possible. Harris estimates we shall have got away from the influence of this depression by nightfall, and that probably the wind and sea will have moderated by then.

There is still the possibility of getting into touch with the depression centred over Iceland by (about) tomorrow afternoon. As a general rule it is foggy and cloudy the more we keep up to the north, the cold currents, meeting the warm currents, causing fog and cloud. On a more southerly course over the Gulf Stream, where there are no cold currents from the north, clearer weather can always be expected.

The clear weather made Gilbert Cooke's job a lot easier. With the sun and the sea visible, fixing a position and plotting a course was more or less straightforward. As Maitland observed in his log:

> There were only three occasions on the outward journey when it was possible to determine our position by means of observation of sun to sea horizon. True bearing sun N 81° W Course 140° steered, 110° made good, speed 57 mph. We have covered 900 miles from New York in 16 hours, and are 1,850 miles from the S coast of Ireland, or exactly one-third of the distance between the two countries.

And with the wind on the ship's tail there were no worries about fuel. The R34 was drinking petrol at a modest rate.

> Our petrol consumption works out at about one gallon per nautical mile made good on four engines – weather clear. Our maximum visibility is very good and, according to the Dip and Distance horizon tables, at our present height, i.e. 1,500 feet., should be about 45 miles.
>
> Wind has dropped considerably, and sea is deep blue. It is interesting to note that, with depressions situated as they are, it would be quite against all the laws of weather forecasting for us to get a head wind anywhere between here and London. The worst condition that we might expect to get would be no wind at all.

All the officers agreed that the quality of information and support that the R34 had received from the US weather service had been superb. Better, they hinted, than anything available on the east side of the Atlantic. That evening Harris radioed back to the USA – 'Many thanks for kind, efficient manner in which weather information has been supplied – deeply grateful. – Guy Harris, Meteorological Officer, R34.'

On the outward journey Maitland had fretted slightly over the fact that the R34 had never spotted a ship on the open sea. There had been radio contact with cargo vessels, liners and warships, but no sightings. The sheer size and emptiness of the Atlantic seem to have both surprised and vaguely unnerved Maitland.

So at 18.15 that Thursday he was pleased to log 'A five-masted schooner under full sail on starboard beam about 5 miles away – the first ship we have yet seen in the open Atlantic on either outward or return journeys'. And he took the opportunity to compare the technologies. 'What an interesting contrast between the old and the new – the sailing ship and the airship!'

We are now over the main eastbound summer route of steamers from New York to Queenstown, so perhaps we may meet an outward-bound liner. The ss *Adriatic*, due New York on 13th, should be somewhere near us, and we are on the look-out for her on our wireless. Getting much colder as we go further east. Harris gives most interesting explanation of the cloud formation to the north and south, and compares the clouds as we see them with the illustration in Claydon's book on *Cloud Studies*, which we have on board.

The return journey was certainly enlivened by the contributions of the R34's American well-wishers. Maitland recorded:

Supper-time fresh boiled eggs and cocoa, preceded by a cocktail mixed by Scott. Apparently some Thermos flasks full of cocktail ingredients had been handed in by some anonymous well-wisher, and we try them as an experiment. Decide that they are just as good in the air as on the ground!

We compare at some length our impressions of American

men and women. I wish our newly made friends could have heard some of the delightful things that were said about them. (Quite a number of charming ladies declared their intention of making the return journey as 'stowaways', and the ship was carefully searched before starting.)

Pritchard goes to sleep under the dining-room table while the second watch come in for their supper. This position (under the dining-room table) seems to be the most sought-after in the ship. The gramophone is a real pleasure on this homeward journey: a magnificent instrument presented to Scott by Mr Edison.

One of our pigeons escaped at Mineola when allowed out for exercise. [The escapee pigeon was afterwards picked up in an exhausted condition by a west-bound steamer 800 miles out in the Atlantic, having made a valiant attempt to fly back to Britain.] And so we have only one on the return journey. He takes his food well, and 'coos' loudly every time the gramophone starts up – his wicker cage being hung on a girder just outside the crew's mess-deck.

British ship ss *Minnekahda* speaks us. She says she is bound for Halifax with troops. During this first day in the Atlantic the sea has been visible the whole time, so that observations for course and speed have been obtained as often as necessary and without any difficulty.

12

Return: Friday, 11 July 1919

In the early hours of Friday morning the R34 was still running before the wind and going well. At 03.20 Maitland reckoned their position as '45° 03′ North, 42° 57′ West, estimated by observations of stars to sea horizon.' Which, if correct, placed the R34 a few hundred miles due south of the southerly tip of Greenland. But it seemed that whether going east–west or west–east there were always problems. That night, one of the Sunbeam 'Maori' engines in the rear car gave up the ghost. Nothing that engineering officer John Shotter and his hard-pressed men could do would bring it back to life.

'The foremost of the two engines in after car is out of action: damaged beyond repair,' Maitland recorded at 04.20. Which was something of a blow. It scuppered the Scott/Maitland plan to make a triumphant flight across London before heading back to East Fortune. 'Scott and myself discuss the situation, and agree we had better make straight for our base at East Fortune, and give up the idea of flying in over London. We change course accordingly and are now making good N 30° E: weather clear – sea moderate.' It was a course calculated to take the R34 more or less straight to central Scotland.

At 06.40 Scott decided to take the ship down to 600 feet in an attempt to get under the gathering clouds which, according to Maitland,

> . . . are now appearing, and threaten to blot out all view of the sea. We find by careful observation that there is a northerly wind below the clouds, that whilst above, on the 3,000-foot level, the wind is from the SW.
>
> The reason for this is interesting: we are over the Gulf Stream on a north-easterly course, and the air over this Gulf

Stream is warmer than the air over the sea immediately to the north. This warm air rises, and its place is naturally taken by the cold air from the north, resulting in a 12-knot convectional wind extending from the surface of the sea up to a height of about 2,000 feet.

Having made this discovery, we remain at the 3,000-foot level above the clouds, where we have a steady wind from the SW. We find it easy to determine the direction of the wind, when flying above the clouds, from their formation. The crests of these curl away from the direction in which the wind is blowing. Scott and Harris are agreed that the wind is stronger in our favour the higher we go up. In spite of this Scott decided to remain on the 3,000-foot level to avoid necessity of losing gas from expansion.

Tomorrow he can go much higher, as the ship will be so much lighter, on account of having burnt another 24 hours' petrol. Beautiful cloudscapes on port beam. Cloud formations, in so far as they indicate weather, are like an open book profusely illustrated, and with a story that changes almost completely every few hours. Away to the NW we see the depression centred over Newfoundland written plainly in the sky, in fantastic and streaky 'Cirrus Ventosus' – a sure indication of what is going on over there, some hundreds of miles away.

At midday a message made the R34 change direction:

Weather report from Air Ministry tells us of an anti-cyclone off SW of Ireland, and so we change course more to the north, with a view to getting round into the westerly wind, which we know must be blowing on the northerly side of it. Noon position, 46° 31′ N, 38° 32′ W. Still above the clouds. Cooke considers the best height at which to take sights to cloud horizon is at about 500 feet above the clouds.

Lunch. Meal-times are always most welcome, as they give the more responsible members of the crew a much-needed interval. The new gramophone is going strong after lunch and, as I was descending the ladder into the forward car, I caught a glimpse of Luck and Harris doing quite a nice one-step together!

Which may have been a minor historical moment: the first-ever outbreak of ballroom dancing thousands of feet in the air over the Atlantic.

According to the R34's wireless log (but not Maitland's) a message came in from the Air Ministry relayed through Clifden. It read: 'Following arrangements have been made for you on arrival: Accommodation available at East Fortune and Pulham, and in emergency Kingsnorth. Airship Officer and necessary landing-party with supply of Petrol is at Fermoy, 15 miles NNE of Cork. Destroyers with steam at one hour's notice are at Berehaven.' Berehaven – now Castletownbere – is a harbour on the coast of West Cork at the entrance to Bantry Bay. The R34 replied:

'Propose to land at East Fortune – one engine completely broken down.' Message from New York – 'At this luncheon given by the Aero Club of America resolutions were passed to the effect that the officers and officials of the Club wish General Maitland and crew of R34 safe and pleasant journey. – Lucas.'

Big glare off the clouds – very noticeable coming down from keel into the forward car. Harris and Cooke climb to top of ship to make observations every two hours; quite a strenuous effort each time, and they at any rate cannot complain for want of exercise. Still at 3,000 feet: in and out of the clouds at intervals. We have not seen the sea since 8.30 this morning. Air speed 32 knots on three engines.

Another weather report from London to say the depression N of Iceland has moved easterly, and that as a result the wind is from the SW over north of Ireland and whole of Scotland. This strengthens Scott in his decision to give up

going to London, and to make for East Fortune instead. It is
sad not to take in London on our return route, but with one
engine lost, and wind in S of England not very favourable,
the decision is a wise one.

Scott brings his ship down to try for a glimpse of the sea,
and so get an idea of our speed; but at 900 feet it is still quite
thick, so he abandons the attempt. We need an instrument
for measuring the depth of the clouds below an airship
without having to reduce height for the purpose; probably a
'Dines' or a 'Marvin' kite meteorograph would be suitable.

The 'Dines' and 'Marvin' kites were simple kites to which
instruments were attached in an attempt to measure temperature, humidity, air pressure and wind velocity of the upper
atmosphere. They were named after their inventors, the Eng-
lishman W.H. Dines and the American C.F. Marvin.

Maitland's fascination with the sky and the clouds never
flagged:

Coming down from the 3,800-foot level to the 900-foot
level, we pass through no less than five distinct and separate
layers of cloud, of which every two layers contain a world in
themselves, with separate sky above and a cloud horizon
beneath. A most fascinating spectacle, and one which im-
presses me more, perhaps, than anything I have yet seen on
either journey.

We have been in these thick clouds for some considerable
time, and there is no means of telling our speed, as they
extend right down to the surface of the water. We assume,
however, from general weather observations, that the wind
is with us; the worst condition we think fair to assume being
no wind at all. There certainly ought *not* to be a headwind
against us. No alternative but to keep plugging away
through these clouds until other weather conditions appear.

We emerge above the clouds for a few blissful moments,
and see a beautiful cloud panorama – range upon range of

alternate white and slate coloured mountains with wide deep valleys, and an occasional glimpse of bright blue sky immediately above. The glare is almost blinding, and we can only look at them for a moment or two at a time. [Reflected glare from the clouds proved a problem. Some of the crew regretted not bringing what they knew as 'tinted glasses'. But before long the ship was . . .] Back again in the clouds, and no visibility whatsoever.

We pick up HMS *Cumberland* on our Marconi spark set. She gives her position and, when plotted on chart, Cooke thinks she should be almost due north of us and, from the strength of her signals, within 30 miles. Durrant tries to get her on the Directional Wireless, but without success. Scott makes the discovery that when he brings his ship down into a cloud she will sometimes tend to dive, and at others tend to climb out of the cloud. Pritchard puts forward the following interesting solution, which seems to fulfil the conditions each time it is observed . . .

Pritchard's theory was later included in his report to the Admiralty (and in Scott's post-flight report). Here's how Maitland described it:

If a cloud is forming, the water vapour in the atmosphere is condensing and giving off heat to the air during the process. The air, therefore, in a cloud which is forming, is slightly warmer than the air above the cloud. The Airship would, therefore, appear to be heavy and tend to dive on entering the cloud. If, on the other hand, the cloud is dissipating, the water in the cloud is evaporating and taking heat from the air in the cloud in doing so. The air in the cloud is, therefore, colder than the air immediately above the cloud, and the Airship on entering the cloud will appear to be light.

The nearer the R34 got to the British Isles the more dismal the weather became. By the early evening the ship was in the familiar mire. 'Passing through wet rain clouds – it has been raining very heavily since five o'clock. Scott tries the 5,000-foot level in the hopes of getting out of it, but with no success, so returns to the 3,000-foot level. Very cold and dark, and all doors and windows shut. Stopping forward engine to replace two broken valve-springs. We ask HMS *Cumberland* for a weather report. She replies, giving her position, and reports: 'Wind NNW – 18 mph – overcast – passing showers – clouds at about 1,000 feet.'

But there was consolation in the American-sourced food, which, it was agreed, was much better than the British variety, as Maitland enthused:

Supper, and a very good one too. We are all equipped with little luxuries, having learnt from experience on the outward journey exactly what is necessary and what isn't. Delicious fresh honey, also 'candies', and chocolates supplied by Sherry's. The gloom does not affect our appetites in the very slightest.

Still pouring in sheets. The wind whistles round the forward car, and it is very dark and dreary – of course we can see nothing. Scott tries a lower level, and an extra-ordinary sight immediately presents itself beneath us. Thousands and thousands of little round clouds like tiny white puff-balls packed closely together, with the blue sea just visible in between them, forming a layer of clouds between us and the sea. This cloud formation is known as 'Ballo cumulus', and is particularly beautiful. Harris has never seen 'Ballo cumulus' so low before: it is usually found at much greater heights.

Dropped a calcium flare, which floated away astern, burning brightly, enabling Cooke to get an estimate of course made good. Our speed is evidently considerable, but as no means exist of taking an angle of depression of the flare, it cannot be calculated. In future we must be equipped with some instrument or other for this purpose.

Flares for use at night are an absolute necessity, and the ones we use are the calcium phosphate flares commonly known in the Navy and Merchant service as 'Holmes' Lights. They will not float in rough weather, and so we attach to each flare a small fabric bag, which can be blown up by air by means of the mouth. Though a clumsy arrangement, it functions well; but, in future, we must have these 'Holmes' Lights fitted with watertight compartment to make certain of their floating in any sea.

The weather refused to relent:

Again in thick cloud and heavy rain. Signals from Clifden Wireless Station sound very loud, which shows we are getting nearer home, and Durrant has just succeeded in getting East Fortune [over 1,600 miles away]. Quite faintly he got the words, 'Saturday evening'. ss *Dominion*, bound for Avonmouth, speaks us and gives her position and barometer reading. She reports us as quite near, though of course she cannot see, or even hear us.

Speaking ss *Orduna*. It is one thing talking to these ships in the Atlantic miles and miles away; but if only we could see them, how much nicer it would be. From ss *Dominion*: 'Shall I fire a gun when I think you are near me? Estimate your speed at 45 mph – Christie. We reply: 'No don't trouble to fire a gun.'

On long journeys like these, it is the engineers upon whom the heaviest strain falls and, on the outward journey, some of them had difficulty in sleeping when off watch. On this return journey we issue them a 'tot' of rum before turning in, with very beneficial effect.

Still pouring with rain; by dropping two more flares drift is estimated to be 10° southward. Height 2,000 feet. Rain is beating down pitilessly against the outer cover, and the whistling of the wind completely deadens the distant hum of our engines. It is indeed a 'dirty' night at sea. For some reason or other I cannot get off to sleep, and lie awake in my hammock with a feeling of confidence and security, but hoping it won't be like this for our landing in Scotland tomorrow evening.

13

Return: Saturday, 12 July 1919

Saturday, 12 July, got off to a mixed start. At 12.45 Maitland noted a distinct improvement in the weather. 'Weather clearing, and sea visible at 2,500 feet.' But 15 minutes later a message came in from the Air Ministry which is recorded in the R34's wireless log but not in Maitland's. The message read: 'Weather conditions at East Fortune extremely doubtful. Steer for Pulham.'

Maitland was preoccupied with the change in the weather. And, yet again, he revelled in the cloudscape that the changing weather produced. At 05.00 he describes a 'Magnificent sunrise; the sun slowly appears above the cloudbank ahead of us in a blaze of golden light, and we head straight into it. Position 52° 20′ N, 22° 35′ W, observation of sun to cloud horizon; 760 miles from East Fortune.'

At 08.40 a message came winging in direct from East Fortune. 'Weather conditions last night on ground . . . 10 to 15 mph. Do not anticipate anything worse tonight. Consider it could be possible to safely house you between 21.00 and 08.00 BST." In other words, it had been a bit blowy but nothing that the airship base couldn't handle. It was a direct contradiction of the Air Ministry's earlier message.

By then the R34 was having one of its all too familiar problems with an engine.

Running on three engines only; changing broken valve-spring on after engine. Air speed 32 knots; Scott takes ship down to 900 feet to sight the water. As speed made good at this height is only 15 knots, however, he returns to 2,800 feet, the surface being now just visible at this height, and speed made good increases to 36 knots.

It is interesting to note that for 24 hours (until 6 a.m. this morning) Cooke has been unable to get a single observation on either sun, moon, star, sea or cloud horizons, and it is quite fair to assume that yesterday's weather is an average day in mid-Atlantic. Clouds beneath us look just like a soft, fleecy white feather-bed, and they fill one with an odd, almost irresistible wish to jump down into them – probably the same sort of sensation experienced by some people when crossing a steep mountain face. We appear to have a slight headwind, but don't think it will last long, as we should soon be getting a helping wind from the depression over Scotland.

Breakfast this morning is a festive meal, as we reckon it should be our last breakfast on board, and we are rather lavish in our issues. East Fortune report weather suitable for a landing up till 8 a.m. tomorrow (Sunday) morning.

Then, just after breakfast:

Signal from Air Ministry instructing us to land at Pulham in Norfolk. This is not understood as, according to the weather reports, conditions seem to be better at East Fortune than Pulham. Besides, the wives, families and sweethearts of the crew are all at East Fortune, waiting to welcome them, so to most them this comes as a great disappointment.

The crew were more than disappointed; they were angry. East Fortune was the R34's home base. It seemed only fitting that the airship should complete her return journey at the point where she started. And so far as the officers and men could see, there was no sensible reason why they should divert to Pulham in Norfolk, hundreds of miles from their base. It was probably the disgruntlement of his men that encouraged Scott to question the order:

Drift observation obtained from about 3,000 feet, and steering course is altered to N 75° E, giving course made

good N 88° E magnetic. Height 5,000 feet. We are now in a
big gap in the clouds, about 20 miles across. Clear blue sky
and sea – making good 35 knots, which should enable us to
land at daybreak tomorrow.

Just after 11.00 a message came in from the airfield at Fermoy
in County Cork:

'Do you intend to land at Fermoy? For I have a landing
party of 500 men if required. – Major Little.' (Major Little is
one of our most experienced airship captains, and has been
sent over to Ireland to land us at Fermoy Barracks, in the
event of our running short of petrol.) We reply: 'No, not
landing at Fermoy.' We have a large supply of petrol left,
and so far this journey has not presented half the difficulties
of the outward voyage. Weather now very cold.

By noon the mood aboard the R34 seems to have changed,
dampened, no doubt, by the weather and the order to make for
Pulham:

Lunch. We are becoming rather impatient to get to our
journey's end. Perhaps it is the strain that is beginning to tell;
anyway, we all feel disappointed at finding we are only
making good 28 knots, and that there is quite a stiff north-
easterly breeze against us. We shall be breakfasting in the air
again tomorrow after all!

Half an hour later the weather had improved. And once again
Maitland was ruminating on the loneliness of the Atlantic.

We are on the 5,000-foot level, with a perfectly blue sky and
deep blue sea; visibility is at its maximum, and at this height,
according to our text-books, we should be able to see a
distance of 81 miles from right forward to right aft, yet –
although this area of visibility works out at 19,200 square

miles – not a ship is in sight. I am afraid that my ambition to see a steamer at close quarters in this gigantic Atlantic will never be realised. If it wasn't for the fact that we have actually been speaking to them all the way across, I should feel inclined to say there are none in the Atlantic at all.

The clear weather didn't last.

Clouds rolling up again. We see some very fine examples of 'Cumulus major'. There is one particularly interesting cloudscape on our port beam – a huge vertical column about 500 feet high, joining a lower strata of cloud to a higher strata. This is caused by an upward vertical current, and beyond its picturesque effect has no special meaning.

Great excitement: two trawlers are sighted on our starboard beam, about 8 miles away, and looking very tiny – one is much nearer than the other. We try and speak the near one with an Aldis lamp, as they carry no wireless, but can get no reply. We are now down to 2,000 feet, and the difference in temperature between this height and 5,000 feet is most marked, viz. 8° F.

Making slightly better headway at this height, viz., 32 knots on four engines – wind NNW, 25° drift. Discussion with Cooke on subject of Aerial Navigation. He thinks that this should not present any insuperable difficulties; and that, with instruments at present available, one should be able to estimate one's position in mid-Atlantic accuracy to within 40 miles. Artificial horizons cannot be relied upon, owing to the necessity of keeping the reflected image continually in sight; and this difficulty is accentuated from a constantly moving platform like an Airship, however steady she may be.

Until Directional Wireless proves thoroughly reliable, a Bubble Sextant should be specially designed, and probably could be made to give an accuracy within about 10 miles. It is extraordinary how seldom we get a view of the sea. On

the outward voyage, out of 17 sights taken with an ordinary
sextant, in three cases only was a sea horizon used – for the
remaining 14 the altitude was measured to a cloud horizon.
On this return voyage it is slightly and, so far, about half the
sights taken have been to a sea horizon.

In the evening, the weather took a turn for the worse.

We run into a sudden squall from the NW, low black clouds
with pelting rain and a rough confused sea; the wind roars
past the control car. All this comes upon us in the space of a
few minutes. Ship very steady. Passed out of the squall.
There appear to be more ahead. Got Clifden on Directional
Wireless N 98° E, Magnetic 76° true, and we cannot be very
far from the west coast of Ireland. The clock is put on
another hour. Another squall strikes us just as suddenly as
the last one.

And then:

Land in sight on our starboard bow; it is from 7 to 10 miles
away, and was first spotted Lt.-Col. Hensley. Great enthusiasm. Scott alters course direct towards it – Cooke gets out
the large chart of the west coast of Ireland, and we have a
keen competition to see who will fix on the exact spot where
we cross the coastline. Two little islands lie right ahead of
us; with our glasses we see the wireless masts at Clifden.
These two islands are undoubtedly the same two little
islands that suddenly appeared out of the fog to the delighted gaze of Alcock and Brown upon the conclusion of
their historical flight. What a strange and happy coincidence!

What Maitland and his colleagues were seeing were the two
uninhabited islands that sit at the mouth of Clifden Bay. It was
their first glimpse of Europe. 'At 8 o'clock precisely we cross

the coastline a little north of Clifden, County Mayo, and our
time from crossing the American coast at Long Island to
crossing the Irish coast is exactly 61 hours, 43 minutes. We
head right in over the mountains, which at this spot are 2,900
feet high. What a wild and rugged coast-line!'

Maitland was plainly delighted by the prospect that
stretched out in front of him. He relished the sight – the
ragged, sea-beaten coastline of County Galway and behind
it the high hills that ranged east into the Irish interior: Mal-
more, Ben Cullagh, Ben Brack, Cregg, Bealnascalpa, Knock-
brack. And among the hills dozens of loughs and loughans,
some substantial, some no more than pools.

A magnificent cloud panorama now appears, high, white
cumulus clouds of weird and fantastic shapes surround us
on all sides. Over the top peep out the mountain summits,
while, through gaps in the clouds, we catches glimpses of
lakes, harbours, islands and green fields; quite the prettiest
picture we have seen on the entire voyage. It seems as if the
elements had reserved their best cloudscapes to welcome us
as we cross over Irish soil.

There was an unlikely welcome home, too.

A two-seater aeroplane from the neighbourhood of Castle-
bar flies successively past, over and under us, waving a
welcome. We are now well away from the mountains, and
over the flat country inland, heading across to Belfast, and
making good 46 mph. Bright full moon.

As things have turned out, it would have been wiser if we
had kept a more northerly course, after getting away from
the helpful influence of the Newfoundland depression. We
would then have been helped, instead of hindered, by this
NNW wind, and so have saved time. Undoubtedly the
captains of future Airship Liners will become wily and
cunning masters of the art of selecting the right wind and

the right height, and, by means of their air knowledge alone, will save many hours upon long sea and land passages.

At 22.00 another message came in from East Fortune, this one reporting on the weather around the Firth of Forth. "Wind indefinite on surface. At 1,500 feet between W and NW, 10 mph. Consider conditions will be favourable for landing you at 10.00 tomorrow.'

Thoroughly confused as to where he was supposed to put the ship down Scott signalled the Air Ministry in London: 'East Fortune report weather conditions favourable for landing tomorrow morning. Request permission to proceed and land at East Fortune. Scott, 20.10.'

But the men from the Air Ministry had made their minds up. The reply was curt: 'Reference your 20.10. Land at Pulham. Acknowledge.'

Scott was not about to give up that easily. At 23.18 he responded with a message marked 'priority': 'Can land at East Fortune 6 a.m. Cannot land Pulham until 10 a.m. One engine completely broken down. Others may fail at any moment. Request Air Ministry may reconsider their decision.' And when he hadn't heard back by 11.30 he radioed: 'Hasten reply.'

But it was no good. London had made up its mind. At five minutes to midnight the reply came: 'Proceed to Pulham. If by doing so you anticipate risk of breakdown, report to Air Ministry.'

There's a note of resignation in Maitland's last entry for that Saturday. 'The reply is to land at Pulham; so we assume there is some special reason, and alter course accordingly. Scott increases height to 5,000 feet, and sets course direct for Pulham. Turn in. We shall need a good night's rest, as tomorrow is likely to be a very tiring day – to say the least of it.'

14

Return: Sunday, 13 July 1919

At 41 minutes past midnight on Sunday, 13 July, Scott signalled East Fortune: 'In accordance with Air Ministry instructions, I am proceeding to Pulham. Please have officers' and ratings' kit sent to Pulham as soon as possible. – Major Scott.' Then at 03.00 he signalled Pulham: 'Probable time of landing, 06.00 GMT.'

That summer night Maitland wrote:

Flying up the Mersey. On our port bow are the lights of Liverpool. We are continually in and out of dense cloud banks, and it is difficult to identify places on the ground through occasional holes in the cloud strata beneath.

Over Nottingham. Wireless message from His Majesty the King: 'I heartily congratulate you all on your safe return home after completion of your memorable and indeed unique Atlantic voyage. – George RI.' From Air Ministry to General Maitland, Major Scott, officers and crew of R34: 'On behalf of the whole Air Force I send you heartiest congratulations on your magnificent achievement in making the double journey across the Atlantic. – Trenchard, Chief of Air Staff.'

From Board of Admiralty to General Maitland and crew of HMA R34: 'Welcome home. The great adventure is beyond all praise. – Board of Admiralty.' From Major-General Seely, Under-Secretary of State for Air: 'I send my heartiest congratulations to you and the crew of R34 on your magnificent achievement of being the first to cross and re-cross the Atlantic by air. We are all very proud of you.' From Prime Minister to General Maitland, Major Scott and the crew of HMA R34: 'Heartiest congratulations on fine feat of airmanship. – Lloyd George.'

Over Pulham. Quite a number of people on the landing ground despite the early hour. Scott makes two circles of the ground, and puts the ship gently down into the hands of the landing-party. Time of landing, 6.57 a.m. Total time of return journey from Long Island, New York to Pulham, Norfolk, is therefore 75 hours and 3 minutes, or 3 days, 3 hours and 3 minutes.

Compared to the reception the R34 received on Long Island the welcome back at Pulham was decidedly muted. It was military and press only. While the Pulham airship base band banged out a selection of cheerful tunes ('The Call of Duty', 'See the Conquering Hero Comes', 'Till the Boys Come Home') the landing party grabbed the trail ropes and began to haul the R34 back to Britain. At which point Scott decided that the ship was a shade heavy and decided to dump some water ballast – soaking most of the landing party. 'It was all very inspiring,' wrote the man from the *Morning Post* sardonically 'and the pity was there were not thousands present to testify their appreciation of the great and lasting achievement.'

The press had been waiting at Pulham since the early hours of a morning which *The Times* described as 'grey with a faint streak of gold in the east, and the heavy clouds that were blowing up from the south-west soon broke into rain'. When the R34 did appear and was finally brought down to land the scrum of reporters and photographers followed it across the landing field and into one of Pulham's huge hangars, where they bombarded the crew with questions.

First to step down from the gondola was Maitland, immaculate in his blue RAF uniform, with a white silk scarf round his neck. He was followed by Scott and the rest of the crew. After a handshake from the base commander, Lieutenant-Colonel Booth, they were whisked away to the officers' mess for breakfast. The post-breakfast press conference, unlike the one at Mineola, was carefully controlled. Only Maitland and

Scott faced the reporters, and most of the talking was done by Maitland (who was, by then, a dab hand at telling the media what he wanted them to hear).

And what he wanted them to hear was that the trip to the USA and back had been wonderful, that the airship was a wonderful creation that had a wonderful future working in cooperation with heavier-than-air aeroplanes. 'On the return journey,' he told the press 'when there was a wind of 45 miles per hour and the sea was running very high, any surface ship would have been all over the place, whereas we were travelling very smoothly with no unpleasant motion whatsoever.'

As for the touch-and-go nature of the outward journey he said 'We were always fully confident that we should be able to make the trip. It was merely a question of the petrol lasting . . .' There was no mention of the fearsome wind barrage off Newfoundland that almost halted the R34 in her tracks, or the terrible buffeting she took in the electrical storms over the Bay of Fundy.

When asked why the R34 had returned to Pulham and not East Fortune he was a bit more candid. 'Not because of any difficulties,' he said. 'Was it not because all you people had come here? As a matter of fact we wanted to go to the other station because we started from there and wished to make the round trip.'

It has never been made clear why the R34 was diverted from East Fortune to Pulham. One theory is that the anti-airship forces inside the Air Ministry – led by Winston Churchill – concluded that the big welcome-home planned for the ship at East Fortune, complete with tearful families and sweethearts for the press to describe and photograph, risked making the R34 and its crew into media heroes. Being a mere 20 miles from Edinburgh, a landing at East Fortune might have attracted crowds from all over central Scotland. Quiet, remote Pulham, deep in the Norfolk countryside, was a more controllable option. But for whatever the reason, the crew of the R34 were servicemen. So Pulham it had to be

Maitland went on to speculate on the time when much bigger airships than the R34 would be ferrying mail and passengers from continent to continent, and in great comfort. Nor would they have to rely on hundreds of men to bring them down. They'd fly to a 200-foot high mooring mast within which passenger lifts took passengers up and down to the ships. (Which, in fact, was a project on which George Scott had been working and for which he was to make a reputation.)

The more taciturn Scott said nothing to contradict Maitland's airier speculations. 'There is no doubt that the airship is the thing for deep sea [*sic!*] work,' he told the journalists 'but such airships must be big and able to sustain a speed of 70 to 80 miles per hour.' As for the best route across the skies over the depression-haunted Atlantic, Scott concluded that 'that question will have to be determined by the weather'.

At the dinner held later that evening in the officers' mess two of the other officers did manage to voice a few words about the trip. When congratulated on his navigational skills Gilbert Cooke pointed out that the coast of the United States was about 3,000 miles long 'and it would have been surprising if we had not hit her'. As for their New York welcome, Guy Harris said 'They would have killed us with kindness if we'd been able to stay long enough'.

But that Sunday ended on an oddly disconcerting note. The R34's bag of mail – which included official greetings to King George, messages of dignitaries, copies of American newspapers etc. – was bundled into a car belonging (for some reason) to the US Embassy's information bureau and driven by one Lieutenant-Commander Ramsay of the US Naval Air Service. Also in the car were one of the Air Ministry's press officers, two mechanics and a journalist called W.A. Mallabar.

The American may have been driving too fast, because outside the village of Capel St Mary near Ipswich he collided with a horse and trap. According to one report, 'The car mounted a fence and fell in a wrecked condition on the other side'. Also in a wrecked condition was Mallabar the journalist, who fractured his skull and was whisked off to hospital. Other injuries were slight. Ramsay and his remaining passengers then found another car and continued on their way to London. It might be argued that the unfortunate Mallabar was the one and only casualty of the entire R34 transatlantic project.

15

Triumph and After

The following morning, Monday, 14 July, Edward Maitland, George Scott and John Shotter took the train to London, where they were met at Liverpool Street by a little delegation of admirers and semi-dignitaries (including Clementine Churchill, Winston's wife, and the Countess of Drogheda). The most senior military officer on the platform was Brigadier-General Ernest Swinton, the Controller of Information at the Air Ministry.

It was another low-key reception. Far too low-key in the opinion of *The Times*, which reported that 'the general public in the station seemed to be unaware of the identity of the visitors, and there was no demonstration'. After some handshaking the R34's officers stepped into a taxi and a government car and drove off to a debriefing at the Air Ministry followed by lunch at the House of Commons with John Seely, the Under-Secretary for Air. Two days later Maitland and Scott got a brief audience with King George V.

But *The Times* took a dim view of the reception the R34 and her crew had received. 'The British and American peoples have been thrilled during the last few days by the wonderful achievement of R34 and her gallant crew', the newspaper opined on 15 July, and went on to assert that, 'London had a right to welcome these men in a style worthy of the occasion. The lack of imagination in officialdom is abysmal . . . Official barriers ought to be swept aside and substantial recognition given to all those, from the commanders to the lowest rigger, who sailed in R34 on her glorious venture.'

Two days later the 17 July issue of *Flight* celebrated the R34's return with a cartoon. Under the caption 'Bridging the Gap' John Bull and Uncle Sam shook hands over a shrunken

Atlantic while an irate German (with waxed, upturned, Kaiser Bill moustaches) looked on in frustration. The editorial declared that: 'By her successful double journey across the Atlantic the airship R34 has . . . demonstrated for the education of the layman that long-distance aerial service for the carriage of passengers and mails is not only a possibility of tomorrow, but the accomplished fact of today.'

But not everyone was quite so enthusiastic. One of the shrewdest of the aviation correspondents of the time was H. Massac Buist, who wrote extensively for the London *Morning Post*. Buist refused to regard the R34 as a triumph of British engineering, described it as 'designed by the British Air Ministry with the aid of Friedrichshafen' (i.e. the Zeppelin works), and was dubious about the hype being generated by Maitland and the Air Ministry.

The day after the R34 landed Buist wrote 'Unfortunately, the performance of the R34 is being made the subject of a certain amount of eulogy of the unwise sort and forecasts calculated considerably to mislead the public'. For the life of him, Buist could not see how passenger airships of the kind envisaged by Maitland would ever make serious money. They were, he wrote 'not a commercial proposition'.

But by then serious money had been committed to airships. The R33 (the R34's sister ship) was already flying, Beardmore's at Inchinnan had the much bigger R36 well under way, and work was about to start on the even bigger R38 at Cardington in Bedfordshire. The airship lobby inside the Air Ministry saw these four ships as the nucleus of a fleet that would sail out and conquer the world, ahead of the Germans, ahead of the French, ahead of the Americans.

But there were critics in parliament. One of the most vocal was Joseph Montague Kenworthy, the newly-elected Liberal MP for Central Hull (who was to become a serious commentator on military matters). Kenworthy stood up in the House of Commons on Thursday, 24 July, to cast cold water on the R34 and its like. 'These airships cost £350,000 each,' he said 'and there are great sheds which will be of doubtful value in the future. The reason is that aeroplanes and seaplanes are advancing in efficiency so rapidly that an airship will have about as much chance with the aeroplane as a sailing ship has today with a cruiser.'

He went on: 'The analogy is this – that the sailing ship was useful for a certain time, and then it became obsolete, and this is the same as the airship, which, I believe, will be dead in spite of a non-inflammable gas or any other improvements. Therefore I do beg the right honourable Gentleman not to spend too much money on airship-building programmes. The money should be spent rather on aeroplanes.'

It is worth pointing out that Kenworthy – later Baron Strabolgi – was not hostile to aviation. Although he had been a naval officer, he constantly criticised the government for pouring too much money into warships instead of building aircraft, which he saw as crucial to the defence of Britain. In the 1920s Kenworthy penned a series of books which warned, among much else, of the spread of world communism, the advent of a far-right regime in Germany, the growing power of Persia (Iran) and the rise of Islamic fundamentalism in the Middle East. One of Joseph Kenworthy's many admirers was H.G. Wells.

The same day that Kenworthy damned airships, *Flight* published a lively attack on what they saw as negative thinking. 'British officialism is an exceedingly peculiar thing,' the magazine opined. 'It has neither soul nor imagination, while its highest priests live in a rut out of which there is apparently no escape.' And the editorial went on to castigate Whitehall for failing to give the R34 the welcome home it deserved and asks 'Have we really any policy in regard to aviation?'

Naturally the manufacturers involved in the flight took the opportunity to bang their own drums. William Beardmore & Co. took out a large display advertisement in *The Times* which featured a (technical) drawing of the airship under the message, 'R34: The first airship to cross the Atlantic, making the round trip inside 11 days.' The ad included the words of a telegram from the Admiralty: 'Hearty congratulations upon the splendid performance of R34, to the success of which the good workmanship and cordial cooperation of your firm have so greatly contributed.'

Amazingly – given the problems that the engines created – the Sunbeam Motor Car Company did the same. They took out a display ad quoting an Admiralty telegram expressing 'Cordial Appreciation of the Skill and Energy. Sincere Congratulations to All Concerned.' The ad went on 'In these words do the Lords of the Admiralty express their opinion of the firm which produced the engines which enabled R34 to make her journey across the Atlantic and back.'

For a while the modest celebrations continued. On Wednesday, 23 July, the officers of the R34 were guests of honour at a dinner hosted by the Royal Aero Club at Prince's Restaurant in Piccadilly. Among the diners: the Duke of Atholl, Sir Hugh Trenchard (Chief of the Air Staff); Major-General John Seely (Under-Secretary for Air); Frederick Handley-Page (aircraft manufacturer); Charles I.R. Campbell (head of airships at the Royal Corps of Naval Constructors); the Countess of Drogheda; and the US Ambassador. There were apologies from Prince Albert (later King George VI) and Winston Churchill.

The following day the R34 was formally handed back to the Admiralty and a week after that, on Thursday, 31 July, she lifted off from Pulham to start the journey back up the coast to East Fortune. But not before making a detour over and around the centre of London, where she arrived late in the afternoon and where her long, elegant silver shape had people pouring out onto the streets to watch her stately progress. She landed back at East Fortune at 06.05 next morning.

Two days previously, Roosevelt Field at Mineola, where the R34 had made landfall in North America, had been laid waste by hurricane-force winds and electrical storms that had swept across Long Island. Buildings on the field were badly damaged and two big aircraft, a Martin bomber and a Handley-Page bomber, which had been sitting on the ground, were tossed about and completely wrecked. If the R34 had still been floating on her moorings that day she would have been torn to bits.

On Monday, 25 August, the press announced the awards for the R34's crew. They were as grudging as the welcome home. There were no knighthoods, although both Alcock and Brown had been knighted within weeks of landing. There was a CBE (Military Division) for Scott, Air Force Crosses for Maitland, Cooke, Harris and Shotter and Air Force Medals for five Other Ranks – Gent, Mayes, Robinson, Ripley and Scull. Most of the crew had to be satisfied with the silver-mounted propelling pencils they'd received from the New York Fire Brigade. But Aircraftman second-class Billy Ballantyne, the R34's stowaway, did escape a court martial, probably on the intervention of Maitland.

By then Scott, Cooke, Harris, Durrant and Shotter had submitted their reports to the Air Ministry (Pritchard's was to the Admiralty). They make interesting reading. Scott's is the longest, 12 foolscap pages, typewritten and single-spaced. He confined himself to a careful account of the return journey and the short stay in New York and avoided straying too far into the territory of his junior colleagues.

But he also set out what he thought should be done (and supplied) on future long-haul flights. He suggested some kind of device for 'obtaining sea-level barometers during a flight', stressed the value of 'cloud forecasting' and suggested a 'virile school of scientists' who were prepared to explore the upper air. He also pointed out that the D.F. (i.e. direction-finding) wireless 'proved to be of very little use', and made it plain that he considered 'the Sunbeam engine to be quite unsuitable for Airship use'.

He felt that the R34's hull stood up to the battering 'extremely well' but that the outer cover left a lot to be desired and should be made from heavier, sterner stuff. He had had 'very little trouble' with the controls (although one rudder cable frayed) but in future the crew accommodation should be situated at the centre of the keel to avoid the nose coming down when meals were being served. He also wanted the hammocks replaced with bunks and the flying suits redesigned to make them more comfortable.

Scott was in no doubt that the engineers had the hardest lot and that 'many of the engineers had difficulty in sleeping when off watch. On the return journey, however, they were supplied with a tot of rum before turning in. This had a very beneficial effect, and should be a standard issue in future extended flights.' He had harsh words for the hand-pumped petrol supply and asked for 'some mechanical method of moving the petrol' in future airships.

And Scott certainly didn't buy into Maitland's line that all was for the best in the best of all possible worlds:

There is a considerable amount of strain upon the entire crew during a flight of this kind, which is not felt at the time, but shows itself in many little ways, such as the intense feeling sometimes displayed over very trivial matters. There is little doubt that a crew doing a lot of long-distance patrols would in time suffer from some form of nerves, unless given a considerable amount of leave.

Scott's report is the most detailed. It even itemised the food and drink carried on both journeys, pointed out that 28 pounds of biscuits were not used on the outward journey and concluded 'The food as a whole was much better on the return journey. The pickles and the tinned fruit being greatly appreciated. It is considered that these items should be incorporated in any lists standardising the food for rigid crews.' Very little was used from the medicine cabinets: some aspirin, some quinine, a few bandages, some lint, iodine and cotton wool and Epsom Salts.

John Shotter's report was surprisingly brief (two pages), but to the point. The 'machinery' in the R34 had left a great deal to be desired. The gear boxes and clutches in the two wing cars had worked well enough but 'the gear box in the forward car is still leaking oil very badly' and the oil pressure was excessive. In the aft car Shotter had 'considerable trouble' with the dog clutches heating and throwing out, 'due, I think, to the inability to synchronise the two engines'.

In fact, the two engines to one propeller arrangement in the aft car gave Shotter and his men more trouble than the other engines put together. 'It seems necessary to devise some method of synchronising these engines, as the vibration is very bad at all speeds, unless you can luckily strike the correct load for each engine, which is difficult in bumpy weather.'

And while the petrol float tanks 'gave no trouble' the rubber hoses in the petrol service 'appear to dissolve and come away internally, in black adhesive form, choking the filters badly, and very difficult to remove from the gauze'. He thought that the petrol service worked well enough but 'the filling system appears far too small, taking up too much time for transferring petrol. The pumps gave a lot of trouble also. All failed, with the exception of one, which was moved from place to place as required.'

Gilbert Cooke contented himself with a day-by-day, hour-by-hour, account of the R34's progress across the Atlantic and back, and the problems of navigating through rain, fog and cloud. For his part Durrant, the wireless officer, estimated that around 20,000 words had been sent and received over equipment that was less than perfect. His main Type 15 transmitter 'showed no sign of strain' but the same could not be said for the 'spark transmitter' and the direction finding wireless on which 'very little work was possible . . .' Durrant seems to have been surprised at the distances (up to 2,000 miles) over which he could transmit and receive.

Perhaps the most interesting of the reports is the one by Guy Harris, the ship's meteorological officer. He begins by pointing out that the ideal conditions in which the R34 set out from East Fortune 'rarely occur' and the bumps met with over the Clyde (which were generated by the high hills to the north) could only be avoided by flying at altitudes of 6,000 feet or more. It was an area, he suggested, that airships would do well to avoid.

He concluded that over the Atlantic 'at all times of the year a large percentage of cloud must be anticipated' and that the shallow depression the R34 ran into off Newfoundland was 'a very fair specimen of its kind' and the fact that they were able to fly above it at 3,500 feet raised 'the very important question' as to the actual danger depth of these depressions.

As for the wind barrage on the east coast of Nova Scotia that more or less stopped the R34 in mid-air, Harris claimed that this was 'typical of its kind, and will probably be met with always with a wind from a westerly quarter along the greater part of the Nova Scotian coast', but as it did not extend far inland it should be possible to outflank the wind to the west (providing a ship had enough petrol).

Harris then ruminated at length over the strange and deceptive skies which the R34 encountered over the Bay of Fundy and the Gulf of Maine. In his opinion the area presented flyers with 'a complicated series of dangers and difficulties and should be avoided by all types of aircraft until an exhaustive survey of both upper air and surface conditions have been made. The dangers from both electrical storms and temperature variations met with by R34 are sufficient proofs.'

He made an interesting comparison between the air over Britain and the air over the Bay of Fundy. British thunderstorms, he said,

. . . give ample warning of their approach by cloud formation, and do not usually extend over a very large area. A series of storms may exist but there are nearly always quiet periods between [them] large enough to allow a ship to escape their violence.

In the Bay of Fundy, however, the squalls which gave the ship such trouble extended at least 50 miles from the outer fringe of the parent storms, and were of much violence. The actual storm itself covered a large area. During the summer months of the year this type of disturbance is frequently met with on the Eastern Coast of America, and constitutes a grave danger to all types of aircraft if caught out in them . . . Long-distance flights or protracted patrols would have to be handled with care during these danger months.

Harris ended his report with a series of suggestions: that priority should be given to investigating the upper air because of its 'vital importance to all kinds of flying'; that cable ships which stay on station for days on end should be equipped with weather instruments and also act as weather stations; that the Atlantic trade winds should be studied for ways of helping airships across the ocean; that aircraft be earmarked for weather investigations in the upper air; that an efficient 'cloud atlas' should be published for the use of aviators; that 'some form of instrument for obtaining barometric readings at sea level' should be devised; that ways of using depressions to advantage should be studied; and that communications between weather stations and weathermen should be improved.

Maitland's report did not appear until the middle of December. In fact, he had to be chivvied by Groves into producing it. 'The behaviour of the Airship was all that could be expected,' he wrote. 'The wear on the structure of the ship herself is inconsiderable and shows that the design is satisfactory.' He agreed with Shotter and Scott that the Sunbeam engines were not up to the job and that they had placed a severe 'mental and physical strain' on the R34's engineers and that a 'great deal' still had to be learned about the outer cover of airships.

But, like Harris and Scott, he regarded decent weather information as being vital and while the information from the battle cruisers *Tiger* and *Renown* had helped it had not been indispensable, although the ships were a source of 'considerable confidence' in the event of things going wrong. And he agreed with Durrant that an efficient direction-finding wireless was essential as 'it may be seldom possible to fix the ship's position by astronomical observation'. He also agreed that there was an 'urgent necessity' for some device to accurately gauge an aircraft's height.

Maitland ended his report by paying due tribute to Scott and the rest of the R34's crew. 'In conclusion I should like to express my high appreciation of the efficient manner in which Major Scott and his crew handled their ship and to point out that the outward journey constitutes the longest duration flight yet accomplished by any aircraft in this or other countries.'

The muted celebrations continued for a while. Maitland's friend Lady Sybil Grant organised an exhibition entitled *Airships: Past, Present and Future* at Prince's Gallery in Piccadilly. Among the paintings, photographs, models etc. were some items from the R34. There was Maitland's pencilled log book, a few navigation instruments, and the pigeon that made the return journey. There were airship souvenirs for sale, music from a 'masked airship band' (*sic*), and all the proceeds went to an aviation charity.

On Wednesday, 24 September 1919, the City of Glasgow and the Scottish branch of the Royal Aeronautical Society threw a lunch to celebrate the R34's achievement. It was presided over by Sir William Beardmore and included most of the dignitaries of the west of Scotland. Representing the R34 were George Scott, Jack Pritchard and John Shotter. Scott delighted his Glasgow hosts when replying to the toast to the R34. He declared that His Majesty's Government would do well to 'support the production of commercial aircraft as much as possible, because any civil airship could in a few days be converted into a war machine.'

On Monday, 12 October, there was a little ceremony at Buckingham Palace when Lady Sybil Grant presented Lizzie Chestnut, one of Sir William Beardmore's workers, to Queen Mary. For her part, Miss Chestnut presented the queen with a plaque of the R34's Lion Rampant figurehead and motto 'Pro

Patria Volans'. That same month Major George Herbert Scott
was awarded the freedom of Dunbar, one of the towns close to
East Fortune.

But the 1920s got off to an ominous start, with the death in
May 1920 of Air Commodore Robert Marsland Groves, one
of the troika of brigadier-generals at the Air Ministry who had
sanctioned the R34 transatlantic project and then steered it
through the opposition. Groves had abandoned his desk at the
Air Ministry and returned to active service with the RAF as Air
Officer Commanding (AOC) the Egypt Group of the RAF's
Middle East Area. He was killed when the aeroplane in which
he was flying crashed at Heliopolis on the outskirts of Cairo.

Edward Maitland, no longer a brigadier-general but an Air
Commodore in the RAF, took every opportunity to promote
the cause of the rigid airship. On Tuesday, 11 January 1921,
for example, he gave a talk at the Royal Society of Arts to an
audience of children, assuring them that 'big airships had a big
and wonderful future'. He told them that within a few years
they'd be able to fly to Australia via Montreal and Vancouver
and do the journey in about 12 days. There would be dining
rooms, comfortable sleeping accommodation and promenade
decks built on *top* of the airships so that passengers could stroll
around in the open air at 3,000 feet.

From the newspaper accounts his lecture went down well.
He entertained the excited children with tales of ballooning
and parachuting and, of course, stories and slides of the R34's
great voyage across the Atlantic and back. And he quoted
Kipling's letter to him in which the great writer had said 'we
are at the opening verse of the opening page of the chapter of
endless possibilities'.

A few months later Maitland was back at the Royal Society
of Arts, but this time trying to enthuse the grown-ups. His
lecture is an intriguing mixture of hard fact, optimistic eco-
nomics, at least one downright fib (about how easy he found it
to sleep in the R34 on the first night) and a paean of praise to
the speed, ease and comfort of airship travel. 'The unit in life is

time, not distance,' he declared 'and the distance between two countries is, in practice, measured by time.'

He went on to paint a word-picture of the next generation of lighter-than-air liners:

The whole of the passenger car will be heated by steam generated from the engine. Air will be admitted at the forward end of the car, where it will be warmed over radiators ... Smoking will be no more dangerous than in a railway carriage, as the car will be completely isolated from engines, tanks etc. A kitchen with at least as good accommodation as any railway restaurant car will be provided, and our experience up to date is that one's appetite in the air is pretty good.

There is a remarkable absence of vibration and noise in the large airship, and the absence of smoke or dirt is also a distinct asset. Compared with transport by sea the almost complete absence of sea-sickness is an important consideration. Being a shockingly bad sailor myself, I can sympathise with others, and I can assure you that the motion in the large airship is slow, so that there is no excuse for sickness.

Maitland even argued that building and running a large fleet of passenger- and cargo-carrying airships would be a useful contribution to shoring up Britain's defences. He told his audience that 'A large air personnel, not required in peace, but of vital necessity in the event of a war, can be kept economically in training by the existence of a commercial air service.'

It is hard not to compare Edward Maitland with 'Uncle Prudent', the fictional anti-hero of Jules Verne's 1886 fantasy novella *Robur the Conqueror*. Uncle Prudent is the leading light in the Weldon Institute of Philadelphia, which is utterly dedicated to the idea of lighter-than-air flight and indeed constructs a huge dirigible, an aerostat with engines fore and aft, which the group names *Goahead* and for which they have high hopes of linking the continents.

But into this lighter-than-air idyll erupts the strange figure of 'Robur' (the Latin word for strong), who has already come up with a heavier-than-air machine which is part-aeroplane, part-helicopter and which he describes as an 'aeronef' and names *Albatross*. At one stage Robur declares to the learned gentlemen of the Weldon Institute that 'As for the future of aerial locomotion, it belongs to the aeronef and not the aerostat. It is to the *Albatross* that the conquest of the air will assuredly fall.'

Despite the obvious superiority of Robur's heavier-than-air machine Uncle Prudent refuses to acknowledge it. Uncle Prudent (like Edward Maitland) is a lighter-than-air man in his bones. The argument is finally settled by a mid-air confrontation over Philadelphia in which Robur's nimble *Albatross* outpaces, outflies and outmanoeuvers Uncle Prudent's aerostat until the *Goahead* breaks apart in the sky. It's an odd, and oddly prophetic tale. And one which, in his literary ruminations, Edward Maitland never mentions.

16

Endgame

Maitland's literary friend Sybil Grant may have been no great shakes as a poet, but some of her verses seem oddly apposite to the airships over which she waxed (literally) lyrical, and the men who flew them. In her collection *Dream Songs* (published in 1915) there is a short four-liner entitled 'I Trust Because I Must'. It runs:

> I trust because I must,
> Then let me not repent
> The great experiment.
> Can fate be so unjust?

The answer to her question was yes, of course. Fate can be cruelly unjust. The 1920s were to expose the limitations of the great airship 'experiment'. In the end the complexities and unpredictability of the atmosphere were to prove just too much for the big lighter-than-air dirigibles. Time after time they were tested and time after time they were found wanting. And at least six of the men who flew the R34 across the Atlantic and back in July 1919 were to have their lives cut short by the shortcomings of the technology they had done so much to help advance.

On a fine evening on Wednesday, 24 August 1921, thousands of people in Hull flocked to the banks of the Humber to watch the stately progress of Britain's newest airship, the R38. Bigger and more advanced than the R34, the R38 had been built by the Royal Airship Works at Cardington in Bedfordshire and was due to be sold to the US Navy. Manned by a crew of British and American airmen and a dozen or so engineers and observers, the R38 had completed two days of trials and was heading for the airship base at Howden, where she was to overnight before returning to Pulham in Norfolk.

The airship had flown over Hull and was cruising at around 1,000 feet over the Humber when she suddenly buckled, went into a slow nosedive and then broke into three pieces, spilling men, parts and debris into the river. The horrified crowd watched as the ship was racked by two explosions that shattered windows all over the city. Then the R38's hydrogen and petrol bloomed into flame and the burning remains settled on the Humber, where the spilled fuel generated a barrage of flames. The last wireless message received from the R38 was terse: 'Ship broken; falling.' Of the 51 men aboard the R38 only five survived, four Britons and one American.

Among the airmen killed that summer evening were three who had battled their way across the Atlantic in the R34: Air Commodore Edward Maitland, then commanding officer of the Howden airship base; Flight-Lieutenant Jack Pritchard; and engineer Aircraftman Second Class Roy Parker. Among the civilian fatalities was Charles Ivor Rae Campbell, Superintendent of the Royal Airship Works, and the man who had led the team that created the R34 out of the wreckage of Zeppelin L33. In a few short minutes the British airship industry had lost two of its most zealous supporters, Edward Maitland and Charles Campbell.

One of the American fatalities was Lieutenant Charles Gray Little, US Navy, who had been an officer on the American non-rigid airship C5 which was wrecked by the wind in Newfoundland in 1919. While training in England to man the R38 Lieutenant Little had married his compatriot Joy Bright, one of the first women to be commissioned in the US Navy. The best man at their wedding in Yorkshire had been the R38's English skipper, Flight-Lieutenant A.H. Wann, one of the five men who survived the R38 crash.

'The controls of the ship were being tested at high speed,' the only American survivor told a correspondent for *The Times*.

'After a few sharp explosions there were two very loud ones and the ship began to fall.' One of the surviving Britons, Leading Aircraftman E.W. Davies said, 'It was all over in a moment. The petrol tanks exploded . . . Some of the poor fellows had no chance whatsoever, particularly those in the control car.'

A hastily convened RAF court of inquiry (held at Howden on the Saturday following the tragedy) came to no firm conclusion as to what had caused the airship to break up in the air. Among the suggestions advanced was that while the R38's structure may have been able to handle a high-speed turn at 5,000 feet where the air is (relatively) thin, at near ground level the stresses on the girders were too much. The British and US governments agreed to share the cost of the destroyed airship.

Whatever caused the R38 to fall apart in mid-air it was enough to prompt the Air Ministry to call a halt to all new airship construction and even research. Which in turn prompted the Royal Aeronautical Society to appeal to the British public for funds to continue researching airships 'pending the time when the resumption of an airship service is decided upon'. Which, in the event, happened in 1924, when the Imperial Airship Scheme rescued the Vickers-built R33 and the Beardmore's-built R36 from mothballs and put them both back in the air.

Edward Maitland and Charles Campbell were among the nine men buried under the R38 memorial at the Spring Bank Cemetery in Hull. They were buried on Friday, 2 September 1921 with full military honours, followed five days later by a memorial service at Westminster Abbey in London. Among the establishment figures in attendance were Air Marshal Sir Hugh Trenchard, the US Ambassador, the Lords Mayor of London and Hull and a little flock of men and women representing the Royal Family and His Majesty's Government.

In August 1922, on the first anniversary of the R38 disaster, *The Times* carried five dedications to Maitland. One read 'Oh, true brave heart, God bless thee wheresoever in His great universe thou art today'. Another one declared 'In ever fond memory of the bravest airman there ever was, my dearest friend . . . Who died trying to save the airship . . . Eddie, I shall always remember your sweet words to me. Bless you. Lily.'

A less poignant but more moving obituary of Maitland appeared in the September issue of *The Aeronautical Journal*. The obituarist made the point that although Maitland was a seasoned parachutist he had made no attempt to save his own skin. The writer found it 'particularly significant that when found after the accident to R38 he [Maitland] was shown to have devoted his last moments to an endeavour to check the fall of the airship rather than saving his life by means of a parachute'.

The bodies of the Americans who lost their lives on the R38 were taken by train from Hull to Devonport Dockyard by an RAF guard of honour then handed over to the Royal Navy. They were returned to the USA aboard the light cruiser HMS *Dauntless*. In a letter to the Lord Mayor of Hull the US Navy expressed its appreciation for the 'sympathy and hospitality we have received from the people in and about Hull'.

Although the R38 disaster was a blow to the US Navy, it was not enough of a blow to stop their airship programme. The construction went on and in June 1923 the Americans walked out the first big rigid airship designed and built in the USA. She was the *Shenandoah* (the Algonquin Indian word for 'daughter of the stars') and she was the first dirigible whose gas bags were filled with inert helium instead of highly-combustible hydrogen.

Built at the Naval Aircraft Factory in Philadelphia and assembled at the US Naval Airship Station at Lakehurst in New Jersey the *Shenandoah* was an impressive piece of work. She was a new generation of airship, the pride of the US Navy. More than 680 feet long with more than 2 million cubic feet of helium in her bags, she was powered by six 300-horsepower

Packard engines. The *Shenandoah* made her first flight in September, 1923.

But from the outset the *Shenandoah* was an unlucky ship. On Monday, 16 January 1924, she was torn from her mooring mast at Lakehurst by a high wind and only saved from disaster by skilful work by the ship's crew and the men on the ground. The damage, however, was extensive. Large sections were torn from the ship's bow, and the upper fin at the stern was left in a bad way. Both the bow section and the tail fin had to be replaced, a process that took more than four months.

When the repairs were complete the *Shenandoah* was flown to San Diego on the Pacific coast and then returned to Lakehurst, where she was taken out of commission for a few months. In June 1925 she was put back to work under the command of Lieutenant-Commander Zachary Lansdowne US Navy, the officer who had acted as US observer on the R34's journey to New York.

By then Lansdowne was the US Navy's most experienced airship officer, and one who took a very dim view of his superiors' enthusiasm for using expensive and vulnerable airships for publicity jaunts across the USA. This was not a good idea, he told them. Airships were best used for reconnaissance work over the ocean and not for public-relations work all over the continental USA, where the weather could be even more unpredictable and dangerous than it was at sea.

But Lansdowne's arguments were ignored and on the evening of Wednesday, 2 September 1925, the *Shenandoah* lifted off from Lakehurst heading for an air show at St Louis, Missouri. Things began to go wrong at 03.30 in the morning, when the airship was over south Ohio and began to buffet alarmingly. Thirty minutes later the *Shenandoah* had broken up in mid-air, killing 14 men in the process, including Zachary Lansdowne. The ship had been taken apart by a 'line squall', common enough in western Ohio and exactly the kind of weather that Lansdowne had warned about.

One of the survivors was Commander C.E. Rosendahl, who reported that:

> A mild storm, suddenly followed by a violent line squall, subjected the ship to enormous and uncontrollable angle strains and to a rapid vertical ascent, which resulted in the ship breaking at about 7,000 feet at the vicinity of frames 130 and 90. The control car was quickly wrenched free in the air, precipitating the occupants. The forward wing cars were wrenched free from the ship's structure in the air.

Other survivors were inclined to blame a sudden expansion of the helium in the ship's gas bags. Chief Rigger James Collier thought the inflation of the helium had stretched the airship's light-metal wires, struts and girders to breaking point and had cracked open the structure with calamitous results. That expansion may have been caused by a shortage of safety valves on the gas bags of the *Shenandoah*, which had been reduced from 18 to 10 in an attempt to save money (helium being 50 times more expensive to produce than hydrogen).

Some of the men were lucky. After the *Shenandoah* had lost her control car and two of her engine cars she broke into two sections in mid-air. There were eight men trapped in the bow section and twenty-one in the remainder. For almost an hour the two separate sections were tossed around in the air by the wind, with the men inside clinging desperately to the girders. The sections gradually lost height as helium drained out of the bags. Astonishingly, only one crewman (in the bow section) lost his life. The other 28 survived, and with only minor injuries.

The ruin of the *Shenandoah* was to mean a second widowhood in four years for Joy Bright. After the death of her first husband, Charles Little, in the R38 over the Humber in 1921 she had married Lieutenant John Hancock, also of the US Navy. Hancock was one of the officers who died in the airship's control car when it separated from the structure of the *Shenandoah* and was sent crashing down to earth.

British airship engineering came to an end just after 02.00 on Sunday, 5 October 1930, when the biggest of all British airships, the government-funded R101, lost altitude on her way to Karachi and sank to the ground in a field near Beauvais north of Paris. Initially there was little damage and none of the 54 passengers and crew seems to have been seriously hurt by the emergency landing. But after the airship had ground to a halt, somewhere in the ship's innards a spark ignited some petrol, the petrol ignited the hydrogen and within minutes the great structure was a mass of flames.

Forty-eight men died, including the Secretary of State for Air Lord Thomson and his valet. But also on board the R101 was Major George Herbert Scott, the man who had skippered the R34 on her return flight across the Atlantic, and Flight-Sergeant William R. Gent, one of the R34's engineers. As one of Britain's most experienced airshipmen, Scott had been appointed to act as the Air Ministry's observer on the flight. Gent, who knew more about airship engines than anyone, was the R101's Chief Engineer. Neither man survived the fire, nor were their bodies ever identified.

The R101 had been heading for Egypt, the first leg of its journey to Karachi, in what is now Pakistan, where Lord Thomson was due to attend an imperial conference. In the R101 the British government had thought they had the vessel that would help link the component parts of the Empire. She was more than 770 feet long, 131 feet in diameter, had a designed speed of 71 mph and was lifted by 5.5 million cubic feet of hydrogen. She was powered by five 'Tornado' diesel engines built by Beardmore's. In her day, the R101 was by far the biggest aircraft in the world.

But her trial flights had been problematic when it was discovered that she didn't have the lift for the weight with which she was burdened. She was taken back into the shed at Cardington, cut in half and another gas bag installed which, of course, meant that the hull had to be lengthened. It was a process which some engineers had warned might weaken the frame. In fact, the R101 didn't even get her airworthiness certificate until the day before she set off for Karachi with 30 passengers (mostly military) and a crew of 24.

Just why the R101 was forced down remains a mystery. A few of the survivors reported the airship twisting and what sounded like the outer cover or some of the gas bags tearing. Whatever it was that ripped the cover and/or the gas bags must have been serious to force more than 5 million cubic feet of hydrogen down onto the ground. Where the spark came from no one knows, but the best guess is that one of the engines was wrenched loose when the ship hit the ground and sparked into hot oil, which lit up the leaking hydrogen.

The wreck of the R101 was treated as a national disaster, maybe because it was an official flight, maybe because it was carrying a senior government minister. The bodies of the 48 dead were shipped back to Britain on HMS *Tempest* and taken by special train to London where they lay in state in Westminster Hall. On Saturday, 11 October, after a grand memorial service at St Paul's Cathedral (attended by the Prince of Wales and the Prime Minister) all 48 coffins were driven to the little village churchyard at Cardington in Bedfordshire and buried in one grave. A year later a big neo-classical memorial was erected over the grave.

There's a bizarre postscript to the R101 tragedy. If spiritualists are to be believed, George Herbert Scott made a posthumous appearance a few weeks before the official inquiry into the wreck. Through an Irish spiritualist called Eileen Garrett the shade of George Scott reputedly told Major Oliver Villiers of the Ministry of Aviation that a crack in one of the girders had torn a 'bad rent' in the ship's outer cover which forced the R101 into a series of dives. And that 'This external pressure, coupled with the fact that the valve was weak, blew the valve right off, and at the same time the released gas was ignited by a backfire from the engine'. This ghostly explanation was more or less the conclusion arrived at much later by the long and very detailed official inquiry.

The end of the R101 was the end of British airships. Her sister ship, the R100, which had already flown the Atlantic without any trouble (to Montreal and back in the summer of 1930) was ordered to be broken up and sold for scrap. Built by Vickers and designed by Barnes Wallis (better known as the creator of the World War II 'bouncing bomb') and Nevil Shute Norway (better known as a popular novelist) the R100's oval cross-section and ridged hull gave it a streamlining that was better than anything yet built. But the scars of the R101 disaster ran so deep that the R100 had to be sacrificed.

The charred but almost intact structure of the R101 lay in France for months before being handed over to a firm of Sheffield steel experts for disposal. There's a sad, but perhaps fitting irony in the fact that the Sheffield firm sold more than 5,000 kilos of Duraluminium from the R101 to Luftschiffbau Zeppelin of Friedrichshafen. It's conceivable that metal from the R101 went into the building of the *Hindenburg*, the biggest airship of all time, which came to grief at Lakehurst, New Jersey in May 1937, killing 36 of its passengers and crew.

The ruin of the *Hindenberg* was both caught on film and witnessed by the radio reporter Herb Morrison. Morrison's description in his famous broadcast is almost incomprehensible in its raw emotion:

> It's burning, bursting into flames a-and it's falling on the mooring mast and all the folks agree this is terrible, this is one of the worst catastrophes in the world. Ohhhh! The flames are climbing, oh, four or five hundred feet into the sky and it's a terrific crash, ladies and gentlemen, the smoke and the flames now. And it's crashing to the ground . . .

The fiery and well-publicised ruin of the *Hindenburg* brought an end to the age of the big airship. After the disaster the company's other (and hugely successful) ship, the *Graf Zeppelin* was taken out of service. This was despite the airship's having flown more than a million miles without incident, including 64 transatlantic flights between Europe and South America and a spectacular round-the-world flight at the end of 1928. The *Graf Zeppelin* was flown to Frankfurt, where she was deflated and used as an exhibition piece until March 1940, when Hermann Göring, then in charge of German aviation, ordered her destruction.

As for the R34 herself, the first of the 'British Zeppelins', at noon on Thursday, 27 January 1921 she lifted off from the airship base at Howden in Yorkshire with a team of RAF trainees. Things started to go wrong when the radio telephone operator lowered his aerials to find that the wireless telephone (WT) set was unserviceable. The problem was compounded when the R34 got lost in fog over the North Sea. By the time radio contact with Howden was established at 19.34 the weather was deteriorating. Then just after midnight on Friday, 28 January, as she was flying low over the north of England, the R34 narrowly missed outright disaster when she scraped over some high ground at Guisborough Moor near Middles-brough.

The accident is described in a letter from one of the helms-men (probably Murray Watson), who flew with the R34 to New York. It is addressed to his friend 'Dear Old Sid'. He wrote:

The whole ship quivered like a whiplash and in the darkness that followed, all was more or less confusion. The keel lights were intact but the fore car was properly upset and girders were buckled in all sorts of shapes. The Douglas castings broke and the forward propeller was smashed completely, also the struts. In the engine room was a regular bed of heather, furze etc. Strange to say the controls were unhurt and we carried on steering with the aid of a hand lamp. So much for the forward car.

. . . The wing cars escaped. The after car propeller was also smashed. Then we were left with two engines to battle against an increasing wind of 18 mph at 1,000 feet. As you can guess, Sid, we were unable to estimate what the damage was until daybreak, and what I have described before is what we found. Our aerial was carried away and we managed on a flying strand of copper wire found in the keel somewhere. Not so bad, Sid?

The R34 then tracked back out to sea to make sure it was clear of any high ground, then turned landward again to find the Humber estuary.

After nine hours we reached the coast, which by the way we could see right from daybreak. We proceeded up the Humber as far as Goole and then turned inland. The wind was all the time increasing. We were travelling crab fashion [sideways?] all the time. Do you know Sid, it was hell steering. I never steered a ship like it in all my life, and I've steered a few times. Fifteen degrees either side even for two hours takes some doing.

The last 20 miles of the R34's flight took three hours running on two engines at full throttle. If one of the engines had failed the ship would have been blown back out to sea and wrecked. The helmsman goes on,

Well, Sid, we reached Howden at about 5 p.m. Friday evening [28 January]. We came down from 600 feet to 300 feet and found the altimeter only 200 feet out. Then the fun began. Drew made a posh landing.

He overshot the landing party and drifted back and down at the same time. As they got hold of us we smashed into the earth, smashing the forward car completely; most marvellous thing of all, all wire suspensions held. Everyone stuck to the ship to the last. The control car was smashed up into the keel and so was the after car. After some ten of these bumps 'abandon ship' was given and the escapes were truly marvellous. I got off with burned fingers.

The ship was moored in an hour and the bows were torn completely off and she sank down in the glare of the searchlights like a dying leviathan of long ago. Do you know, Sid, it nearly made me cry to hear her wrench herself asunder. Two years, Sid, and then to tear herself to pieces before our very eyes. All the crew were heartbroken. To see her go. And now, nothing.

Once it was plain that the R34 was beyond repair, the painful process began of taking her apart. The hydrogen was vented out into the atmosphere and the fabric of the outer cover and the gas bags was removed and most of it burned. Everything that was valuable and/or reusable – instruments, steering mechanisms, engines etc. – was stripped out and carted off. What was left of the elaborate Duraluminium skeleton was smashed to pieces, mainly with heavy hammers and sharp axes, to be sold for scrap. To the men who had flown in her to America and back it was a painful sight.

The wreck of the R34 was reported in *Flight* magazine on Friday, 3 February 1921 almost as an obituary. 'It is with the greatest regret we have to report the total wreckage of the "R34", the rigid airship which made that historic voyage to America and back on the summer of 1919.' The magazine went on to criticise the government as 'penny wise and pound foolish', claiming that 'there is little doubt that had the Station (i.e. Howden) been properly equipped with a mooring mast and various other handling gear, the cost of the installation would have been nothing as compared with the loss of a quarter of a million or so craft'.

But the days of the military airship were over. In September 1921 the Air Ministry announced that the aerodrome at Renfrew was to close and in October 1922 the airship base at Inchinnan – land, workshops, barracks and airship sheds – was taken over by the Disposal and Liquidation Commission. The commission sold the works to the firm of Murray McVinnie & Co., who had already dismantled the airship sheds at

East Fortune (parts of which had gone to build a new bus garage in the town of Dunbar). The plant and remaining equipment at Inchinnan were auctioned in May 1923 and the great airship shed, in which the R34 had been created, was taken apart and sold off by the year's end. What was left was bought by the India Tyre & Rubber Company.

William Beardmore & Co., the firm that had built the R34, did not thrive in the post-war period. The fact that the ill-fated R101 had been equipped with Beardmore aero-engines did not help. Beardmore himself (Lord Invernairn) may have been an enterpreneur of great energy and imagination, but he was no economist. The post-war recession hit Beardmore's hard and when problems emerged William Beardmore's response was to throw money at them. Not all of the money was his own.

In 1928 the financial tangle in which his sprawling empire was enmeshed brought down the wrath of Montagu Norman, the Governor of the Bank of England, who more or less forced the company to dismantle itself. Norman did point out, however, in a letter to the Securities Management Trust in 1930, that 'The present structural and other defects of Beardmore's are in a large measure due to Lord Invernairn's endeavour to meet the wishes of the Government during the war'.

Beardmore himself was drummed out of office and retired to sulk in his strange, turreted mansion at Flichity near Croachy in the hills east of Loch Ness where he died, aged 80, in April 1936. After his death it took his lawyers three years to sort out his calamitous financial affairs. He is buried in the grounds of Flichity, under a granite boulder inscribed 'William Beardmore, Baron Invernairn of Strathnairn, 1856–1936, a brain of steel and a heart of gold. This stone commemorates his great National Service 1914–1918'.

It was a bad year for veterans of the R34 project. A few months after Beardmore's death, Archie Campbell, the works manager who had overseen the construction of the R34 and whose daughter Jessie had married George Herbert Scott, drowned in a boating accident in the Gare Loch in Argyll.

He had been fishing on the loch near his home at Mambeg with his son and grandson when their boat overturned, pitching all three into the water. The 70-year-old Campbell died saving his son, who could not swim. The son and the grandson survived.

One long-lived member of the 31-strong crew who flew the Atlantic and back in July 1919 was the stowaway Billy Ballantyne. In July 1979, wheel-chair bound and an old man of 82, he turned up at East Fortune to mark the sixtieth anniversary of the flight. But he was on good form and impressed the folk who met him with his 'cheeky chappie' demeanour. He told anyone who was interested that he had 'absolutely no regrets' about having risked a court martial by stowing away in the R34's rigging. He was, he said, determined to be part of the history of flying.

The last known survivor of the Atlantic crossing was Corporal E.P. Cross, one of the engineers assigned to the R34's forward car. After he left His Majesty's service he emigrated to the USA and settled, ironically, in Long Island, not far from Mineola where the R34 made its triumphant descent. Cross died in the 1990s, having donated some papers and photographs of the flight to the Cradle of Aviation Museum at Garden City, Long Island.

It is now almost 100 years since the R34 made its stately progress across the Atlantic and back again. Since then, of course, aviation has progressed to an extent which was beyond the imagination of the prophets of that time. Even Herbert George Wells never dreamed of the day when 500 people could climb into an aeroplane and be whisked across to New York at 30,000 feet in six hours, in comfort, while watching full-colour films and being fed and watered. And for a return ticket that costs less than a week's wage. And the idea of making the journey at twice that height and at twice the speed of sound, as the late Concorde used to do, and in the process arriving in New York shortly before you left London, would have confounded Jules Verne.

All of which seems to suggest that the lighter-than-air vessel, the airship, is a thing of the past, aviation's equivalent of *Tyrannosaurus Rex*. Well, maybe. But there may be life in the old idea yet. The Zeppelin Company at Friedrichshafen is still turning out modestly sized semi-rigids in which tourists are flown around the Bodensee. Airship Industries produced a series of models (the 500, 600 and 1000) which have done away with landing problems with 'vectored thrust' power plants, that is, engines that can swivel into vertical position for take-off and landing and back to horizontal for level flight. And the Goodyear company's 'blimp' seems to turn up at every major sporting event to function as a camera platform.

More importantly, perhaps, given that so much innovation begins with the military, the US Air Force has been looking at plans for a giant transport airship (an HLAV or 'Heavy Lift Air Vehicle') inflated with helium and capable of carrying 500 tons of men and equipment 'intercontinental distances'. If the price of aviation fuel soars and governments around the world start slapping taxes on it (as the international Green lobby is demanding), then lighter-than-air craft like the R34 may look like the future and not the past.

But whatever happens in the future, the R34's return transatlantic flight in July 1919 was a genuinely historic event. It was a fine piece of flying by a skilled crew in charge of a fine piece of Scottish engineering. In his book *Great Flights* the historian Edwin Colston Shepherd paid this tribute to the men of the R34:

> The crew had taken all the chances that go with a first attempt and had made them look small and ordinary by their diligence and attention to detail. The accidents of later years showed how great their achievement was . . . Nothing can rob the feat of its own inherent greatness and none can dispute the courage of men who did so fine a job so greatly and well.

Crew of the R34

Officers

Major G.H. Scott	Captain
Captain G.S. Greenland	Second Officer
Second Lieutenant H.F. Luck	Third Officer
Second Lieutenant J.D. Shotter	Engineering Officer
Major G.G.H. Cooke	Navigator
Lieutenant G. Harris	Meteorological Officer
Second Lieutenant R.F. Durrant	Wireless Operator
Lieutenant-Commander Z. Lansdowne	US Navy Observer (outward)
Lieutenant-Colonel W.N. Hensley	US Army Observer (return)
Brigadier-General E.M. Maitland	Special Duties
Major J.E.M. Pritchard	Special Duties

Other Ranks

Sergeant Major W.R. Mayes	First Coxswain
Flight-Sergeant W.J. Robinson	Second Coxswain
Sergeant H.M. Watson	Rigger
Corporal R.J. Burgess	Rigger
Corporal F. Smith	Rigger
Leading Aircraftman J.N. Forteath	Rigger
Leading Aircraftman E.P. Browdie	Rigger
Corporal H.R. Powell	Wireless Operator
Aircraftman First Class W.J. Edwards	Wireless Operator
Flight Sergeant W.R. Gent	Engineer
Flight Sergeant N.A. Scull	Engineer
Flight Sergeant R.W. Ripley	Engineer
Sergeant A.G. Evenden	Engineer
Sergeant J. Thirlwall	Engineer
Corporal E.P. Cross	Engineer

Corporal J.H. Gray	Engineer
Leading Aircraftman G. Graham	Engineer
Leading Aircraftman J.S. Mort	Engineer
Aircraftman Second Class R. Parker	Engineer
Aircraftman Second Class J. Northeast	Engineer
Flight-Sergeant E.E. Turner	Engineer (return)
Flight-Sergeant W.I. Angus	Engineer (return)

Aircraftman Second Class W.W. Ballantyne

Stowaway (outward)

Remains of the R34

Following the destruction of the R34 in January 1921, what was left of the airship and its contents disappeared into corners all over Britain. Just how much remains, no one seems quite sure, although it is not very much. But some items are in public view or can be seen after making the necessary arrangements.

Museum of Flight, East Fortune, East Lothian
The museum is part of the National Museums of Scotland and lies about 20 miles east of Edinburgh. From the R34 it contains: the Lion Rampant bowplate; a fragment of gas bag with goldbeaters' skin; Major Jack Pritchard's plate camera and binoculars; one of the airship's pennants; the face plate of the ship's altimeter; one of the gas valves; a water ballast valve; a small piece of one of the ship's Duraluminium girders ; a pocket watch that was awarded to John Shotter; the R34's bottle of 'medicinal' brandy, which was given to the medical officer at East Fortune after the flight.

The museum also holds a decent collection of R34 photographs (many of them by Pritchard) and a few of Beardmore's elegant working drawings of the R34. Outside the Nissen hut which now houses (among other things) the artefacts from the R34 there is a plaque, erected in 1957, commemorating the flight. An identical one was erected at Mineola in Long Island at the same time.

National Library of Scotland, Edinburgh
In its large collection of manuscripts the NLS holds the hand-written original of Brigadier-General Edward Maitland's log, including a few cablegrams from New York. Maitland had given the book and its content to his friend Sybil Grant as a

token of his regard for her support. She later donated it to the NLS. She was the daughter of the Earl of Rosebery, one-time Liberal prime minister.

Fleet Air Arm Museum, Yeovilton, Somerset
Most of the R34's crew originally served with the Royal Naval Air Service, the forerunner of the Fleet Air Arm, so it inherited a few items. Among them a walking-stick made from the R34's timbers; a helm indicator plate; the watch bill for the crossing; three 'souvenir' maps of the flight (two of them signed by George Herbert Scott); the original of Scott's report; a water-colour painting by Russell Flint of the R34 under construction; some press cuttings about the stowaway, Billy Ballantyne.

Royal Aeronautical Society, London
The society's material on the R34 takes the form of papers, reports and newspaper cuttings, photographs and glass slides. It also holds a collection of Edward Maitland's own papers and the diary of Lieutenant Harold Luck, the R34's third officer.

Royal Aeronautical Society, Farnborough
The society's 'satellite' library at Farnborough contains six large bound volumes of press cuttings (UK and USA) under the inaccurate title 'Voyage of R34 from England to America and back'.

Royal Air Force Museum, Hendon
When the Royal Air Force was formed in 1918 most of the airmen serving with the Royal Flying Corps and the Royal Naval Air Service became officers and men of the RAF. That included the crew of the R34, some of whose documents found their way to the RAF Museum at Hendon. Most interesting, perhaps, are the papers of the R34's hard-pressed engineering officer, Lieutenant (later General) John Shotter. The museum also has the report of the ten-man R34 advance party that was sent out to the USA to instruct the Americans on how to land a large rigid airship.

British Rigid Airships

HMA1
Built by Vickers Ltd at Barrow-in-Furness, Cumberland. Also known as *The Mayfly*. Length 512 feet; gas capacity 663,000 cubic feet; powered by two 180-horsepower engines. Launched 24 September 1911. Never flew. Wrecked at hangar in 1911.

HMA9
Built by Vickers Ltd at Barrow-in-Furness, Cumberland. Length 526 feet; gas capacity 846,000 cubic feet; powered by four 180-horsepower engines. The HMA9 was the first British rigid airship to fly. Commissioned in November 1916, she spent most of her life in handling and mooring trials. Between October 1917 and June 1918 she was based at Pulham in Norfolk, where she was dismantled and scrapped.

HMA23
Built by Vickers Ltd at Barrow-in-Furness, Cumberland. First of the four '23-class' airships. Length 535 feet; gas capacity 942,000 cubic feet; powered by four 250-horsepower engines. Launched 26 August 1917.

HMA24
Built by William Beardmore & Co. at Inchinnan near Glasgow. Length 535 feet; gas capacity 942,000 cubic feet; powered by four 250-horsepower engines.

HMA25
Built by Sir W.G. Armstrong Whitworth & Co. at Selby, Yorkshire. Length 535 feet; gas capacity 942,000 cubic feet; powered by four 250-horsepower engines.

HMA26

Built by Vickers Ltd at Barrow-in-Furness, Cumberland. Length 535 feet; gas capacity 942,000 cubic feet; powered by four 250-horsepower engines.

R27

Built by William Beardmore & Co., at Inchinnan, near Glasgow. Commissioned 29 June 1918. Length 539 feet; gas capacity 942,000 cubic feet; powered by four Rolls-Royce 300-horse-power 'Eagle' engines. The R27 had a short and disastrous life. After a few hours' flying she was destroyed by fire in a hangar at Howden on 16 August 1918. In the fire one airman lost his life.

R29

Built by Sir W.G. Armstrong Whitworth & Co. at Selby, Yorkshire. Commissioned 20 June 1918. Length 539 feet; gas capacity 942,000 cubic feet; powered by four Rolls-Royce 300-horsepower 'Eagle' engines. Based at East Fortune near Edinburgh, the R29 was the only British dirigible that could claim to have attacked and sunk a German submarine (U-115) in the North Sea. The ship was superseded by the new '33-class' airships and scrapped in October 1919.

R31

Built by Short Brothers at Cardington, Bedfordshire. First of two '31-class' airships. Length 615 feet; gas capacity 1.5 million cubic feet; powered by six Rolls-Royce 300-horse-power 'Eagle' engines. Designed by the Swiss-German defector Müller, the R31 was based on the German Schütte-Lanz construction. Her main girders were made from laminated plywood held together with 'kaltlein' (cold glue). The R31 was commissioned on 6 November 1918, just before the armistice was signed. On her way to East Fortune airship base she put into a hangar at Howden in Yorkshire for repairs and never came out again. She was slowly destroyed by a leaking hangar roof and finally dismantled in October 1919.

R32

Built by Short Brothers at Cardington, Bedfordshire. Length 615 feet; gas capacity 1.5 million cubic feet; powered by five Rolls-Royce 300-horsepower 'Eagle' engines. Commissioned 3 September 1919 to the Royal Navy as fast scout ship, then transferred to the Royal Air Force in October 1919. Later used as a test ship by the National Physics Laboratory and for training US crews for the R38. On 27 April 1921 the R32 was tested to destruction at Howden.

R33

Built by Sir W.G. Armstrong Whitworth & Co. at Selby, Yorkshire. Length 643 feet; gas capacity 1.95 million cubic feet; powered by five 250-horsepower engines. Launched 6 March 1919. A very successful airship, the R33 was the first to carry out the in-flight launch of an aeroplane.

R34

Built by William Beardmore & Co. at Inchinnan, near Glasgow. Length 643 feet; gas capacity 1.95 million cubic feet; powered by five 250-horsepower Sunbeam 'Maori' engines. Launched in December 1918. In July 1919 it became the first aircraft to fly the Atlantic from east to west and the first aircraft to make the return flight. Damaged on a training flight over the north of England and dismantled and scrapped at Howden airship base, Yorkshire, in January 1921.

R35

Partly built by Sir W.G. Armstrong Whitworth & Co., at Selby, Yorkshire, but scrapped after the order was cancelled.

R36

Built by William Beardmore & Co. at Inchinnan, near Glasgow. Length 675 feet; gas capacity 2.1 million cubic feet; powered by five Sunbeam 'Maori' engines; accommodation for 50 passengers in 131-foot long passenger car. Launched

2 April 1921. One of the most successful British airships. The first British airship to have a civilian registration: G-FAAF. But in 1925 the R36 ran into a mooring mast at Pulham in Norfolk, suffered damage and never flew again. She was dismantled and scrapped in June 1926.

R37
Built by the Royal Airship Works at Cardington, Bedfordshire. Length 672 feet; gas capacity 2.1 million cubic feet; powered by five Sunbeam 'Cossack' 323-horsepower engines. The R37 was being built in the same shed as the R38 and was 90 per cent complete when all work on her was halted early in 1921. Later that year she was dismantled and scrapped.

R38
Built by the Royal Airship Works at Cardington, Bedfordshire. Length 695 feet; gas capacity 2.7 million cubic feet; powered by six Sunbeam 'Cossack' 323-horsepower engines. A heavily-armed ship with 14 Lewis guns, four 520-pound bombs and eight 230-pound bombs. Contract originally cancelled by the British government but was then taken up, for $2.5 million, by the United States Navy as Airship ZR11. Launched 23 June 1921. Broke up in mid-flight and crashed in the River Humber on fourth trial on 24 August 1921, killing 44 British and American servicemen. There were five survivors.

R39, R40, R41
Airships that were in the same class as the ill-fated R38 but never built. Orders were cancelled after the armistice of November 1918 and the signing of the peace treaty in June 1919.

R80
Built by Sir W.G. Armstrong Whitworth & Co. at Selby, Yorkshire. Length 535 feet; gas capacity 1.2 million cubic feet; powered by four 230-horsepower engines. Launched 29 July, 1921. Designed by Barnes Wallis, the R80 was one of the

most streamlined British airships. She was to be used for training American airmen preparing to man the R38. After the R38 disaster the R80 was taken out of service. She was scrapped in 1925.

R100

Built by the Airship Guarantee Company Ltd (a wholly-owned subsidiary of Vickers Ltd) at Howden, Yorkshire. Designed by Barnes Wallis and Nevil Shute Norway. The R100 was seen as a 'sister ship' to the R101. Length 719.5 feet; gas capacity 5.1 million cubic feet; powered by six 650-horsepower engines. With only 13 longitudinal girders the R100 was lighter than any airship of its size. It also had a remarkably luxurious interior. Launched June 1930 and after a few trial flights made a return flight to Montreal, Canada, between July and August, 1930. After the R101 disaster in October 1930, the R100 was 'deflated' on 11 December 1930, and then dismantled and scrapped on 16 November 1931.

R101

Built by the Royal Airship Works at Cardington, Bedfordshire. Length 777 feet; gas capacity 5.5 million cubic feet; powered by six 650-horsepower Beardmore 'Tornado' engines. Launched October 1929 at 735 feet with a gas capacity of 4.9 million cubic feet. After trial flights it was decided the ship did not have enough lift so an extra gas bag was fitted which extended the length by 42 feet and the gas capacity by 600,000 cubic feet. The R101 was the largest aircraft ever flown. Crashed near Beauvais in France on 5 October 1930, on her way to India via Egypt, killing everyone on board except three crewmen. One of the fatalities was the Secretary of State for Air, Lord Thompson of Cardington.

R102, R103, R104

A new class of British airship that was conceived (in August 1930) but never realised. The class was designated 'Project H'.

Length 822 feet; gas capacity 7.5 million cubic feet; to be powered by seven Beardmore 'Tornado' engines. Each of the ships was expected to carry 150 passengers to every corner of the British Empire. Project H was abandoned in the wake of the R101 disaster.

Bibliography

Abbot, Patrick, *The Story of R34*, Adams & Dart, 1973

Brooks, Peter W, *Zeppelin: Rigid Airships 1893–1940*, Putnam, 1993

Burne, Charles R.N, *With the Naval Brigade in Natal, 1899–1900*, Edward Arnold, 1902

Chamberlain, Geoffrey, *Airships, A history of Cardington airship station and its role in world airship development*, Lavenham Dalton, 1984

Clayden, Arthur William, *Cloud Studies*, London 1905

Duggan, John, *Airships in International Affairs 1890–1940*, Palgrave Macmillan, 2001

Grant, Sybil, *The End of the Day*, Hodder & Stoughton, 1922

Hartcup, Guy, *The Achievement of the Airship: A History of the Development of Rigid, Semi-Rigid, and Non-Rigid Airships*, David & Charles, 1974

Hurst, K.A., *William Beardmore: 'Transport is the Thing'*, National Museums of Scotland, 2004

Jamison, Tom, *Icarus Over the Humber*, University of Hull Press & Lampada Press, 1994

Jeans, T.T., *Naval Brigades in the South African War 1889–1900*, Kessinger Publishing, 1901

Kipling, Rudyard *With the Night Mail*, The Windsor Magazine, 1905

Maitland, Edward M., *The Log of HMA 34: Journey to America and Back*, Hodder & Stoughton, 1920

Mowthorpe, Ces, *Battlebags: British airships of World War I*, Tempus, 1995

Mowthorpe, Ces, *Skysailors*, Tempus, 1998

Raleigh, Walter, *The War in the Air,* Volume 1, Oxford University Press, 1922

Robinson, Douglas H., *Giants in the Sky: A History of the Rigid Airship*, G.T. Foulis & Co., 1973

Robinson, Douglas H., *The Zeppelin in Combat: A History of the German Naval Airship Division 1912–1918*, University of Washington Press, 1980

Shepherd, Edward Colston, *Great Flights*, London, 1939

Swinton, Ernest, *Eyewitness: Being Personal Reminiscences of Certain Phases of the Great War including the Genesis of the Tank*, Hodder & Stoughton, 1932

Swinton, Ernest, *Over My Shoulder: An Autobiography*, George Ronald, 1951

— *The Study of War: An Inaugural Lecture as Chichele Professor of War 1926*, Clarendon Press, 1926

Ventry, Lord & Kolesnik, Eugene M., *Airship Saga,* Blandford Press, 1982

Wells, Herbert George, *The War in the Air,* Bell & Co., 1908

Whale, George, *Airships: Past, Present and Future*, 1966

Whitehouse, Arch, *The Zeppelin Fighters*, 1966

Official Sources

Although newspaper and magazine accounts of the R34's epic transatlantic flight abound, the real tale lies in the reports, official diaries, memoranda, accounts of conferences, letters, telegrams, flying orders, sailing orders, transport orders, radio logs, etc., most of which (although not all) lie in the National Archives in Kew. There are so many such files and documents that to attribute every quote and reference would make for some very heavy going, to say the least. The ones listed below are the most important.

AIR1/110/15/33/18

Contains the official post-mission reports of Edward Maitland, George Herbert Scott, Gilbert Cooke, John Shotter, Geoffrey Harris and Ronald Durrant. They comprise assessments of the performance of the airframe, the engines, the instruments, the radio equipment, the fuel system and the effects of the journey on the crew. They highlight the short-comings of the equipment and the problems thrown up by the hugely variable Atlantic weather.

AIR1/455/15/312/32

Contains letters from the commander of the station at East Fortune worrying about his ability to handle the R34, the appointment of 'control' officers to handle the flight from London, warnings from the Admiralty that the R34 and the attendant cruisers may have to be pulled out if the Germans failed to sign the Peace Treaty, and documents on the (tem-porary) transfer of the R34 from the Admiralty to the Air Ministry. Also in that file: letters from the US Navy and US Army offering landing facilities, a memo from the UK's Air Attaché in Washington fretting about the role of the Aero Club of America and a note on the R34 from the US Ambassador in London to Lord Curzon, the British Foreign Secretary. There are also details of the precise location of the landing field at Mineola, Long Island, New York.

AIR1/2421/305/18/5

Contains details of the fitting of the Sunbeam Motor Com-pany's 'Maori' engines to the R34.

AIR1/2424/305/25

Contains an assessment of the R34, its crew and its mission by Brigadier-General R.M. Groves, the Deputy Chief of the Air Staff. There are also entries from his diaries with accounts of meetings with the senior politicians and the top brass of the Air Ministry and the Admiralty. The file also contains the R34's 'flying orders', instructions to ships on how to assist the R34 in an emergency, details of the 12-man 'advance party' that was sent to the USA ahead of the flight, and mention of the 'special conference' of manufacturers, shipowners, politicians and military men to advance transatlantic air travel.

AIR2/725
Contains the publicity arrangements for the flight, as organised by Brigadier-General Ernest Swinton. There are memoranda on who is to take the photographs, who will write the 'narrative' of the east–west flight, and how the pictures and information will be distributed to the US and UK press. Also contains Air Ministry press releases on the flight and letters from manufacturers anxious to be mentioned in the publicity.

AIR2/726
Contains telegrams from Brigadier-General Swinton to Brigadier-General Groves, and papers discussing the need for censorship and the difficulty of controlling information in the USA.

AIR5/894
Contains papers and correspondence on the final flight, damage to and ultimate loss of the R34 at the air station at Howden in Yorkshire in January 1921.

Other Material
Other official files worth consulting are to be found within AVIA6, T1, TS28, ADM188 and ADM273.

Index

238   *The Flight of the Titan*